Refiguring the Postmaternal

This book explores the concept of the 'postmaternal' as a response to changing cultural, political and economic conditions for motherhood and responds to Julie Stephens' contention that gender-neutral feminism has led to a forgetting of the maternal within feminist memory. In *Confronting Postmaternal Thinking: Feminism, Memory, Care* (2011) Stephens identifies a significant cultural anxiety about caregiving, nurturing and human dependency that she calls 'postmaternal' thinking. She argues that maternal forms of care have been rejected in the public sphere and marginalised to the private domain through an elaborate process of cultural forgetting, in turn contributing to the current dominance of a degendered form of feminism.

This book argues that refiguring postmaternalism requires opening up the maternal beyond the category of mothers and the nuclear family. The chapters in this edited volume contribute to the field of maternal studies by investigating the connections between maternalism, feminism and neoliberalism through diverse feminist theories, cases and methodologies. We challenge Stephens' diagnosis of the 'forgetting' of certain forms of maternal practices from feminism's history by highlighting the ongoing contested place of the maternal in feminist scholarship and activism for the last five decades. We argue that the memorialising of the maternal in feminist scholarship needs to reflect its diverse legacies in the analyses of black feminism, socialist feminism and ecofeminism in order to destabilise the association of the maternal with neoliberalism and the depoliticisation of feminism. This book was originally published as a special issue of *Australian Feminist Studies*.

Maria Fannin is Reader in Human Geography in the School of Geographical Sciences at the University of Bristol, UK. Her research focusses on the social and economic dimensions of health, medicine and technology, particularly in relation to reproduction and women's health. She is currently researching the multiple forms of value attached to human placental tissue in the biosciences, medicine and alternative health practices. Her work has appeared in *Body & Society*, *Feminist Theory* and *New Genetics & Society*.

Maud Perrier is Senior Lecturer in Sociology at the University of Bristol, UK. She has written about class and contemporary motherhood and the relationship between neoliberalism, work, care and feminisms. She is currently researching women food social entrepreneurs in Sydney, Australia, with Elaine Swan. She has published in *Sociology*, *Sociological Review*, *Sociological Research Online*, *Continuum: Journal of Media and Cultural Studies*, *Humanities*, *Gender and Education* and *Feminist Formations*.

Refiguring the Postmaternal
Feminist Responses to the Forgetting of Motherhood

Edited by
Maria Fannin and Maud Perrier

LONDON AND NEW YORK

First published 2018
by Routledge
2 Park Square, Milton Park, Abingdon, Oxon, OX14 4RN, UK

and by Routledge
711 Third Avenue, New York, NY 10017, USA

Routledge is an imprint of the Taylor & Francis Group, an informa business

© 2018 Taylor & Francis

All rights reserved. No part of this book may be reprinted or reproduced or utilised in any form or by any electronic, mechanical, or other means, now known or hereafter invented, including photocopying and recording, or in any information storage or retrieval system, without permission in writing from the publishers.

Trademark notice: Product or corporate names may be trademarks or registered trademarks, and are used only for identification and explanation without intent to infringe.

British Library Cataloguing in Publication Data
A catalogue record for this book is available from the British Library

ISBN13: 978-0-8153-9205-7

Typeset in Myriad Pro
by codeMantra

Publisher's Note
The publisher accepts responsibility for any inconsistencies that may have arisen during the conversion of this book from journal articles to book chapters, namely the possible inclusion of journal terminology.

Disclaimer
Every effort has been made to contact copyright holders for their permission to reprint material in this book. The publishers would be grateful to hear from any copyright holder who is not here acknowledged and will undertake to rectify any errors or omissions in future editions of this book.

Contents

	Citation Information	vi
	Notes on Contributors	viii
	Introduction: Refiguring the Postmaternal *Maria Fannin and Maud Perrier*	1
1	Postmaternal, Postwork and the Maternal Death Drive *Lisa Baraitser*	11
2	The 'Good' Attached Mother: An Analysis of Postmaternal and Postracial Thinking in Birth and Breastfeeding Policy in Neoliberal Britain *Patricia Hamilton*	28
3	A Vision for Postmaternalism: Institutionalising Fathers' Engagement with Care *Junko Yamashita*	50
4	Belly Casts and Placenta Pills: Refiguring Postmaternal Entrepreneurialism *Maud Perrier and Maria Fannin*	66
5	Embodied Care and Planet Earth: Ecofeminism, Maternalism and Postmaternalism *Mary Phillips*	86
6	Postmaternal Times and Radical Feminist Thinking *Alison Bartlett*	104
7	Shape-shifting Around the Maternal: A Response *Julie Stephens*	119
	Index	131

Citation Information

The chapters in this book were originally published in *Australian Feminist Studies*, volume 31, issue 90 (December 2016). When citing this material, please use the original page numbering for each article, as follows:

Introduction
Refiguring the Postmaternal
Maria Fannin and Maud Perrier
Australian Feminist Studies, volume 31, issue 90 (December 2016) pp. 383–392

Chapter 1
Postmaternal, Postwork and the Maternal Death Drive
Lisa Baraitser
Australian Feminist Studies, volume 31, issue 90 (December 2016) pp. 393–409

Chapter 2
The 'Good' Attached Mother: An Analysis of Postmaternal and Postracial Thinking in Birth and Breastfeeding Policy in Neoliberal Britain
Patricia Hamilton
Australian Feminist Studies, volume 31, issue 90 (December 2016) pp. 410–431

Chapter 3
A Vision for Postmaternalism: Institutionalising Fathers' Engagement with Care
Junko Yamashita
Australian Feminist Studies, volume 31, issue 90 (December 2016) pp. 432–447

Chapter 4
Belly Casts and Placenta Pills: Refiguring Postmaternal Entrepreneurialism
Maud Perrier and Maria Fannin
Australian Feminist Studies, volume 31, issue 90 (December 2016) pp. 448–467

Chapter 5
Embodied Care and Planet Earth: Ecofeminism, Maternalism and Postmaternalism
Mary Phillips
Australian Feminist Studies, volume 31, issue 90 (December 2016) pp. 468–485

CITATION INFORMATION

Chapter 6
Postmaternal Times and Radical Feminist Thinking
Alison Bartlett
Australian Feminist Studies, volume 31, issue 90 (December 2016) pp. 486–500

Chapter 7
Shape-shifting Around the Maternal: A Response
Julie Stephens
Australian Feminist Studies, volume 31, issue 90 (December 2016) pp. 501–512

For any permission-related enquiries please visit:
http://www.tandfonline.com/page/help/permissions

Notes on Contributors

Lisa Baraitser is a Reader in Psychosocial Studies at Birkbeck, University of London, UK. She has published widely on motherhood and feminist and psychoanalytic theory, and runs the research network MaMSIE (Mapping Maternal Subjectivities, Identities and Ethics). Her recent work is on the relations between temporality, gender and care.

Alison Bartlett teaches at The University of Western Australia. She has widely published on maternity, 1980s peace camps and Australian feminist histories. She is the author of *Breastwork: Rethinking Breastfeeding* (2005) and recently edited *Things That Liberate: an Australian Feminist Wunderkammer* (with M. Henderson, 2013).

Maria Fannin is Reader in Human Geography in the School of Geographical Sciences at the University of Bristol, UK. Her research focusses on the social and economic dimensions of health, medicine and technology, particularly in relation to reproduction and women's health. She is currently researching the multiple forms of value attached to human placental tissue in the biosciences, medicine and alternative health practices. Her work has appeared in *Body & Society*, *Feminist Theory* and *New Genetics & Society*.

Patricia Hamilton completed her PhD in Women's Studies and Feminist Research at the University of Western Ontario, Canada in 2017. Her PhD thesis examined black mothers' engagements with attachment parenting. Drawing from interviews with black mothers living in Britain and Canada and employing an intersectional feminist theoretical framework, the study explored how black mothers used (and rejected) attachment parenting to assert themselves as good mothers. Her current research interests focus on how race impacts breastfeeding promotion and the intersectional politics of parental leave.

Maud Perrier is Senior Lecturer in Sociology at the University of Bristol, UK. She has written about class and contemporary motherhood and the relationship between neo-liberalism, work, care and feminisms. She is currently researching women food social entrepreneurs in Sydney, Australia, with Elaine Swan. She has published in *Sociology, Sociological Review, Sociological Research Online, Continuum: Journal of Media and Cultural Studies, Humanities, Gender and Education* and *Feminist Formations*.

Mary Phillips is a Reader in Organisation Studies at the University of Bristol, UK. Her research focusses on transformative, and particularly feminist, alternatives to the neo-liberalist agenda on planetary flourishing. Her recent anthology, *Contemporary Perspectives on Ecofeminism*, was published by Routledge in 2015. She is also active in green politics and a member of both the Green Party and Frome Anti-Fracking.

NOTES ON CONTRIBUTORS

Julie Stephens is an Honorary Professor in Humanities and Social Sciences at Victoria University, Australia. She is author of *Confronting Postmaternal Thinking: Feminism, Memory, and Care* (2011) and *Anti-Disciplinary Protest: Sixties Radicalism and Postmodernism* (1998). Her research is informed by feminist theory, social movement theory, memory studies and the emerging area of maternal studies. She also has a research and clinical interest in the theory and practice of psychoanalysis.

Junko Yamashita is Senior Lecturer at the School of Sociology, Politics and International Studies, University of Bristol, UK. Her expertise is in comparative analysis of East Asian and European Social policy, especially in relation to care and gender.

INTRODUCTION

Refiguring the Postmaternal

Maria Fannin and Maud Perrier

In *Confronting Postmaternal Thinking: Feminism, Memory, Care* (2011) Julie Stephens identifies a significant cultural anxiety about care-giving, nurturing and human dependency she calls 'postmaternal' thinking, based on analysis of offline and online cultural texts and oral histories about maternal experiences. Stephens argues that maternal forms of care have been rejected in the public sphere and marginalised to the private domain through an elaborate process of cultural forgetting, in turn contributing to the current dominance of what Stephens terms a degendered form of feminism. Stephens argues that an alternative politic where human dependency and vulnerability – rather than market performance – are imagined as the primary connection between people has been forgotten. This is manifest in the realm of social policy through the reduction and in some cases elimination of social supports for women as mothers. In the cultural sphere, Stephens cites the anxieties over motherhood and mothering articulated in the genres of popular and advice literature aimed at professional women, and in the conflicted memoirs of young women recounting their experiences as children of feminist mothers. The postmaternal thus describes for Stephens the contemporary condition of forgetting, obscuring, or rendering culturally illegible the maternal in both social policy and histories of feminism, whereby women's claims as mothers are no longer seen as political.

Stephens situates her diagnosis of the postmaternalism of contemporary social policies in Europe, Australia and North America as one of the defining characteristics of neoliberal policy-making. In this sense, Stephens' book makes an important contribution to theorising neoliberalism as a cultural and political formation. The forgetting of the vulnerability, intimacy, emotion and affective labour entailed by mothering is an important yet undertheorised dimension of how neoliberal policies transform social responsibilities for dependent others into 'burdens' to be borne by individuals. Stephens' critique of this forgetting of maternal thinking, and her return to theorists of care such as Sara Ruddick for inspiration, extends to the telling and retelling of histories of feminist politics in relation to experiences of mothering.

The aim of this special issue, *Refiguring the Postmaternal*, is to explore the concept of the 'postmaternal' as a critique of and response to changing cultural, political and economic conditions for mothering and motherhood (Kawash 2011; Giles 2014; Wilson and Yochim 2015). Our initial interest in bringing together critical reflections on Stephens' book emerged from our inquiry into alternative models of feminine and feminist relationalities and the ways that metaphors of maternity and sorority have tended to dominate feminist theorizations of women's relationships (Fannin and Perrier, forthcoming). Stephens' analysis of the deep cultural anxieties around public expressions of maternalism resonated with our experiences as researchers of birth and mothering respectively; however, we also found the repertoire of the maternal limiting and sought ways of describing relations of care between women that didn't rely on the metaphor of motherhood. The concept of the postmaternal seemed to speak to some of these concerns, to social policy domains as well as the memories and practices of intergenerational feminism and feminist politics. It has been diversely deployed in feminist scholarship to analyse new reproductive technologies (Michaels 1996), representations of women's midlife (Gullette 1995, 2002, 2003) and American welfare reform in the 1990s (Howe 2002). In Stephens' book, the postmaternal is offered as a way to diagnose the 'forgetting' of certain forms of feminist practices from feminism's history, inviting a broader reflection on how feminism is remembered, memorialised, preserved, contested and rewritten. In this collection of articles, we use Stephens' contention that gender-neutral feminism has led to a forgetting of the maternal within feminist memory as a starting point for outlining what we see as the most salient set of empirical and conceptual questions facing feminist scholars of the maternal today.

A new maternalism?

The maternal was a central concern of 1970s feminist scholarship with the work of Sara Ruddick, Adrienne Rich and later Ann Oakley standing out as early attempts to make motherhood count as a topic worthy of academic study and to map out the conditions under which motherhood could be empowering outside of patriarchy. While the place of the maternal within feminist scholarship has shifted since these landmark texts, it certainly hasn't disappeared. The scholarship on motherhood is characterised by efforts to capture the differences and divisions in mothers' experiences (Ribbens 1994; Reynolds 2005; Gillies 2007), to record women's ambivalent relationships towards motherhood (Baraitser 2009), to document the continuing unequal division of childcare and the transformations motherhood brings to women's identities (Miller 2005; Thomson et al. 2011) and to critically interrogate dominant discourses of good motherhood and their effects (Hays 1996; Tyler 2011).

We can discern significant divergences between those feminists who, as inheritors of Rich and Ruddick, still remain committed to a re-valorisation of the maternal and mothering as a feminist strategy and those who prioritise deconstructing the over-association of femininity with maternal identity and labour. In this special issue we attempt to connect these two distinct lineages of feminist work on motherhood to construct a more thorough analysis of and response to the ongoing devaluing of both maternity and care in post-austerity crises. Specifically, we seek to connect the postmaternal to wider debates in feminist theory about postfeminism and the depoliticization of feminism: to what extent does the postmaternal represent a particular manifestation of neoliberal feminism or can it provide an alternative vision of maternity for 21st century feminism?

Discussions of the maternal in the last few years have been very rich but there have been no theoretically informed discussions of how the relationship of the maternal to feminism as a movement and a cultural formation has shifted in the last decades which is our aim in this special issue.[1] *Refiguring the Postmaternal* thus asks important conceptual questions about the relationship between contemporary feminism and maternity which had been hitherto ignored in contemporary maternal scholarship. It echoes and develops other feminist analyses of the ways that the organisation of care has become increasingly individualised and privatised in post-welfare western states: the large proportions of professional mothers and enduring gendered division of care labour have resulted in a care deficit being met by working-class and migrant women (Hochschild 2003; Fraser 2013; McDowell 2013). Reflections on Sara Ruddick's work and the work of other theorists of care continue to inform and inspire feminist theories of affect and labour (Ruddick 1990; Akalin 2015). Consideration of the 'maternal' as a concept also informs research into reproduction, gender, care and parenting, in particular given the efforts of scholars to trace the impact of neoliberal economic and social policies in these domains (McRobbie 2013; Adkins and Dever 2014). These latest analyses provide an update on the classic feminist contribution that the concept of 'social reproduction' made to understanding the gendered division of labour and signal the persistence of the feminist project of radically transforming the work and care conundrum today. Lisa Adkins and Maryanne Dever's (2014) call for feminists to rethink the conceptualisation of women's reconfigured waged and unwaged labour under the post-Fordist sexual contract suggests that significant theoretical transformation has yet to happen in this area. This special issue contributes to this debate by capturing some of these transformations through our attention to the building of alternative practices, spaces and economies of care beyond the maternal.

In thinking about how 21st century feminist theory can approach the question of maternity we have found Angela McRobbie's (2013) reflections in 'Feminism, the Family and the New 'Mediated' Maternalism' a helpful reminder of how socialist feminism aimed to transform reproductive work and paid work by providing state-funded childcare that would both collectivise care and denaturalise the gendering of care. Whereas Stephens characterises liberal feminism as having rejected the maternal, McRobbie argues that a particular model of professional maternal citizenship is folded back into neoliberal political economies to become a key mechanism of its success (2013, 136). Stephens' argument sometimes presents a conflict between 'the glorification of market work and the devaluing of family work' (Williams 2001, 41 quoted in Stephens 2011, 21), however we argue this opposition neglects to consider how the provision of state-funded childcare would enable mothers to combine both care work and paid work without devaluing either. McRobbie shows that in the UK the longstanding political relationship between post-war social democracy and state-funded nursery care has been under attack since New Labour:

> to understand the new family values of the present moment it is necessary to look back to the New Labour period and to the way in which previous historical affiliations between social democracy and feminism which aimed to support women as mothers were dismantled and discredited. This opened the pathway for the present day demonisation of welfare which suggests that relying on support or subsidy is somehow shameful. (2013, 128)

The necessity of remembering such feminist demands is key to refiguring postmaternalism at a time when the erosion of welfare support has reached a point where its value as a social good risks being erased from our collective imaginaries. In post-Brexit Britain parents' and carers' rights are in further jeopardy given senior government minister Andrea Leadsom's call to reduce maternity leave entitlements for small businesses and with EU nationals being required to take out private insurance during parental leave to secure permanent residency in the UK (Bienkov 2016; O'Carroll 2016).

Postmaternal thinking

In May 2015, we convened a workshop on 'Postmaternal Thinking' held at the University of Bristol. The starting point for this workshop was a collective reading of Julie Stephens' *Confronting the Postmaternal* and the presentation of reflections and responses to the concept of the postmaternal by participants. We asked participants to consider Stephens' diagnosis of the cultural forgetting of maternal thinking in light of their own empirical research and to consider their own work in light of a set of questions posed by Stephens' book: What is or should be the concept of the postmaternal? What theoretical resources does the concept of the postmaternal provide for ongoing and future feminist research? How is neoliberalism refiguring maternity and mothering, and what are feminist and/or maternalist responses to this? How might the analysis of the postmaternal travel to other geo-political spaces beyond Euro-American and Australian contexts? And finally, how useful is the concept of the postmaternal in helping feminist scholars revisit afresh the problem of essentialism and ethics of care debates?

These questions are particularly timely given the changing political currency and competing meanings of the postmaternal in contemporary western societies facing so-called austerity crises. For example, recent changes by the Conservative-Liberal Democrat coalition in the UK replaced maternity leave with shared parental leave from 5th April 2015 – interestingly this policy still depends on mothers giving their consent to share the parental leave entitlement with their partners (Grabham 2014). We found Stephens' contention that adult women are predominantly defined as workers first and foremost compelling given the neoliberalisation of welfare policies around the globe. Additionally, debates over the effects of the 2008 global economic recession on fertility rates have been read as a signal of women 'taking advantage' of unemployment to have children. Such societal changes around the place of motherhood suggest that the idea of the postmaternal is now ripe for (re)definition by feminist scholars.

The workshop on 'Postmaternal Thinking' signalled the importance of considering Stephens' and other feminist scholars' examination of the changing policies and practices of mothering in the context of contemporary social and political conditions. The articles in this special issue come up with different responses to how feminist politics in a postmaternal age might be imagined and enacted. They draw from a range of disciplines, including management studies, cultural studies, psychology/psychosocial studies, social policy, sociology and human geography and wider academic literatures on gender, care, parenting, affect and the writing of feminism's histories. They revisit the old dilemma of the de-valorisation/revalorisation of the maternal drawing on fresh insights from different contexts including Canada, Australia and the UK. They are connected by their efforts to analyze the postmaternal using diverse feminist methods and theories – such as radical feminism, psychoanalysis, black feminism and ecofeminism – and argue that such analyses are particularly needed politically in times of neoliberal and austerity crises. The articles are also connected in their attempt to return to well-known 'blind spots' in maternal studies which have long been argued to result in divisions rather than solidarity between mothers, leading to the exclusion and repudiation of black, working-class and single mothers amongst others. The edited collection charts how such differences and divisions between women are reconfigured in a neoliberal postmaternal landscape.

Although our starting point was a collective reading of Stephens' book, concerns over the 'forgetting' and reconfiguring of the maternal resonate with other scholarly debates in feminist theory and the retelling of feminism's history as a one of generations or 'waves' (Kevin 2005; Hemmings 2011). As the feminist scholarship on alternatives temporalities demonstrates, claims to moving 'beyond' or 'after' a particular social formation make implicit the underlying presumptions of linear or chronological experiences of time that structure conventional reflections on historical change (Bastian 2011). Stephens' analysis of the Euro-American and Australian contexts for mothering needs to be understood contextually rather than as representations of mothering practices in other places and at other times. We contend that the cultural contexts in which Stephens' notion of the postmaternal is articulated may reflect a particular view of motherhood – one that invites comparison and contextualization outside the dominant Euro-American and Australian frame. We see this special issue as a forum in which to explore more carefully the presumptions made about research on 'mothering' that tends to posit its universality rather than emphasising how mothering and parenting are practices shaped by temporal and geographical specificity.

Our reflections on the postmaternal bring to the fore how the study of maternity, motherhood and mothering continues to be divided between scholars interested in the psychoanalytical and psychological aspects of mothering and those interested in the social construction of motherhood across different groups of women: thus the terminology of the *maternal* has tended to be confined to humanities scholars interested in cultural representations and individual experiences, whereas *mothering* and *motherhood* are preferred by social scientists. This special issue brings these perspectives together to analyse the cultural formation of postmaternalism and deploys a variety of feminist methodological and empirical resources including archives, interviews, policy, manifesto and memoir writing to imagine alternative postmaternalisms.

Lisa Baraitser's article opens this special issue with the important and critical reminder that mothering cannot be reduced to care and nurturance and includes feelings of hatred, aggression and frustration. She insightfully traces maternalism's connection to feminist socialism through her juxtaposition of psychoanalytical readings of maternity and Kathi Weeks' book *The Problem with Work* (2011). Baraitser writes of mothering as letting go and bearing the time of another's unfolding. This opening up of what constitutes maternal practice involves expanding who participates in mothering and where mothering takes place. This is a refrain found throughout the subsequent articles in this special issue, where Sara Ruddick's exhortation to consider the practices of mothering opens up the possibility for alternative figures of the maternal.

A refigured concept of the postmaternal also opens up how presumptions of what constitutes 'good' mothering reflect the racial hierarchies that underpin calls to re-orient mothering practices through dualisms of 'traditional' and 'modern' or 'natural' and 'technological'. Patricia Hamilton's article skilfully excavates the debt attachment parenting owes to late colonial research on non-Western mothering as well as to the individualistic ethos of neoliberal parenting, in which mothers are expected to make wise personal choices on behalf of their children. Hamilton suggests that analysis of the postmaternal condition of Euro-American mothering also needs to take into account the presumption that the contemporary period is a postracial one, in which racial and class inequities are imagined as having been overcome.

Highlighting the elasticity of maternal practice as it is instantiated in social policy, Junko Yamashita argues for taking up Sara Ruddick's provocative claim that men could be mothers. Yamashita's analysis of how social policy models have grappled with the practice of care suggests that the recent transformation of maternity leave in some social welfare states (e.g. the UK) to shared parental leave opens up the opportunity for expanding maternal practice to fathers. She reads Stephens' diagnosis of the 'unmothering' of the public sphere as a reconfiguring of mothering that will make good on the efforts of Ruddick and other feminist scholars to imagine a more open-ended reorientation of social and cultural forms of mothering to include fathers' care.

Indeed, expanding maternal thinking and practice beyond the mother–child dyad informs our article included in this special issue on the 'maternal entrepreneurs' who are attempting to shape self-employment in the pregnancy, birth and parenting economy around the practices of mothering, or as one interviewee described her work, around 'mothering the mothers'. This article highlights the presence of maternal practice beyond maternal relationships and the private sphere, such as the carework carried out with and for other mothers. It also seeks to open up the analysis of mothering to include the how precarious, part-time and self-employed work cultures of the neoliberal economy are also sites for the production of new forms of collective imaginaries around mothering, recalling Angela McRobbie's account of 'mediated maternalism' discussed earlier in this article.

This refigured concept of maternalism as social and collective is explored in more depth in Mary Phillips' article on the possibilities of an ethics of care beyond the human. Phillips returns to key ethics of care texts and ecofeminist literatures to show that recognition of vulnerability and interdependence should not limit itself to maternality but include an imaginary of embodied emotional attachments to landscapes, animals and ecosystems beyond our doorstep. She argues that a concept of embodied care for nature and non-human others offers a more inclusive vision on which to build care ethics than a narrow appeal to maternalism.

Alison Bartlett's article reminds us of the ways radical feminism transformed motherhood through its critique of the nuclear family. Taking up Stephens' contention that the telling of feminist history occludes the complexity of feminist practice, Bartlett draws on research on women's peace movements in the UK and Australia to complicate the notion of the postmaternal, showing how experiments with alternative social formations of mothering (collective, queer, ecofeminist) multiplied the possibilities for maternal practice and seemed to prefigure what Stephens' diagnoses in her book as the 'postmaternal'. Bartlett closes her article with 'a manifesto for postmaternal times', a reminder of the momentous transformations to being maternal over the latter half of the twentieth century and a call to stay with the undecidability of what the *post*maternal will become.

This special issue on *Refiguring the Postmaternal* concludes with a response by Julie Stephens. Her careful and generous reading of these articles emphasises the necessity of limits: limits to the neoliberal fantasy of an endless horizon of personal choices *and* the limit as instantiated in the unavoidable vulnerability and dependency of infants and newborns. Stephens' response raises generative questions about the continued difficulties in feminist scholarship of reconfiguring maternalism, including more affirmative modes of maternal ambivalence. We are grateful to her for taking up the invitation to response to the articles collected here. We hope the questions raised by her response will inspire further work on how social policies, cultural practices and political activism are refiguring the maternal in postmaternal times.

In conclusion, all of the articles take on and expand Stephens' diagnosis that gender-neutral feminism has led to a forgetting of the maternal within feminist memory by reconnecting the maternal with its varied and ambivalent place in feminist histories. They engage with the concept of the postmaternal in order to extend, interrogate and enter into dialogue with Stephens' conceptual and empirical starting points and her methodological approaches to the study of popular culture and feminist history. They demonstrate how envisioning alternative postmaternal futures requires opening up the maternal beyond the category of mothers to reflect the diversity of maternal practices and their contestations. This opening out of the postmaternal is also critical if feminism is to reflect and engage the ever-rising number of childless women and men in the global north whose involvement in relations of care cannot be captured by maternalism. They highlight the necessity of postmaternal studies that are attuned to power differentials amongst mothers and between men and women, as neglecting this strand of scholarship on mothering would result in a different but equally problematic kind of cultural forgetting to the one on which Stephens is focused.

The contributions in this special issue show both the relevance of the term postmaternal to analysing the problematics of work and care in western neoliberal economies from feminist perspectives and offer up the postmaternal as a useful concept to articulate what alternative futures for maternalism in the twentieth century might look like. They interrogate how the postmaternal is configured and refigured as a conceptual tool for feminist scholarship, and in doing so, explore contemporary transformations in the practice of mothering, the metaphors of maternity, and the gendering of maternity, childrearing and family in social policy and beyond. The articles brought together here contribute to ongoing debates in feminist theory over essentialism and the ethics of care, especially in light of how anxieties over essentialism may continue to obscure the complexity of previous feminist work on embodiment, the maternal, and the 'forgotten' histories of ecofeminism over the last four decades. Following the much discussed affective turn in feminist scholarship, this special issue signals the recent return in feminist theory to issues of relationality, autonomy and interconnectedness beyond their resonance and association with essentialism. It also make an important contribution to the field of maternal studies by investigating the connections between maternalism, feminism and neoliberalism and by deploying rich and diverse feminist resources to refigure postmaternalism in creative ways.

By responding to Stephens' diagnosis of the 'forgetting' of certain forms of maternal practices from feminism's history, the articles here highlight the importance of remembering the contested place of the maternal in feminist scholarship and activism for the last five decades. They show that the process of remembering and memorialising the maternal in feminist scholarship needs to reflect its central location in diverse bodies of feminist scholarship and make visible its legacies in the analyses of black feminism, socialist feminism and ecofeminism beyond that of Sara Ruddick's *Maternal Thinking*. Through these performances of remembering they destabilise the association of the maternal with postfeminism and with the depoliticization of feminism.

Note

1. A recent discussion of austerity and mothering can be found in Jensen and Tyler's special issue of *Studies in the Maternal* on 'Austerity Parenting: new economies of parent-citizenship' (2012). However, this special issue does not explicitly discuss feminism's relationship to the maternal.

Disclosure statement

No potential conflict of interest was reported by the authors.

Notes on Contributor

Maria Fannin is Reader in Human Geography in the School of Geographical Sciences at the University of Bristol, UK. Her research focuses on the social and economic dimensions of health, medicine and technology, particularly in relation to reproduction and women's health. She is currently researching the multiple forms of value attached to human placental tissue in the biosciences, medicine and alternative health practices. Her work has appeared in *Body & Society, Feminist Theory* and *New Genetics & Society*.

Maud Perrier is Senior Lecturer in Sociology at the University of Bristol, UK. She has written about class and contemporary motherhood and the relationship between neoliberalism, work, care and feminisms. She is currently researching women food social entrepreneurs in Sydney, Australia with Elaine Swan. She has published in *Sociology, Sociological Review, Sociological Research Online, Continuum: Journal of Media and Cultural Studies, Humanities, Gender and Education* and *Feminist Formations*.

ORCID

Maria Fannin http://orcid.org/0000-0002-8922-2499
Maud Perrier http://orcid.org/0000-0001-8531-5092

References

Adkins, Lisa, and Maryanne Dever. 2014. "Gender and Labour in New Times: An Introduction." *Australian Feminist Studies* 29 (79): 1–11.
Akalin, Ayşe. 2015. "Motherhood as the Value of Labour." *Australian Feminist Studies* 30 (83): 65–81.
Baraitser, Lisa. 2009. *Maternal Encounters: The Ethics of Interruption*. London: Routledge.
Bastian, Michelle. 2011. "The Contradictory Simultaneity of Being with Others: Exploring Concepts of Time and Community in the Work of Gloria Anzaldúa." *Feminist Review* 97 (1): 151–167.

Bienkov, Adam. 2016. "Andrea Leadsom called for minimum wage and maternity pay to be scrapped for small business." *politics.co.uk*, July 5. http://www.politics.co.uk/news/2016/07/05/minimum-wage-maternity-pay-scrapped-plans-andrea-leadsom

Fannin, Maria, and Maud Perrier. Forthcoming. "Birth Work, Accompaniment and PhD Supervision: An Alternative Feminist Pedagogy for the Neoliberal University." *Gender and Education*.

Fraser, Nancy. 2013. *Fortunes of Feminism: From State-Managed Capitalism to Neoliberal Crisis*. London: Verso Books.

Giles, Melinda Vandenbeld. 2014. *Mothering in the Age of Neoliberalism*. Bradford, ON: Demeter Press.

Gillies, Val. 2007. *Marginalised Mothers: Exploring Working-Class Experiences of Parenting*. Routledge: London.

Grabham, Emily. 2014. "Legal Form and Temporal Rationalities in UK Work–Life Balance Law." *Australian Feminist Studies* 29 (79): 67–84.

Gullette, Margaret Morganroth. 1995. "Inventing the 'Postmaternal' Woman, 1898-1927: Idle, Unwanted, and Out of a Job." *Feminist Studies* 21 (2): 221–253.

Gullette, Margaret Morganroth. 2002. "Valuing 'Postmaternity' as a Revolutionary Feminist Concept." *Feminist Studies* 28 (3): 553–572.

Gullette, Margaret Morganroth. 2003. "Can America Catch up to the Wonderful Midlife Mother? Postmaternal Characters in Contemporary Culture." *Journal of the Motherhood Initiative for Research and Community Involvement* 5 (1): 82–90.

Hays, Sharon. 1996. *The Cultural Contradictions of Motherhood*. New Haven: Yale University Press.

Hemmings, Clare. 2011. *Why Stories Matter: The Political Grammar of Feminist Theory*. Durham, NC: Duke University Press.

Hochschild, Arlie Russell. 2003. *The Managed Heart: Commercialization of Human Feeling*. Berkeley: University of California Press.

Howe, Renate. 2002. "Post-Maternalism and the End of Welfare." *Australasian Journal of American Studies* 21 (2): 111–116.

Jensen, Tracey, and Imogen Tyler. 2012. "Austerity Parenting: New Economies of Parent-Citizenship." *Studies in the Maternal* 4 (2). doi:10.16995/sim.34.

Kawash, Samira. 2011. "New Directions in Motherhood Studies." *Signs: Journal of Women in Culture and Society* 36 (4): 969–1003.

Kevin, Catherine. 2005. "Maternity and Freedom: Australian Feminist Encounters with the Reproductive Body." *Australian Feminist Studies* 20 (46): 3–15.

McDowell, Linda. 2013. *Working Lives: Gender, Migration and Employment in Britain, 1945-2007*. London: Wiley-Blackwell.

McRobbie, Angela. 2013. "Feminism, the Family and the New 'Mediated' Maternalism." *New Formations* 80: 119–137.

Michaels, Meredith W. 1996. "Other Mothers: Toward an Ethic of Postmaternal Practice." *Hypatia* 11: 49–70.

Miller, Tina. 2005. *Making Sense of Motherhood: A Narrative Approach*. Cambridge: Cambridge University Press.

O'Carroll, Lisa. 2016. "Spanish UK resident feared insurance rule would force her to leave" *The Guardian*, December 30. https://www.theguardian.com/uk-news/2016/dec/30/spanish-uk-resident-fears-insurance-loophole-will-force-her-to-leave

Reynolds, Tracey. 2005. *Caribbean Mothers: Identity and Childrearing in the UK*. London: Tufnell Press.

Ribbens, Jane Ribbens. 1994. *Mothers and Their Children: A Feminist Sociology of Childrearing*. London: Sage.

Ruddick, Sara. 1990. *Maternal Thinking: Toward a Politics of Peace*. London: Women's Press.

Stephens, Julie. 2011. *Confronting Postmaternal Thinking: Feminism, Memory and Care*. New York: Columbia University Press.

Thomson, Rachel, Mary Jane Kehily, Lucy Hadfield, and Sue Sharpe. 2011. *Making Modern Mothers*. Bristol: Policy Press.

Tyler, Imogen. 2011. "Pregnant Beauty: Maternal Femininities Under Neoliberalism." In *New Femininities: Postfeminism, Neoliberalism and Identity*, edited by Rosalind Gill and Christina Scharff, 21–36. Basingstoke: Palgrave.

Weeks, Kathi. 2011. *The Problem with Work: Feminism, Marxism, Antiwork Politics, and Postwork Imaginaries*. Durham, NC: Duke University Press.
Williams, Joan. 2001. *Unbending Gender: Why Family and Work Conflict and What to Do About It*. Oxford: Oxford University Press.
Wilson, Julie A., and Emily Chivers Yochim. 2015. "Mothering Through Precarity: Becoming Mamapreneurial." *Cultural Studies* 29 (5–6): 669–686.

Postmaternal, Postwork and the Maternal Death Drive

Lisa Baraitser

ABSTRACT
The term 'postmaternal' has recently emerged as a way to articulate the effects of neoliberalism on the public devaluing of caring labour [Stephens, Julie. 2011. *Confronting Postmaternal Thinking: Feminism, Memory, and Care*. New York: Columbia University Press]. This term suggests a valorisation of values associated with care and mothering that have traditionally been gendered and rely on a heterosexist matrix for their intelligibility. Marxist feminist writers during the 1970s struggled with the question of the particular form of care that reproduction entails, and this feminist archive has been recently extended to a discussion of 'post-work' [Weeks, Kathi. 2011. *The Problem with Work: Feminism, Marxism, Antiwork Politics and Postwork Imaginaries*. Durham: Duke], in which calls for the valuing of unpaid work as a viable form of labour have been reanimated. In this article I examine the relation between these two analytic categories – 'postmaternal' and 'postwork'. Both categories require that we re-think some of the most trenchant issues in feminist thought – the sexual division of labour, the place of 'reproduction' in psychic and social life, and the possibilities for a new feminist commons.

Introduction

Over the last few years I have written a series of 'maternal anecdotes', short, not-quite-stories about odd and resistant experiences prompted by motherhood, which I have 'over-mined', we could say, for theoretical insights, by paying a huge amount of attention to what were otherwise rather mundane incidents in the everyday life of a particular mother (Baraitser 2009a, 2009b, 2011, 2013, 2014). This overmining was a strategic practice, an attempt to generate theory out of an autoethnography that took my own experience of the dislodgements and estrangements of motherhood as a starting point for an investigation into what we might really mean by a 'maternal subject'. I wanted to see what kind of theory could be generated out of a deliberate and profound attention paid to the maternal-ordinary. I was aiming at an intervention into an entrenched set of debates and questions in feminist, psychoanalytic and queer theory concerning the figure of the mother in both social and psychic life; whether 'the mother' constituted an analytic category in the way that 'woman' once did; how to conceptualise the putative, if now precarious relations between femininity and maternity;[1] and what happens to the category of the maternal, and experiences of motherhood, when theories are underpinned by an implicit repudiation of reproduction, care, vulnerability and dependency (see, in particular, Edelman 2004). I did not, however, want to substitute this repudiation with a version of maternalism – an assertion, as Julie Stephens puts in *Confronting Postmaternal Thinking* (2011) of the public and social importance of motherhood, and the nurture and care of children as a model for the public good. Instead I worked away at a theory of maternal ethics that could step aside from figurations of maternal care as either vital necessity, or a form of female masochism, by trying to account for what I called 'maternal alterity' (Baraitser 2009a). My interest was in whether maternal encounters (encounters between those who identify as 'mothers', and those whom we come to name and claim as our 'children') could hold open the potential for a radical form of ethics running counter to capitalist modes of productivity, temporality and exchange, without this form of ethics necessarily re-suturing femininity to an ethic of care. I drew not only on Levinas' trenchant account of the subjective productiveness of an encounter with otherness (1998), but on Badiou's account of love that 'treats' the condition that there are two radically 'disjunct' positions of experience that cannot know one another (2000), as well as a long history of feminist metaphysics that has argued in different ways for the 'not-one'.[2] I was concerned with thinking maternal ethics as an encounter a mother may have with an irreducible otherness in the figure of the child, who remains resistant to the effects of that encounter, and therefore may call forth what we could then, with more surety, name as a 'maternal subject'. Maternal alterity also meant listening out for the 'call' of many other 'others', signalling both the multiple histories of collective practices of childcare, and in a more materialist vein, our relations with non-human others involved in the complex processes of maternal labour. This concerned paying attention to the ethicality of 'stuff', as in Heidegger's (1962) notion of 'Zeug'; 'things' and their thingness, as Bennett (2010) would have it, 'tool-beings', to use Harman's (2007, 171–205) evocative Heideggerian term, and the inanimate 'dumb' materiality that Lacan (1992) links with the Real of the maternal body, but is, of course, far from dumb. So I wrote about the ethics of encounters between mothers and baby clothes, blankets, quilts, bottles, teats, milk powder, sterilisers, breast pumps, feeding spoons and bowls, juice bottles and bibs, pacifiers, mobiles, rattles, nappies, wipes, changing mats, creams, powders, cribs, cots, baskets, baby monitors, prams, buggies, carry cots, slings, back packs, car seats and, as O'Rourke (2011) has put it 'so ever infinitely on'.

> While I was doing this work, something strange happened; something I should, of course, have foreseen, should have been mindful of right from the start. My children … grew up. My oldest child is now seventeen, and looking out into the world, his back to the small group of us who have born, carried, cajoled, taught, and supported him, still occasionally inclined towards us when he needs to be, and recently turning in an ironic way when he leaves the house, to wave, a half-jokey reminder that one day soon, when I'm not looking, he will just turn the corner at the end of the street, and simply walk away. I neither dread nor savour it. He will continue to be someone I think of as 'my child' after he is gone, as I will continue to inhabit lives other than the one named 'mother', just as I will go on mothering other children. He will continue to be 'my child' should I have the profound misfortune to outlive him. But he is leaving. I am 'postmaternal'.

What might 'postmaternal' mean? In this article, I shall be departing from Julie Stephens' use of this term. Stephens' 'postmaternal' describes the manifestation of a generalised public anxiety about the values associated with maternal models of care, and the repudiation of the maternal in public and private(ised) life that she calls 'unmothering', particularly in discourses that operate in areas of the global north where neoliberal principles have dominated state interventions in the labour market (2011, 15, 132). Her argument is that the cultural ideals central to the workings of neoliberal institutions, work arrangements, and conceptualisations of the self, require a kind of 'forgetting' of the core dependencies of all human experience. This leads to a cultural hostility to what Richard Sennett calls the 'dignity of dependence' (Stephens 2011, 7). Without wanting to fully embrace a position of maternalism, even in its more recent neomaternalist evocations, Stephens nevertheless wants to 'confront' this repudiation of dependencies that she names as 'postmaternal thinking' through a practice of actively remembering feminism's own 'nurturing' mothers, returning us to the possibilities of making political claims based on universal needs for care, nurturance and the management of vulnerability.

My aim here is to open up the notion of the 'postmaternal' through bringing it into some kind of proximity with Weeks' (2011) concept 'postwork'. 'Postwork' is a rather different attempt to respond to some of the same problematics that Stephens identifies in the ways work and care (or social reproduction) have become so separated from one another, and draws on 1970s Marxist feminist texts about wages for housework to reanimate a utopian demand for a postwork politics. In bringing these two terms into relation with one another I'm seeking to think with and against the postmaternal, by suggesting, with Weeks, that there is a strategic need for making certain demands in the name of both social reproduction and work, that go beyond the neomaternalism (albeit a feminist one) that underpins Stephens' analysis of the postmaternal discourses that surely do surround us. However, the thrust of my argument is that we also need to continue to prize open the implications of using mothering to signify the tripartite conjunction of care, nurture and the management of states of dependency when we make arguments about work and care in public life. Mothering may include practices of care and nurturance, but it also concerns the daily management and experience, for those who mother, of hatred, aggression, guilt, fear, frustration, violence and despair, that have some relation, even if a retroactive and indirect one, to early experiences of being mothered (Kraemer 1996; Lewis 2009; Parker 1995; Stone 2011). I aim, therefore, to track across psychoanalytic and social theory, trying to keep open the meanings of 'the maternal', not simply in order to de-gender or denaturalise care, but to remind ourselves of the implications of 'forgetting' that love and hate are always bound up with one another. If we think about the maternal as a principle or model in social and psychic life that speaks to this impossibility of love without hate, an impossibility that has the potential to mobilise guilt, gratitude, and reparative wishes (if we follow Melanie Klein's thinking about early object relations), then we might instigate a pathway from a social analysis of the 'unmothering' of society, to a more nuanced understanding of both motherhood, and broader ideas about the social good. Weeks seeks to address the problem of waged labour, and its implications for social reproduction by exploring the notion of a basic income for the common production of value. 'Postwork' undoes the relation between wage and labour through an analysis of social reproduction in neoliberal conditions, calling not just for the common production of value but for a basic income for the common reproduction of 'life' (Weeks 2011, 230). Weeks' appeal to sharing the responsibility for reproducing 'life' rather than value maintains a relation between work and reproduction that is neither maternalist, nor occludes the possibility of such labour emanating from a demand for a form of *reparation*, understood both in the sense of financial recompense and in the sense of 'repair'. This may provide us with a more radical model for rethinking a feminist maternalism that includes, but is not subsumed by, a politics of care. One element of my argument is that whilst the notion of sharing the reproduction of 'life' may serve us well as a figuration of the maternal that allows care to circulate as everybody's business, we need to make sure that such a project also entails an engagement with what works *against* life, the 'hostility to life', as Derrida (1995) puts it, or in Freud's terms, simply the death drive.

Secondly, my concerns here are with the temporality of the death drive in relation to maternal practice. Postwork calls on us to understand the temporal dimensions of the relationship between work, reproduction and care. Denaturalising the 8-hour day, or, for that matter, denaturalising the regime of 'total work' that is the outcome of the precaritisation of labour, in order to open up unfettered time that is required for care, may be one element of a broader operation that seeks to reconfigure the privatisation and gendering of care. But maternal practice (as distinct from maternal labour) is not simply synonymous with care. It entails a form of emotional labour in which this labour itself comes to matter to us, causing us to return again and again to the scene of love and hate. The 'again and again', I argue, might be understood as the temporality of a 'maternal death drive'; a repetitive return, not exactly to a state of nothingness, as Freud's death drive implies, but to a state in which we can tolerate the knowledge that we hate what we also love, and therefore that we may desire to repair the damage done to the loved object. Maternal time emerges from this account as the time it takes for the capacity for reparation to be established and maintained – the 17 years that it takes the mother–child pair in the anecdote above, to wave ambivalently both hello and goodbye to each other. A postwork notion of care requires not just the reorganisation of the social reproduction of 'life' but the time it takes to live out the complexities of caring relations, and the development of capacities that may enable the reparation of psychic life.

Love, guilt and reparation

If we frame the question in another way, what else might the postmaternal signify *other* than a public expression of anxiety about what Stephens assigns as the maternal values of care, nurture and dependency? In *Love, Guilt and Reparation* (1998, 306–343), Melanie Klein tells us that anxiety about maternal care, nurture and our dependency on the maternal body in very early life – the relationship, that is, with a feeding-object of some kind, that could be loosely termed 'breast' – is a result of both the frustrations of that breast (its capacities to feed but also to withhold or disappear at whim), and what the infant does with the hatred and aggressive feelings stirred up by those experiences of frustration which rebound on the infant in the form of terrifying persecutory fantasies of being attacked by the breast itself. Klein's conceptual infant swings in and out of mental or psychic states that she calls 'sadistic', full of envious rage and aggressive raids on the maternal body, in an attempt to manage the treacherous initial experiences of psychical and physical survival. Where Freud saw the drive as a mental representation of instinctual wishes or urges, Klein moves us closer to a more thing-like internal world permeated less with representations and more with dynamic aggressive phantasies of biting, hacking at, and tearing the mother and her breasts into bits, and attempts to destroy her body and everything it might, in phantasy, contain (1998, 308). Libido, of you like, gives way to aggression in Klein's thinking, so that the defences themselves are violent in their redoubling on the infant in the form of persecutory anxiety – splitting the world and the self into good and bad to keep them separate; experiences of self and objects as powerless or omnipotent with nothing in between; greed for good things which are swallowed up but constantly vulnerable to contamination by the bad; projection of unacceptable parts of the self into the other whom one then tries to control. One's own greed and aggressiveness, in other words, becomes itself threatening in Klein's account of the inner world of infants, and these experiences, along with the maternal object that evokes them, have to be split off from conscious thought. Coupled with this are feelings of relief from these painful states of 'hunger, hate, tension and fear' (Klein 1998, 307) through a temporary feeling of security that comes with gratification of both our early self-preservative needs, and what Klein calls 'sensual desires' (307). These 'good' experiences form the basis for what we could think of as love. It is only as the infant moves towards a tolerance of knowing that good and bad 'things', and experiences, are bound up in the same person (that is, both (m)other and self) that guilt arises as an awareness that we have tried to destroy what we also love. Whilst this can overwhelm the infant with depressive anxiety that also needs to be warded off, there is a chance that this guilt can be borne and that a temporary state of ambivalence can be achieved that includes the desire to make good the damage done. Care and nurturance emerges, in other words, out of the capacity to tolerate the proximity of love and hate towards the mother, not the other way around. To use the term maternal to simply signify care, nurturance and dependency effectively splits off this whole dynamic psychic terrain.

I argue that the 'postmaternal', then, could be used to raise wider psychosocial issues than those encapsulated by the unmothering of society, if unmothering is predominantly thought about as the public repudiation of nurturance, care and dependency. Perhaps postmaternal thinking, as a psychosocial phenomena, is a way of signalling the proximity of love and hate towards maternal figures that continues to inhabit and animate life 'post' our early experiences of being mothered, and itself forms part of our mothering practices and attitudes towards our children, and towards 'the mother' as a public figuration? If we read the postmaternal through the anecdote above, perhaps we are always dealing with a precarious psychic attachment to motherhood itself, played out at both individual and collective levels, suggesting that we constantly inhabit maternal and postmaternal subject positions simultaneously, as ambivalence is achieved, breaks down, and has to be shorn up again. Or maybe we are never really postmaternal, whether or not we have borne and raised children, in all the multiple ways that we might bear and raise children, and with all the multiple singularities in the call to a 'we', who may be implicated in this form of relational labour.

What comes after the maternal?

These questions about what might work against life or generativity within the very experience of reproduction for both mothers and those whom they mother, suggests we may also need to ask what kind of labour the term 'post' does, in relation to the maternal, that may alert us to the particular temporalities of motherhood. Motherhood, from one perspective, appears to involve a kind of retroactive gathering up of maternal experience, in all its ambivalence, in the name of a futurity that is not one's own. Perhaps more precisely, however, motherhood seems to offer a form of living in the elongated suspended time of staying alongside another's erratic, unprincipled and unpredictable growth and change whilst managing one's own experiences of love and hate as they veer in and out of relation to one another.

The function of the prefix 'post' has been much discussed in relation to other attempts to temporalise critical frameworks in the sense of a gesture towards moving past, or transcending some earlier 'exclusivity of insight', (Appiah 1991, 342) as well as a refusal or struggle to transcend traumatic, yet resistant aspects of cultural and critical formations: postfeminism, postmodernism, poststructuralism, postcolonialism, posthumanism, posttheory, to name a few (Cohen, Colebrook, and Hillis Miller 2012). In the early 1990s Kwame Anthony Appiah described postmodernism, for instance, as an attempt at retheorising the multiple differences that reflect the underlying dynamic culture of modernity, in order, as he put it, 'to clear oneself a space', a space for critical thinking and reflection about what gets sidelined, requisitioned, commodified and silenced in dominant discourses and practices of an era. He saw the 'post' in postcolonialism, especially in its literary forms, as signalling both the refusal and impossibility of clearing that space in any simple way, the 'post' signifying a desire to move beyond and a simultaneous acknowledgement of how the past makes us who we are and cannot be easily transcended (Appiah 1991, 346). One of the lessons of the postcolony, he claims, is that we are all already contaminated by one another, both temporally and spatially, making the distinction between colonialism and postcolonialism unstable.

Similarly, Peter Osborne, in his key book, *The Politics of Time* (2011), worked through the semantic and conceptual difficulties of speaking about modernity and postmodernity as distinctive historical periods, highlighting this tension between a desire for transcendence and the inevitability of remaining attached to what came before. Despite 'modernity' specifically signalling a period of 'new time consciousness' that inaugurates a series of breaks or ruptures in the development of societies, he argued, this narrative presumes a homogenous continuum of historical time, 'across which comparative judgements about social development may be made in abstraction from all qualitative temporal differences' (Osborne 2011, 1). 'Modernity', Osborne explained, becomes fixed as a discrete historical period within its own temporal scheme, and left stranded in the past. If the 'modern', Osborne argued, in its primary sense, is simply that 'pertaining to the present and recent times', or 'originating in the current age or period', then 'postmodernity' is the name for a 'new' modernity, a kind of conceptual paradox that throws both terms into crisis. A similar tension is produced by the contested term postfeminism, gesturing in one sense to the backlash against second-wave feminism, and in another to a permanent internal critique within feminist discourses, in an attempt, again, to clear that space, to unsettle assumptions about what 'feminism' signifies, and therefore to claim itself as a site for feminist politics.

Stephens, in proposing the term postmaternal, is as much concerned with turning back to prior feminist discourses, and to processes of memory and feminist forgetting, as she is with the deep cultural anxiety around public expressions of what she calls 'maternal values'. Part of her claim is that one of the dominant stories that as feminists we tell ourselves concerns feminist demands for autonomy that have resulted in an illusion of self-sufficiency fuelled by the feminisation of the workplace. This chimes with Angela McRobbie's notion of the 'postfeminist sexual contract' (2007) that invests in the figure of the young woman as a highly educated, genderless, independent and flexible skilled worker, which holds until the point that women become mothers, and it is then that they are left scrabbling around without the support of feminist theories that can help to unpack the contract itself, which often pits women against other women in an attempt to continue to hold together work and care. The postfeminist sexual contract is a form, then, of post-maternal thinking, in Stephens' use of the term, reinforcing narratives that paid work, and giving birth to the 'motherless self' are linked (Stephens 2011, 59). In addition, feminists' retelling of stories about their own mothers reveals, Stephen's claims, a cultural forgetting of the nurturing mother, as in the 'highly contradictory reworkings and responses to the second-wave feminist idea of women "giving birth to themselves"' (2011, 44). Stephens is concerned to track counter-narratives to these stories, listening out for forgotten or repressed versions of the nurturing mother in feminist her-stories that can help to recalibrate the dismissal of nurturance more generally as a force for good.

However, forgetting is a complicated process. Derrida reminds us, in *Archive Fever* (1995) that the feverishness of our desires to work against forgetting through processes of archiving are always being undone at a level that leaves no trace. We do not, in other words, simply forget our nurturing mothers in the practice of compiling feminist archives. Rather, we could say that we destroy the very trail of hatred and aggression that is aroused when we come into proximity with nurturance. We ward off the contamination of nurturance by hatred, through a destructive process of forgetting which itself leaves no trace. I read Stephen's 'post', therefore, less as the enactment of space clearing, and more in the sense of 'against', remaining in the binary relation of remembering and forgetting, rather than an attempt to understand and make visible the workings of the death drive in the feminist archive.

Working in the binary is not at all without value. The postmaternal thinking that Stephens seeks to confront is an amplification of old cultural ambivalences about nurture, care and dependency that *do* coalesce around the social representation of the mother, a form of thinking that works against 'maternal thinking', as Sara Ruddick first described it in *Maternal Thinking: Towards a Politics of Peace* (1989). In that founding text for maternal studies, Ruddick argued that maternal labour is a specific form of thinking, available to men and women equally, that can foster the growth, preservation, and socialisation of a child. The conjunction of 'maternity' with 'thinking' was, at the time, a deliberate move within the discipline of philosophy to disaggregate the insistence that thinking belonged to a masculine realm, and domestic labour proceeded from some instinctual impulse, somehow outside of the workings of the intellect. Ruddick drew attention to the judgments, metaphysical attitudes and values that mothers affirm, as the central practice of child raising. In replacing 'labour' for 'thinking' Ruddick was responding to a strain in Simone de Beauvoir's writing, in which reproductive labour remains immanent, and the mundane and monotonous labour of turning infants into human beings is characterised as meaningless biology (Beauvoir 1948). Ruddick's intervention was to therefore transform an earlier feminist rendition of motherhood and domestic labour as non-productive and unable to accrue value. By articulating the values themselves that are necessary for maternal practice to develop, she reaffirmed maternity whilst skirting the issue of essentialism. Maternity is not labour, but a discipline, a collective practice that develops in response to certain demands, and which is shaped by interests in preserving, reproducing, directing and understanding individual and group life. Maternity, for Ruddick, was only ever a social practice, available to men and women, and offered to a range of 'others' whom may or may not be our biological children. However, due to what she saw as the ongoing conditions of patriarchy that skew women's relation to power and powerlessness, the development of maternal thinking in women remains particularly nuanced. Ruddick therefore located her own thinking as part of a shared feminist project to construct an image of maternal power that worked against the tendency for motherhood to be sentimentalised and devalued.

Stephens draws heavily on Ruddick for her account of a maternal thinking that stands against the 'postmaternal thinking' she identifies as growing out of the aggressive individualism of the 'new capitalism' (Stephens 2011, x). She is concerned with the figuration of mothering, and its dereliction in public life, as a way of speaking about dependency, vulnerability and the interconnectedness of lives more generally. The argument is partly underpinned by Fraser and Gordon's (1994) early genealogy published in *Signs* that charted the historical shift in discourses of dependency in the European pre- and post-industrial world and its impact on the then contemporary U.S. discourses of welfare dependency.[3] Using this genealogy Stephens shows how a social commitment to the ethics of care is historically and culturally bound, and is therefore open to political change. At the heart of postmaternal thinking, then, is the idea that under neoliberal conditions no form of dependency is immune from being experienced as 'disgraceful and aberrant'. The maternal in a postmaternal regime is a failure of subjectivity. If self-sufficiency is paraded as moral virtue, and being dependent, or caring for someone who is dependent, is widely understood as infantilising, this, she argues, will produce pervasive cultural anxieties about mothering.

However, if the 'maternal' in the postmaternal only signifies care, nurturance and the management of states of dependency, then despite the importance of the forms of remembering that Stephens calls for, we perform our own kind of forgetting of the long history in maternal studies that traces the relations between love and hate as they play out in relation to mothers, and within experiences of mothering. I'm referring here to a deep strand of 'maternal thinking', that includes de Beauvoir's own complex and ambivalent accounts of mothering in *The Second Sex* ([1949] 1997), Rich's (1976) work of making visible the impossible paradoxes of holding together contradictory feelings towards children under conditions of patriarchy, through to the work of Parker (1995), who draws out an account of mothering that focuses less on Klein's description of infantile experiences of love and hatred towards early part-objects, and more on mothers' own psychic development as mothers, that entails managing intense, and at times unmanageable ambivalence towards their children. This work was influential for a whole generation of feminist scholarship – literary, sociological, psychological – that took up maternal ambivalence as a crucial way to de-idealise motherhood, and drew attention to the anxieties and aggressions that it mobilises. This focus on ambivalence has found its way into the public sphere through the literary output of authors such as Rachel Cusk, the graphic novels of Alison Bechdel, and through the work of numerous visual artists who have been working at the interface of motherhood and creative practice in the last two decades (see e.g. Bechdel 2012; Cusk 2007; Liss 2013).

The tension between maternal and postmaternal thinking, then, revolves around how we understand 'care'. The philosopher Adrianna Caverero talks of the 'inclined self' and 'maternal inclination' as a kind of leaning out of the self, towards the other, in a relation of nonreciprocal dependency (Cavarero 2010, 195). Using the mother–child relation as a model, she understands care as a dilemma provoked by the utterly dependent other, in which the 'mother' chooses to give or receive care. We have seen how this choosing, from a Kleinian perspective, has, in part, its antecedents in the ways we have managed our aggression towards our internal objects and their relations, and the resultant guilt and desire to repair what we imagine we have damaged. In developments of Klein's thought, care emerges out of the management not only of the dilemmas of love and hate, but a more basic nameless dread, that in its turn requires containment by another who can react without retaliation to the dread that temporarily comes to reside in them, through a process the psychoanalyst Wilfred Bion (1984) calls 'reverie'. This notion that care has something to do with the shared management of intolerable and destructive states of mind, coupled with our reliance on both the practices and good will of others, describes the contours of a psychosocial reading of the ethics of care. In the philosopher Joan Tronto's early work with Berenice Fisher, she saw care as:

> […] a species activity that includes everything that we do to maintain, continue, and repair our 'world' so that we can live in it as well as possible. That world includes our bodies, our selves, and our environment, all of which we seek to interweave in a complex, life-sustaining web. (Fisher and Tronto 1990, 103)

For Tronto, caring reaches out beyond the limits of the relational self to include forms of action not limited to human action, not exclusively dyadic, but rather a broad spectrum of ongoing, culturally constrained practices and dispositions that have to do with maintaining, continuing or repairing the world. But from a psychosocial perspective, care has to also be understood through its ties to guilt, destructiveness, and a core fear for survival, the survival both of ourselves and of others. Reparation, we could say, is the on-going shared management of these states. By shared, I mean to move away from the idea that we develop the capacity to care only out of a drive for the preservation of the ego, and for our own individual survival. As Butler (2014) has reminded us, in her engagement with Klein, destructiveness in a relational theory is not simply separated from love. Love or care are always already ambivalent, being experienced as distinct from destructiveness at the very point that we can recognise that the two have come together. In other words, if, in what Klein calls the depressive position, we can acknowledge we have in phantasy hated and destroyed what we love and depend on, then we might also be able to recognise that we might want to preserve, repair, and care for that very same thing. Klein writes 'There is … in the unconscious mind a tendency to give [the mother] up, which is counteracted by the urgent desire to keep her forever.' As Butler puts it, individuality is never complete, and dependency never really overcome. It is only in the context of an ungoingly unresolved relation between love and destructiveness that Butler's statement on dependency can be understood:

> […] it is a matter of recognizing that dependency fundamentally defines us: it is something I never quite outgrow, no matter how old and how individuated I may seem. And it isn't that you and I are the same: rather, it is that we invariably lean towards and on each other, and it is impossible to think about either of us without the other. (Butler 2014)

In summary, whilst postmaternal thinking is a helpful way to articulate the dereliction of dependency, and the care it elicits, in the social sphere, mothering is a practice that is always already bound up with the particular psychic outcomes of dependency which include the urgent desire to retain and repudiate its source. Maternal care, from this perspective, is the name for the collective management of hate that emerges at the very point that we can recognise that love and hate can be directed towards the same (maternal) object.

Postwork

What I've described as the 'psychosocial' evokes a non-reduceable relation between psychic and social spheres, one defined by the 'permeability, impingement, resonance, and phantasmatic excess', as Butler puts it, of one sphere on the other (Butler 2015). I'm approaching 'the maternal' as a particularly tender site for these impingements, due to the ways that both psychic and social life emerge in and through relations to maternal practice, as I've described above. My discussion therefore seeks to keep open a question about how the maternal circulates in social form, and how the social forms the maternal takes are invested in, attached to, and transformed in psychic life. It is a discussion that moves between psychoanalysis, and social theories that can help us understand how the organisation of labour, time, care and reproduction have material effects that may congeal in the psychic labour of the mother, and how this psychic labour may in turn reorganise the relation between labour, time, care and reproduction.

I therefore want to make what might appear to be a rather abrupt turn from Klein to a Marxist feminist analysis of social reproduction, through an engagement with Kathi Weeks' argument in *The Problem with Work: Feminism, Marxism, Antiwork Politics and Postwork Imaginaries*, in which 'postwork' emerges as a category around which certain utopian demands that relate to wage, labour and social reproduction can revolve. Weeks is concerned with the now almost total privatisation of employment in countries of the global north, and the general acceptance of waged work as the primary mechanism for income distribution that remains ubiquitous and unchallenged.[4] Although she does not particularly dwell on the details of what the problem of work currently is, we can surmise that she is speaking to the almost total encroachment of time by work in post-Fordist conditions that has been noted by many scholars elsewhere (see e.g. Berardi 2011; Lübbe 2009; Sharma 2014; Southwood 2011; Virilio 1999; Wajcman 2014; Wright 2009). Part of the problem with subsuming time by work is the squeezing out any kind of unfettered time that might include time to be with others, including children, beyond what we can define as the 'labour' of care.

Weeks uses the term 'work' to refer to 'productive cooperation organised around, but not necessarily confined to, the privileged model of waged labour' (Weeks 2011, 14). Wage labour, in her reading, is the central mechanism of capital's production and leads to the privatisation of both work and family life. Taking up Marx's assertion that waged work, for those without other options, is a system of forced labour, waged work becomes naturalised in capitalist conditions, coming to seem necessary and inevitable (7). Instead, waged work, Weeks argues, is a social convention and disciplinary apparatus rather than an economic necessity (8). It produces goods, services, income, capital and disciplined governable social and political subjects. It is also crucially the mechanism through which gender is enforced, performed, and endlessly recreated (9).

Whilst a protestant work ethic continues to ideologically drive our relationships with work in post-industrial contexts, (and western feminism, Weeks argues, has its own tendencies to mystify and moralise about work, producing its own version of the work ethic), Weeks is interested in mining an alternative history, firstly a history of the refusal to work, and then of what she calls a postwork politics. This parallel history to the work ethic could take in nineteenth century working class 'labourist' versions of the work ethic that championed the worth and dignity of waged work (Weeks 2011, 59), through to a history of 'bad subjects' whose class consciousness was articulated through a deliberate avoidance of the 'space, time and demands of wage labour' (79). There were segments of the black working class, for instance, in postwar America, who visibly refused to be good proletarians, seeking meaning and pleasure in the times and spaces of nonwork (Kelley 1994 cited in Weeks 2011, 80). But most importantly Weeks focuses on the wages for housework movement in the early 1970s, a movement that coalesced around a number of Marxist and socialist feminist theory texts published in Italy, the U.K. and the U.S., that insisted that work, whether waged or unwaged domestic work, was not something women should aspire to, but something they should try to escape from, and by example, begin the process of abolishing the capitalist relations between work, wage and social reproduction. Much of Weeks' energies in *The Problem with Work* (2011) are devoted to drawing out some specific implications of this aspect of the demands made by the wages for housework movement, despite distancing herself from their core demand of payment for housework itself. In doing so she argues for the contemporary necessity of a renewed demand for basic income and a demand for shorter hours to counter the work ethic that drives what Cederström and Fleming (2012) have described as 'total work'.

The arguments that circulated in Marxist and Socialist feminist literatures in the period that Weeks is interested in, between 1972 and 1976, tended to either aim at equal access to waged work for women through an acceptance of the lesser value accorded to unwaged domestic labour, or aimed at revaluing unwaged forms of household-based labour including housework and caring work (Sandford 2011). Margaret Benston and Peggy Morton, for instance, framed the argument in terms of women working in the home for capital – either with the family being understood as a production unit for housework and child-rearing, or as an economic unit that maintained and reproduced labour power (Benston and Morton 1980; Cox and Federici 1976). If socially necessary labour time remained invisible, and yet propped up the capacity for male workers to generate waged labour, women remained the invisible class that capitalism exploited and relied on. According to Weeks, both strategies, however, failed to challenge the dominant legitimating discourse of work. Each drew on a version of the work ethic to claim essential dignity and special value of women's waged or unwaged labour.

Instead, the texts Weeks examines, particularly Mariarosa Dalla Costa and Selma James' *The Power of Women and the Subversion of the Community* (1973) and Nicole Cox and Silvia Federici's *Counter-Planning from the Kitchen: Wages for Housework, A Perspective on Capital and the Left* (1976), argued that the problem lay in the ways the ideology of the family compensated for the failures of the living wage. The argument hinged on an analysis of the double-edged mechanism of the wage, that both facilitates accumulation of capital, but also keeps workers focused on fighting for more money, power and less work in order to fulfil their own autonomous needs and desires. This constant tussle over the wage obscures those involved in social reproduction, through pitting worker against capitalist without addressing the mechanism of everyone's oppression – the wage. The refusal of work was therefore as central to the wages for housework project as it was to the better-known autonomist tradition. Counter to its populist reception, Weeks draws out how the naming of domestic labour as work was not meant to valorise it, but was 'the first step towards refusing to do it' (Federici 1980 cited in Weeks 2011, 124). The demand was certainly for money, but for money that was precisely not to be exchanged for labour, either domestic or otherwise. The demand for money was to buy *time* – the time to do things for one's pleasure, especially to choose to be with others, including children; to eat as one pleased; to have sex outside of the confines of the heterosexual matrix; to 'live' beyond waged work and housework. In the words of Cox and Federici: 'For our aim is to be priceless, to price ourselves out of the market, for housework and factory work and office work to be "uneconomic"' (Cox and Federici 1976 cited in Weeks 2011, 132). Crucial to the wages for housework demands was the call for more unconstrained or undetermined time – time for sociality, intimacy and experimentation beyond the constraints of a heterosexist social matrix that was operationalised through the family.

Time and postwork

There is clearly a way in which this now reads as deeply anachronistic in conditions in which it is our very capacities for pleasure beyond work that capital has had to evoke and invade, in order to re-inject 'life' into the 'dead-zone' of work in an attempt to keep labour 'living' (Cederström and Fleming 2012). As Cederström and Fleming have argued (2012, 10), capitalism draws in discourses of the social, the experimental, the aesthetic and the relational to motivate a generation of workers who *already know* that capitalism is fundamentally destructive to both society and nature. Hence the reflexive injunction to enjoy but also to 'rest', to take time off, to 'take care' of the self and the planet, to find a life-work 'balance', to 'spend' time, to find 'quality' in the dead time of perpetual work. 'Life' as many have noted, *is* capital, which squeezes the space of heterogeneity and the capacity to refuse total work.

And yet, as Stephen Wright argues in his essay on 'time without qualities' we desperately need an analysis of 'public time' that moves us away from the individualised injunctions to spend 'quality time', and produces a more collective response to the 'crisis' of the present (Wright 2009). 'Might one not think of public time', he asks 'as carving out breathing spots, intervals, transitory breaches in the very core of collective existence, time slots still unfettered by moral or political discipline?' (Wright 2009, 129). Here seamless time begins to show its cracks. If time now has various capitalised qualities, in other words, then what is a time without qualities, a time that is 'available', 'an undisciplined time, a public time whose ideological and moral density is tolerably low'? (Wright 2009, 130). These intervals would constitute the equivalent to the strange in-between spatial zones in cities – derelict sites, empty parking lots, those bedraggled non-spaces that Ian Sinclair is so fond of tracking on the edge of London (Sinclair 1997). Drawing on Jacques Rancière's insistence that the sphere of democracy is always under construction, an *interval*, that is, between legal and social identity, then that sphere is *temporal,* and the sort of public time Wright refers to as 'without qualities', unqualified and unquantified, is the very condition of the possibility of democracy, of a sharing of public life. In returning to the wages for housework debates, we could say that Weeks gestures, though not explicitly, towards the need to rethink not just how to share out labour but how to share time; an issue, then, of generationality rather than intergenerationality, of lateral as well as vertical relations, and of the propping up of institutions and practices that make such relations viable. Although maternal time can feel relentlessly interrupted, especially for those with small children, and those who mother over elongated periods of their lives, devoid of these illusory breathing spots, Wright is drawing attention to transitory and momentary appearances of time without qualities that is by definition a public time.

From value to 'life'

At the end of *The Problem with Work*, Weeks' argument drives towards the notion of a basic income and a call for shorter working hours. Calls for basic income have circulated since the sixteenth century,[5] and in the contemporary period arguments about uncoupling income from the wage system have been part of national debate since the 1960's in the U.S., and the 1980's in Northern Europe. The idea behind the basic income is that a universal basic payment is made for participation in the production of *value*, above and beyond what wages can measure and reward. Weeks' real innovation, however, which she mentions in the closing pages of the book, and therefore remains an intriguing opening rather than a fully worked through theory, is to rethink the common production of value, and substitute for value the common reproduction of life. The 'life' that Weeks substitutes for 'value' is the life alluded to in the colloquial phrase 'get a life'. She acknowledges that 'life' does not lie outside of biopower, and is neither exterior to work, nor captured by the notion of life that proliferates in vitalist philosophies that emerge from a Spinozist tradition of thought. Rather 'life' refers to the notion of striving for a 'full life' that is 'common to and shared with others without being the same as others' (Weeks 2011, 232). A 'full life' would include, but not be subsumed by reproduction or work. By considering life as a counterpoint to value, she suggests a political project that might frame the antiwork critiques and post-work imaginaries represented by demands for basic income and shorter hours:

> Perhaps more important from the point of view of my argument, the collective effort to get a life can serve as a way both to contest the existing terms of the work society and to struggle to build something new. (Weeks 2011, 233)

Postwork, as an extension of the refusal of work, is then 'a utopianism that replaces socialism as the horizon of revolutionary possibility and speculation'. The call is not for more conventional 'family time', or the time to care and nurture others, but for the denaturalisation of both the 8-hour day, and the privatisation and gendering of reproductive labour. Weeks notes the collective endeavour in getting a life – lives are relational, and cannot be acquired, possessed or held onto at the level of the individual: 'A life [...] always exceeds what we have, and its getting is thus necessarily an incomplete process' (Weeks 2011, 233). Postwork is a speculative horizon that resists closure or appropriation and remains committed to difference, futurity and excess.

The maternal death drive

Although Weeks does not explicitly situate her notion of 'postwork' within contemporary discussions of the problem of time, I think postwork is political to the extent that it suggests we re-think the relations between time, work, reproduction and care. Challenging the infiltration of work into every experience of time, as well as denaturalising the privatisation and gendering of care suggests the possibility of a social sphere in which we can all have a more fluid and shared relation to both work and reproduction, one in which time can be less 'qualified' in Stephen Wright's sense, by the time of labour, thought in both its productive and reproductive modes. However, as Stella Sandford has noted, discussions about social reproduction tend to occlude the specific emotional labour of motherhood that is not subsumed by the more general tasks of domestic work and social reproduction, and have to do with the ways that the product of this labour comes to *matter* to the one labouring, and is no longer a question of 'indifference' that is at the heart of Marx' analysis of labour in *The Grundrisse* (Sandford 2011). After all, mothering does not always feel fluid, transferable, or 'full'. It can leave us feeling drained and empty, angry and depressed, and full of anxiety, in ways that may be difficult to share out. And yet this mattering can mean that we go back for more, whether under paid or unpaid conditions, and may drive the ways we choose to make ourselves available to the 'again and again' that is required to 'get a life'. I am naming the particular repetitions of this return to the 'again and again' of the site of mattering, the 'maternal death drive'. Lives tend to unfurl, in other words, in relation to other lives, and that unfurling requires the time that it takes for love and hate to come to be understood as residing together, in the same other. It is an understanding that constantly breaks down and has to be re-established, repetitively, again and again in the context of maternal care. Both mother and child come back, again and again, to the scene of love and hate. I would agree that we can and should collectivise care; we can and should denaturalise the gendering of that care; and we can and should pay everyone a basic income for their part in that care. However, what we earlier called 'maternal care' is not synonymous with a generic concept of care, but the name for the collective or public management of hate that emerges at the point that we can recognise that love and hate can be directed towards the same (maternal) object. The maternal death drive is then the name for the repetitive time that it takes for the emergence of a desire to repair the damage we have done to the other whom at that moment we realise we also love. It requires that someone will go on attempting to manage their own emotional states in relation to the emotional storm that accompanies 'getting a life'.

It is here that I think the potential in the notion of 'reparation' emerges. Holding onto Weeks' utopian vision is vital if we are to move beyond the ongoing divisions and privatisations of work and reproduction. There should be 'reparation' for the common reproduction of life in the form of the basic income. But in addition, I would augment this vision with a call for the recognition of the time that it takes for the emergence of the capacity for reparation in psychic life, for love and hate to have some proximity to one another in an ongoing motion of veering towards and away from one another that is the permanent reminder of their relation. Roszika Parker has argued for the recognition of holding together our love and hate for our children, and sees this as a developmental achievement for mothers that she thinks of as a maternal depressive position, separate from that established in our own infantile lives, and emerging through the specific experience of mothering (Parker 1995). What I am arguing for here is the recognition of a form of waiting time that is the condition for the establishment of reparation. If we return to the anecdote at the beginning of the article, there is the odd realisation that time has passed that can only be retroactively understood as having been the time of another's unfolding. This time cannot at the time be grasped as 'passing'. It is what allows that ambivalent gesture of the wave – a gesture that is both greeting and leaving. The wave symbolises the capacity for reparation – I have inevitably hurt what I also love, and I can bear it, and now it's time to go, which is also a form of return. The postmaternal, in this reading, is animated by the maternal death drive, the capacity to wait, to bear time.

Conclusion

The 'post' in the postcolonial is an activity of space clearing, as Appiah would have it, an impossible process of clearing a space for critical thinking about what is radically repressed in a particular cluster of discourses and practices. The impossibility is not just a function of the dispositif, but has to do with our spatial and temporal contamination of one another, so that clearing a space itself becomes simultaneously an imperative and a fantasy. I have attempted here the impossible task of clearing a space to think about what else the 'postmaternal' may signify beyond the 'unmothering' of the public sphere. Through an engagement with Klein, the postmaternal emerged as the contamination of love and hate in psychic life that could be seen across the shared field of mother–child relations. Its emergence requires the time that it takes to 'get a life', a repetitive return to the site of emotional contamination, and the mattering of emotional labour. Its outcome is the ambivalent wave, hello, goodbye, a gesture that suspends the movement of coming and going at the very point that the child disappears around the corner of his own childhood. I am, indeed, postmaternal.

Notes

1. Parker (2012) notes that where once paternity was the question and maternity the given, new forms of motherhood that are not tied to a female body are shifting this old certainty.
2. I am thinking here of the contributions of Luce Irigaray, Christine Battersby, Elizabeth Grosz, Adriana Cavarero and Bracha Ettinger.
3. Fraser and Gordon showed how pre-industrial usages of the term in seventeenth-century Europe, for instance, carried no moral opprobrium, given that the majority of men and women in agrarian societies were wage labourers, serfs or slaves, making dependency the norm. What it did carry was a sense of inferiority, an indication of a place in the classed hierarchical ordering of such social groupings around landowners and their subordinates. The dependencies of women and children related more to their place on this social ladder, than on the gender or emotional dependency. It was only with the rise of industrial capital that a splitting of dependency into social, political and economic forms was affected. As dependency no longer referred simply to a social relation, it could also designate, for the first time, an individual character trait, producing a moral and psychological register, that we could say has persisted in contemporary discourses of the 'undeserving poor'. As wage labour became increasingly normative, it was those excluded from wage labour who came to personify dependency – the pauper, the 'colonial native' and 'slave' and the newly invented figure of 'the housewife' (316).
4. Weeks is writing in the U.S. context, and her analysis is largely about work in post-industrial economies in the global north.
5. See www.basicincome.org for a history of the basic income.

Disclosure statement

No potential conflict of interest was reported by the author.

Notes on contributor

Lisa Baraitser is a Reader in Psychosocial Studies at Birkbeck, University of London, UK. She has published widely on motherhood and feminist and psychoanalytic theory, and runs the research network MaMSIE (Mapping Maternal Subjectivities, Identities and Ethics). Her recent work is on the relations between temporality, gender and care.

References

Appiah, Kwame Anthony. 1991. "Is the Post- in Postmodernism the Post- in Postcolonial?" *Critical Inquiry* 17 (2): 336–357.

Badiou, Alain. 2000. "What is love?" In *Sexuation*, edited by Renata Salecl, 263–284. Durham: Duke University Press.

Baraitser, Lisa. 2009a. *Maternal Encounters: The Ethics of Interruption*. London: Routledge.

Baraitser, Lisa. 2009b. "Redundant Groupings and the Ethico-Political Subject: Mothers Who Make Things Public." *Feminist Review* 93: 8–26.

Baraitser, Lisa. 2011. "Maternal Publics: Time, Relationality and the Public Sphere." In *Critical Explorations Through Psychoanalysis*, edited by Ayden Gulerce, 221–240. Basingstoke: Palgrave Macmillan.

Baraitser, Lisa. 2013. "Mush Time." *Families, Relationships, Societies* 2 (1): 149–155.

Baraitser, Lisa. 2014. "Time and Again: Repetition, Maternity and the Non-reproductive." *Studies in the Maternal* 6 (1): 1–7. http://doi.org/10.16995/sim.3.

Beauvoir, Simone de. 1948. *The Ethics of Ambiguity*. Translated by Bernard Frechtman. New York: Citadel Press.

Beauvoir, Simone de. (1949) 1997. *The Second Sex*. Translated by H. M. Parshley. London: Vintage.

Bechdel, Alison. 2012. *Are You My Mother? A Comic Drama*. Boston: Mariner Books.

Bennett, Jane. 2010. *Vibrant Matter: A Political Ecology of Things*. Durham: Duke University Press.

Benston, Margaret, and Peggy Morton. 1980. *The Politics of Housework*. London: Allison and Busby.

Berardi, Franco Bifo. 2011. *After the Future*. Baltimore: AK Press.

Bion, Wilfred. 1984. "A Theory of Thinking." In *Second Thoughts*, edited by Wilfred Bion, 110–119. London: Maresfield Reprints.

Butler, Judith. 2014. "The Death Penalty." *London Review of Books* 36 (14): 31–33.

Butler, Judith. 2015. "Forward: Tracking the Mechanisms of the Psychosocial." In *Psychosocial Imaginaries: Perspectives on Temporality, Subjectivities and Activism*, edited by Stephen Frosh, vi–xii. Basingstoke: Palgrave Macmillan.

Cavarero, Adriane. 2010. "Inclining the Subject: Ethics, Alterity and Natality." In *Theory After 'Theory'*, edited by Jane Elliott and Derek Attridge, 194–204. London: Routledge.

Cederström, Carl, and Peter Fleming. 2012. *Deadman Working*. Hants: Zero Books.

Cohen, Tom, Claire Colebrook, and J. Hillis Miller. eds. 2012. *Theory and the Disappearing Future*. London: Routledge.

Cox, Nicole, and Silvia Federici. 1976. *Counter-Planning from the Kitchen: Wages for Housework: A Perspective on Capital and the Left*. Brooklyn, NY: New York Wages for Housework Committee.

Cusk, Rachel. 2007. *A Life's Work: On Becoming a Mother*. London: Faber and Faber.

Dalla Costa, Mariarosa, and Selma James. 1973. *The Power of Women and the Subversion of the Community*. 2nd ed. Bristol: Falling Wall.

Derrida, Jacques. 1995. *Archive Fever: A Freudian Impression*. Translated by Eric Prenowitz. Chicago: University of Chicago Press.

Edelman, Lee. 2004. *No Future: Queer Theory and the Death Drive*. Durham: Duke.

Federici, Silvia. 1980. "Wages Against Housework." In *The Politics of Housework*, edited by Ellen Malos, 253–261. New York: Allison & Busby.

Fisher, Berenice, and Joan Tronto. 1990. "Toward a Feminist Theory of Caring." In *Circles of Care: Work and Identity in Women's Lives*, edited by Emily Abel and Margaret Nelson, 35–62. Albany: State University of New York Press.

Fraser, Nancy, and Linda Gordon. 1994. "A Genealogy of Dependency: Tracing a Keyword of the U.S. Welfare State." *Signs: Journal of Women in Culture and Society* 19 (2): 309–336.

Harman, Graham. 2007. "On Vicarious Causation." In *Collapse Volume II*, edited by Robin Mackay, 187–221. London: Urbanomic.

Heidegger, Martin. 1962. *Being and Time*. Translated by John Macquarrie and Edward Robinson. Oxford: Blackwell.

Kelley, Robin. 1994. *Race Rebels: Culture, Politics, and the Black Working Class*. New York: Free Press.

Klein, Melanie. 1998. "Love, Guilt and Reparation (1937)." In *Love Guilt and Reparation and Other Works 1921–1945*, 306–343. London: Vintage.

Kraemer, Susan. 1996. "Betwixt the Dark and the Daylight of Maternal Subjectivity: Meditations on the Threshold." *Psychoanalytic Dialogues* 6: 765–791.

Lacan, Jacques. 1992. *The Seminar of Jacques Lacan, Book VII: The Ethics of Psychoanalysis (1959–60)*. Translated by Dennis Porter, edited by Jacques-Alain Miller. New York: Norton.

Levinas, Emmanuel. 1998. *Otherwise Than Being, or, Beyond Essence*. Translated by Alphonso Lingis. Pittsburgh: Duquesne University Press.

Lewis, Gail. 2009. "Birthing Racial Difference: Conversations with My Mother and Others." *Studies in the Maternal* 1 (1): 1–21. http://doi.org/10.16995/sim.112.

Liss, Andrea. 2013. "Maternal Aesthetics: The Surprise of the Real." *Studies in the Maternal* 5 (1): 1. http://doi.org/10.16995/sim.32.

Lübbe, Hermann. 2009. "The Contraction of the Present." In *High Speed Society: Social Acceleration, Power and Modernity*, edited by Hartmut Rosa and William E. Scheuerman, 159–178. University Park, PA: Pennsylvania State University Press.

McRobbie, Angela. 2007. "Top Girls? Young women and the Post-Feminist Sexual Contract." *Cultural Studies* 21 (4–5): 718–737.

O'Rourke, Michael. 2011. "'Girls Welcome!!!' Speculative Realism, Object Oriented Ontology and Queer Theory." In *Speculations II*, edited by Michael Austin, Paul J. Ennis, Fabio Gironi, and Thomas Gokey, 275–312. Brooklyn: Punctum Books.

Osborne, Peter. 2011. *The Politics of Time: Modernity and Avant Garde*. 2nd ed. London: Verso.

Parker, Rozsika. 1995. *Torn in Two: The Experience of Maternal Ambivalence*. London: Virago.

Parker, Andrew. 2012. *The Theorist's Mother*. Durham: Duke.

Rich, Adrienne. 1976. *Of Woman Born: Motherhood as Experience and Institution*. London: Virago.

Ruddick, Sara. 1989. *Maternal Thinking: Towards a Politics of Peace*. London: Women's Press.

Sandford, Stella. 2011. "What Is Maternal Labour?" *Studies in the Maternal* 3 (2): 1–11.

Sharma, Sarah. 2014. *In the Meantime: Temporality and Cultural Politics*. Durham: Duke.

Sinclair, Ian. 1997. *Lights Out for the Territory*. London: Granta.

Southwood, Ivor. 2011. *Non-stop Inertia*. Hants: Zero Books.

Stephens, Julie. 2011. *Confronting Postmaternal Thinking: Feminism, Memory, and Care*. New York: Columbia University Press.

Stone, Alison. 2011. *Feminism, Psychoanalysis, and Maternal Subjectivity*. London: Routledge.

Virilio, Paul. 1999. *Politics of the Very Worst*. Translated by Michael Cavaliere. New York: Semiotext(e).

Wajcman, Judy. 2014. *Pressed for Time: The Acceleration of Life in Digital Capitalism*. Chicago: Chicago University Press.

Weeks, Kathi. 2011. *The Problem with Work: Feminism, Marxism, Antiwork Politics and Postwork Imaginaries*. Durham: Duke.

Wright, Stephen. 2009. "Time Without Qualities: Cracking the Regime of Urgency." In *Public Spheres After Socialism*, edited by Angela Harutyunyun, Kathrin Horschelmann, and Malcolm Miles, 129–132. Bristol: Intellect Books.

The 'Good' Attached Mother: An Analysis of Postmaternal and Postracial Thinking in Birth and Breastfeeding Policy in Neoliberal Britain

Patricia Hamilton

ABSTRACT

In the last 20 years, a new parenting philosophy has garnered increasing attention and popularity. Coined by William Sears in the early 1980s, attachment parenting (AP) proposes that secure attachment between parent and child is necessary for optimal development and therefore 'good' parenting. Simultaneously, neoliberalism, a socio-political context defined by market logic, has emerged as the dominant global trend. In this article, I examine the correspondence between AP, and the broader ideology of intensive mothering it expresses, and the parenting-related policies advanced by the neoliberal state. Specifically, I focus on how birth and breastfeeding policy in Britain aligns with AP, contextualising the emergence of AP and its appearance in contemporary state policy as the result of two features of neoliberalism: postmaternal and post-racial thinking. I draw attention to the experiences of black mothers and, through this lens, reveal the raced, gendered and classed dimensions of 'good' parenting. In my examination of these policies, I argue that postmaternal and postracial thinking have enabled the emergence of AP, an approach that individualises child-rearing and relies upon an uncritical appropriation of the so-called traditional practices of racialised women.

Introduction

Parenting today is defined by a growing list of ever more specific decisions and duties (Edwards and Gillies 2011), often made in the early years of child-rearing. Increasingly individualised, these choices, which include infant feeding options and sleeping positions, have taken on tremendous significance in neoliberal society, a socio-political context defined by market logic (Larner 2000). The significance invested in child-rearing practices is even more immense as these choices are understood as having the potential to shape future societies. A new parenting paradigm, attachment parenting (AP), has emerged to guide child-rearing choices and has grown in influence with the entrenchment of neoliberalism. In this article, I examine the correspondence between AP, and the broader ideology of intensive mothering it expresses, and parenting-related policies advanced by the neoliberal state. This process is illuminated by examining motherhood through the perspective of black women, revealing the raced, gendered and classed dimensions of 'good' parenting that neoliberal ideology seeks to disguise.

Coined in the 1980s by American paediatrician William Sears and his wife, Martha, a registered nurse, AP has attracted an increasing amount of attention across the globe. AP builds on the foundation of attachment theory, developed by psychologists John Bowlby and Mary Ainsworth in the 1950s (Bretherton 1992). While attachment theory's most central tenet is every child's need for 'committed caregiving' from one or a few adults (Bretherton 1992, 770), the Sears' articulation of this notion emphasises particular parenting *techniques* and it is increasingly their vision of attachment that dominates popular culture. In 2012, *Time* magazine ran a cover story on William Sears, featuring an image of AP enthusiast Jamie Lynne Grumet breastfeeding her three-year-old son. The story, provocatively headlined 'Are you mom enough?' generated a great deal of controversy and commentary and thrust AP into the mainstream. In the same year, AP gained a foothold in the United Kingdom with the founding of AP UK and the establishment of a number of Facebook groups by AP followers.

This period in contemporary British history is also marked by successive governments' fortification of the neoliberal project since the election of Margaret Thatcher in 1979 (Hall 2011). More recently, Conservative-led governments have implemented austerity policies since 2010. Initiated partly in response to the 2008 global economic recession, the Conservatives' austerity measures are a tangible demonstration of the global dominance of neoliberal ideology. The austerity program aims to reduce public expenditure, particularly focusing on 'reducing welfare costs and wasteful spending' (HM Treasury 2010, 5) and has disproportionately affected women (Fawcett Society 2012) and people of colour (Khan 2015). This approach to public spending also shapes the government's promotion of 'good' child-rearing practices which, more recently, have focused on the importance of early interventions (Gillies 2012). While the promotion of breastfeeding, for example, predates the Conservative government's tenure, these programs have now taken on a more explicitly individualised and consumerist ethos. For example, in 2013, the Nourishing Start for Health pilot scheme was launched, an initiative to encourage the breastfeeding rates of low-income mothers by rewarding them with shopping vouchers. More recently, former Prime Minister David Cameron announced the expansion of a scheme to offer parenting classes to reinforce his claim that families, rather than the state, 'are the best anti-poverty measure ever invented' (2016).

This article will advance a critique of such policies, focusing on birth and breastfeeding policy in particular, as an indicator of AP's favoured position, and will address the following three questions: how does AP align with the policies promoted by the British neoliberal state? How does the emergence of AP in state policy reflect the claim that neoliberalism relies upon a disavowal of the maternal (Stephens 2011)? Finally, how does the correspondence between AP and policy rest on the dismissal of race and racism? Before exploring these questions, I first address how both postmaternal and postracial thinking have enabled the emergence of AP, an approach that individualises child-rearing and relies upon an uncritical appropriation of the so-called traditional practices of racialised women.[1]

Neoliberal posts: postmaternal thinking and the postracial

In the 20 or so years since 'neoliberalism' emerged as a key conceptual tool to analyse our current globalised socio-economic context (Peck, Theodore, and Brenner 2009), it has generated a great deal of scholarly interest and debate over how best to conceptualise and for some scholars, resist it. Critical scholars in particular have made important contributions to the efforts to critique and resist neoliberalism and indeed, to draw attention to the complexity and incoherence of the concept itself and how it appears in the state, among other institutions (see Bezanson and Luxton 2006; Hall 2011; McRobbie 2013; Spence 2012 for examples). From motherhood studies to political science, feminists and critical race scholars have examined the race, gender and class dimensions of neoliberal ideology and developed sophisticated analyses of how neoliberalism functions *through* race, gender and class while purporting to be beyond them (Duggan 2003).

The central focus in this article is on neoliberalism's (and by extension, postmaternalism and postracialism) appearance in the state, primarily NHS health policy.[2] Often theorised as requiring the shrinking of the state, I follow Loïc Wacquant in his claim that neoliberalism *produces* a new kind of state which performs the necessary functions of circulating and upholding neoliberal values, including individualism, self-governance and the celebration of the market (2012, 74). The neoliberal state monetises welfare and redefines citizenship through the lens of self-sufficiency all the while evading meaningful recognition of the raced, gendered and classed structures that govern society. This article is concerned with two features of neoliberal governance that reveal these structures; the postmaternal and the postracial.

Theorised by Stephens (2011), the postmaternal describes the processes by which practices and policies associated with mothering are disavowed (x). Stephens argues that this disavowal is made possible by the advent of neoliberalism which asserts individualism and self-sufficiency as defining characteristics of good citizenship. Such measures of citizenship place mothers in the precarious position in which their participation in the waged labour force is demanded while their reproductive and care labour is required to perpetuate neoliberal production but is undervalued and essentialised (Vandenbeld Giles 2014). These contradictions manifest themselves in public policy which, reconfigured by neoliberal governmentality, bids 'farewell to maternalism' (Orloff 2006, 231), reducing or limiting the supports previously available to support mothering and cultivating new kinds of maternal subjectivity shaped by neoliberal notions of consumption and choice (Craven 2007).

Such a gendered critique of neoliberalism points out that the devaluing of care has particular consequences for women, broadly increasing their responsibilities in both the private and public sphere and foregrounding economic productivity as a defining feature of good citizenship. By measuring women's citizenship through this lens, their contributions, performing the essential function of social reproduction, are relegated to the private sphere, hidden away from the all-important market (Arat-Koc 2006). This privatisation of maternal responsibility is fertile grounds for the emergence of AP which emphasises individual child-rearing decisions as a solution to the 'social and emotional diseases that plague our society' (Sears and Sears 2001, ix).

Stephens explains the emergence of postmaternal thinking as a consequence of what she calls cultural forgetting. Bolstered by neoliberal investment in the myths of autonomy and self-sufficiency, this cultural forgetting not only enables the myth of the impossible unencumbered self (2011, 7) but also affects the tools we take up to resist postmaternal thinking, demonstrated in the way second-wave feminism is remembered, namely as a movement whose main aim was increasing women's participation in the labour force.

In this article, I draw attention to another kind of neoliberally produced cultural forgetting that occurs alongside and is intertwined with the disavowal of the maternal; the denial of race.

As Lentin and Titley (2011) argue, in our current neoliberal context '[r]ace has been semantically conquered, but it remains deeply ingrained in the political imaginaries, structures and practices of "the West"' (49). This absent presence enables the dismissal of racism as legitimately shaping the experiences of people of colour while simultaneously mobilising race, especially blackness, as a signifier of failed citizenship (Roberts and Mahtani 2010). Although neoliberalism requires imagining racism as a historical problem that has been overcome, race continues to play a significant role in the construction of the 'ideal neoliberal citizen' (Roberts and Mahtani 2010, 249) and in the very organisation of the state (Kapoor 2013).

In our contemporary postracial context, the jettisoning of race as a legitimate framework through which to analyse and address inequality and the reality of people of colour's lives is enacted through appeals to progress and fairness. If racism has been overcome, any attention to the disadvantaged experiences of racialised people is deemed suspect (Kapoor 2013). The disappearance of race is also enabled through the process of culturalisation in which demands that racialised people adopt 'Western values' are framed not as neo-imperial imposition but rather as a polite request for integration: 'it is the cultural norms, values, traditions and lifestyles of outsiders which are now held to be problematic, rather than physiognomy' (Lentin and Titley 2011, 50). The perceived failure of people of colour to meet the standards of neoliberal citizenship is read, then, not as a consequence of entrenched racism but as a result of poor choices. Further, any capacity to organise to resist these persistent but disguised forms of discrimination and oppression is precluded by the closing down of race as a site of shared community and the accusation of racism 'against those who invoke it to point to its historical legacies and to use race for any kind of progressive purpose' (Kapoor 2013, 1035).

Considering the interaction between postmaternal and postracial thinking facilitates an intersectional analysis of motherhood that attends to its gendered and raced dimensions. Developed from black feminist theory, intersectional analysis views oppression as multiple and mutually constitutive (Collins 2000; Crenshaw 1989; Dill and Zambrana 2009). Thus, an examination of motherhood through only a gendered lens would be incomplete and could not account for the experiences of women who live at the intersection of gender and other social locations. Intersectionality calls for attention to the overlapping, interlocking nature of gender, race, class and other social locations that shape both the institution and experience of motherhood. While postmaternal thinking rightfully draws attention to the gendered consequences of the neoliberal restructuring of the welfare state in its focus on the devaluation of maternal care, the concept does not address how race, especially racial difference, is mobilised to justify this restructuring and exacerbates marginalised women's ability to meet the prescripts of 'good' motherhood (Bloch and Taylor 2014). For black mothers in the Global North, this impossibility is marked by the contrast between 'the myth of the primitive or Third World woman' (Johnson 2008, 901) who is a 'naturally' capable attachment parent and their pathologised status in the West. My analysis of the state's alignment with certain principles of AP and the postmaternal and postracial consequences of such alignment brings these two points of cultural forgetting together.

The emergence of AP

AP is a 'child-centric parenting technique in which children's needs are ideally met on the child's schedule rather than that of the parent' (Liss and Erchull 2012, 132). The central tenet of attachment parenting is the promotion of 'secure attachment' (Dear-Healey 2011, 383) between mother and child, facilitated by activities such as natural birth, extended breastfeeding, babywearing and co-sleeping. Despite its name suggesting otherwise, AP is a prescriptive doctrine for women. As Arendell (2000) argues, what we call motherhood, the 'social practices of nurturing and caring for dependent children' (1192), can be performed by anyone but historically has consistently been a task assigned to women. AP, with its nostalgic reference to a past in which infants received biologically beneficial care, relies upon and expands this assignment, emphasising practices that can only be performed by mothers such as birth and breastfeeding. In its emphasis on the importance of building a secure relationship between *mother* and child, attachment parenting 'both assumes and reinforces the traditional gender-based division of labour' (Arendell 2000, 1194) and idealises a parenting relationship in which mothers are 'totally responsive to an infant or child's emotional needs' (Dear-Healey 2011, 392).

Examinations of the phenomenon of AP are few. However, given AP's dependence on the mainstream success of attachment theory,[3] there is much to learn from the thriving body of work that examines and critiques the theory of attachment and maternal deprivation as articulated by Bowlby, Ainsworth and others (especially from a feminist perspective, see Hays 1998 and Contratto 2002 for examples). Scholars have made significant contributions to critiquing how attachment theory has historically and contemporaneously been taken up in ways that perpetuate conservative gender ideology and support neoliberal welfare-cutting policies (Duschinsky, Greco, and Solomon 2015). Despite these and other long-standing critiques of attachment theory (Eyer 1992), 'attachment' and 'bonding' continue to inform the state's thinking about what qualifies as good child-rearing (Allen and Duncan Smith 2008; Field 2010; Lowe, Lee, and Macvarish 2015).

How might this enduring emphasis on attachment be understood by parents? The philosophy of AP provides one translation of attachment theory into practice but there have been few studies of how parents take up the philosophy of AP, especially of how AP's promotion of particular parenting activities might more closely align with the state's neoliberal politics. Of the research on AP that has been carried out, I identify two important gaps. First, there is a dearth of literature in this field focused on the impact of race and other markers of difference. Studies of AP report that the majority of its adherents are white, middle-class women but offer little explanation for these raced and classed realities (Green and Groves 2008; Liss and Erchull 2012). Secondly, few studies have located their analysis of AP in a neoliberal context (exceptions include Bobel 2002; Bueskens 2001; Reich 2014). Without attention to these dimensions, the ways in which AP is utilised by neoliberal states in the promotion of 'good' parenting and the raced, classed and gendered dimensions of this promotion can be overlooked.

My analysis of AP responds to these gaps and interprets AP as one, particularly poignant example of the dominant ideology of intensive mothering (Faircloth 2013), an ideology that defines good parenting as the ability to invest significant levels of physical, emotional and financial resources into child-rearing (Hays 1996). The physical resources AP requires are evident in the philosophy's emphasis on embodied parenting activities; AP promotes 'more touch, less stuff' (Sears and Sears 2001, 12) facilitated through skin-to-skin contact, breastfeeding on demand, babywearing and bed-sharing. AP also requires emotional investment in one's children; parents are expected to submit themselves completely to the needs of their children and develop the capacity to read and respond to their children's cues. Finally, the Sears' advice to take extensive maternity leave and hire domestic help as well as their implicit preference for mothers who do not work outside the home (2001) suggest that access to financial wealth eases the practice of AP. While many AP enthusiasts might be drawn to the practice by its purported rejection of consumerism and elevation of the mother–child relationship as sacred, the existence of a burgeoning AP industry (Phipps 2014) as well as the practice's predominantly middle-class membership suggests otherwise.

Like AP, intensive mothering requires mothers to continue to be the primary caregiver, guided by experts who will advise on best child-rearing practice. For attachment parents, the Sears are the experts whose copious books and exhaustive website can answer every parenting query. The contradiction at the centre of intensive mothering is the insistence that women dedicate copious amounts of energy to raising children while simultaneously remaining committed to their economic productivity. This contradiction is captured by the concept of postmaternal thinking; the elevation of waged work as a signifier of good citizenship requires the evacuation of maternal and caring values from the public arena while concurrently heightening care responsibilities in the private sphere. The notion that children *require* this level of attention and care collides with the expectation that parents ought to engage in paid work to support their offspring.

Thus, AP is 'good' intensive mothering taken to its logical conclusion; AP fulfils the remit of what intensive mothering requires, 'emotionally demanding, financially draining, labor-consuming child-rearing' (Hays 1996, 4), albeit concentrated in the early years and with a particular focus on physical attachment between mother and child. That the women who manage to practice AP are seen as 'ridiculous' or 'extreme' reveals the contradiction Hays identifies; between the expectation that women dedicate themselves completely to 'good' parenting and the neoliberal demand to maintain economic productivity.

These contradictions created by intensive mothering are racialised in two ways. First, the ideology of intensive mothering emerges as a consequence of the neoliberal decimation of state support for child-rearing, a phenomenon largely captured in the adoption of welfare-to-work policies and their particular effects on parents. Such decimation is made possible by drawing on 'racialized anxieties' (Kandaswamy 2008, 707) that position people of colour as outsiders to the nation, undeservedly depleting ever-dwindling resources (Tyler 2010). In the construction of ideal neoliberal citizenship, blackness is associated with 'anti-market behaviors' (Roberts and Mahtani 2010, 249) thus enabling the mobilisation of anti-blackness to garner support for public spending cuts. The discursive construction and cultural deployment of racialised figures such as the 'welfare mother' (Collins 2000) or the 'baby mother' (Reynolds 2005) operate as justification for the enactment of neoliberal policies.

Second, through the elision of race as a reasonable explanation for inequality, women of colour's inability to meet the standards of intensive mothering is framed as a result of their individual failings rather than a consequence of the withdrawal of state support and the ongoing effects of structural, gendered racism. Through reducing its provision of services and material aid, the state not only achieves its aim of a reduced welfare bill but responsibilises those who rely on said services (Gillies 2012) and contributes to the production of parental and particularly maternal subjects for whom accepting greater responsibility for the well-being of their children is an indication of 'good' intensive motherhood. The ideology of intensive mothering thus operates through postmaternal and postracial thinking; it is contingent on both race and class privilege and the withdrawal of state support for all but a few caring activities.

As an example of this ideology, AP adds yet another dimension to this debate in its embrace of 'nature'. AP enthusiasts argue that attachment is achieved through adherence to AP tools, drawn from the philosophy's belief in the fundamental power of 'nature'. As the AP International states, for its adherents, AP involves a return to the 'instinctual behaviors' of our ancestors (2014).

In their belief in the notion that AP is merely the expression of the natural, AP enthusiasts often problematically conflate instinctual desires with the current parenting practices of people in the Global South. From Mongolia to Kenya, racialised women in the Global South are constructed as better mothers because they continue to (naturally) be attuned to their babies' desires, unlike their European and North American counterparts. Aside from the homogenisation of women in the Global South and the absence of critical attention to the legacies and realities of poverty, colonialism and global economic inequity, this perception also puts racialised women in the Global North in a precarious position in that the culture of their 'homeland' should predispose them to AP philosophy and therefore locate them as 'good' mothers. However, the historical and ongoing pathologising of mothers of colour (Collins 2000; Roberts 1997), particularly black mothers, in the Global North forecloses this possibility and overlooks the particularities and complexities of maternal practices.

AP and intensive mothering in policy

In the fourth of their numerous books and parenting manuals on the subject, *The Attachment Parenting Book*, Sears and Sears (2001) identify seven 'tools' essential to the practice of AP: 'birth bonding, breastfeeding, babywearing, bedding close to baby, belief in baby's cry, balance and boundaries and beware of baby trainers' (4). The Sears' emphasis on baby care reflects broader societal investments in the potential transformative significance of the early years of a child's life. They argue that these baby Bs enable the building of a close, life-long bond between parent and child and make frequent reference to the tools' 'biological' grounding. In this section of the article, I will analyse the ways in which two[4] of these tools, birth bonding and breastfeeding, appear in British public policy arguing that the British state's correspondence with AP techniques and more broadly, intensive mothering, reflects the postmaternal and postracial thinking endemic to neoliberal governance.

Like the states that came before it, neoliberal state intervention in women's maternal practices has a long history. Reflecting Wacquant's (2012) conceptualisation of the neoliberal state as a 'space of forces and struggles' (73), recommendations about childbirth, bonding and infant feeding in particular have been the subject of vigorous debate with the state going back and forth about what constitutes 'good' mothering. While the championing of 'natural' birth and breastfeeding that characterises contemporary British policy can be traced back to at least 1970 (Carter 1995) and emerges independently of the rise of

AP, I will focus on the promotion of these activities since 2006, when the National Institute for Health and Care Excellence (NICE) first began issuing public health guidance (Kelly et al. 2010). NICE is a non-departmental public body, first established by the New Labour government in 1999 in an attempt to address the 'postcode lottery' that resulted in patients in different parts of the country receiving unequal treatment. Today, NICE provides guidance and advice to support the National Health Service (NHS) including publishing guidance on the promotion of public health and is thus responsible for promoting breastfeeding, 'natural' or 'normal' birth and close bonding between mother and child.

Birth bonding

The Sears identify the moments after childbirth as playing a crucial role in the establishment of secure attachment, a phrase that echoes the criteria established by attachment theorist Mary Ainsworth. While they include disclaimers to allow for medical necessity and tiredness, they nonetheless describe a number of 'tips', some with clearer class implications than others, to ensure bonding between mother and baby including skin-to-skin contact, the postponement of medical procedures that require separation, breastfeeding, maternity leave and the employment of a cleaner or housekeeper (Sears and Sears 2001, 37). NICE (2014) guidance also emphasises bonding, recommending skin-to-skin contact, delaying separation 'unless these measures are requested by the woman' (73) and encouraging the initiation of breastfeeding within an hour of birth. Further and most significantly for this analysis, NICE's bonding recommendations are couched in broader advice that encourages 'low-risk' women to give birth 'at home or in a midwife-led unit' (2014, 7). According to their evidence, in such settings women are more likely to avoid interventions or 'unnecessary medical routines' (Sears and Sears 2001, 38) that can disrupt the bonding process.

My intention here is not to claim that such guidance is incorrect, both the Sears and NICE describe their recommendations as evidence-based, but rather to analyse how such recommendations correspond with and are framed in ways that reflect neoliberal ideology, particularly postmaternal and postracial thinking. When what is understood as 'best for mothers' aligns with neoliberal rationality, the risks to mothers are manifested in the gradual narrowing of 'appropriate' choices and the withdrawal of structural supports for child-rearing. The first evidence of this neoliberal influence is in NICE's clinical practice director, Mark Baker's summary of the benefits of such a recommendation. Baker is quoted in *The Guardian*: 'Surgical interventions can be very costly, so midwifery-led care is value for money while putting the mother in control and delivering healthy babies' (3 December 2014).

Baker's analysis communicates three points: first, it points to cost-cutting as a primary motivation, revealing the well-established economic bent favoured by neoliberal governance. Second, it suggests that saving money and the promotion of (neoliberal) maternal autonomy and child health are goals with equal value, further revealing the far-reaching intrusion of economics into all avenues of social life. Finally, the attention to maternal autonomy contributes to the celebration of self-governance central to neoliberal citizenship (Bryant et al. 2007). The specific kind of maternal autonomy mothers are intended to embrace is constructed for the purposes of reinforcing neoliberal values and reproducing the same decision making in others. Baker's explanation demonstrates the twin duties performed by the neoliberal state – the cutting of welfare spending is accompanied by an investment in 'health-related technologies, programs, and healthcare and public healthcare arrangements that aim to produce new kinds of citizens' (Polzer and Power 2016, 13), such as the rise of prenatal genetic counselling (Samerski 2009) and the much-discussed shopping-vouchers-for-breastfeeding promotion scheme mentioned earlier. Among other goals, such programs and technologies contribute to an ideal of 'good' motherhood that prioritises a narrowed definition of choice that supports some women and excludes others (Craven 2007).

In this way, responsibility for good health outcomes is shifted to individuals, in this case, individual women, making the right choices while also contributing to the marginalisation of those women unable to fulfil the remit of maternal autonomy and optimal child health, whether through their own 'poor' choices or the realities of increasing racial, classed and gendered inequities (Bloch and Taylor 2014). For the remainder of this section, I will discuss the promotion of this kind of birth as first, the co-optation[5] of feminist health activists' efforts to resist medicalisation especially through the very same language of maternal autonomy and choice, and secondly, as an indication of the productive power of the new public health discourse, both reflecting the neoliberal values I describe above.

'Natural' birth as a response to medicalisation

NICE's identification of maternal autonomy as an important factor in the development of birthing guidance is testimony to the success of feminists and birth activists who, since the 1970s, have criticised the medicalisation of childbirth and called for maternal choice and autonomy. However, as Phipps (2014) points out, the medical community's embrace of 'straightforward births' (NICE 2015) has involved less 'protecting women from the process of medicalization' and more '[the] neoliberalized practice of using "normal birth" as an indicator and target' (Phipps 2014, 107). The neoliberal promotion of 'normal' birth constructs such a birth as advantageous to women as citizens while also contributing to cost-cutting efforts and legitimating a model of 'good' motherhood that celebrates pain and sacrifice (Baker 2010). It also aids in the production of neoliberal maternal autonomy in which mothers are 'empowered' to choose, as long as they choose parenting decisions that fiscally save the state money and ideologically contribute to the circulation of neoliberal values such as self-governance. This new vision of maternal autonomy builds on the arguments made by feminist critiques of medicalisation and reflects the growing 'symbiotic relationship' (McRobbie 2013, 124) between neoliberalism and (liberal) feminism. That the state has embraced the promotion of 'natural' birth reflects not only its tendency to co-opt 'resistant counter-discourses' (Polzer and Power 2016, 14) but also reveals the limits of liberal feminism's very articulation of freedom and the consequences of centring this version of feminism as the defining feature of women's activism (Stephens 2011, 29). Neoliberal maternal autonomy and citizenship gestures towards feminism, channelling women's newfound educational and employment skills into the home where they might professionally manage their families (McRobbie 2013). Measured by performances in key 'signal moments' concentrated in the early years of mothering, this model is only available to certain women as it is intensely individual and effaces gendered and raced realities (Kukla 2008).

The fight for more empowered and autonomous experiences of pregnancy and childbirth rests on a critique of medicalisation. However, like much of mainstream feminist activism, this critique has largely been advanced by and in the interests of white, middle-class women (Brubaker 2007; Johnson 2008). Underpinned by a 'return to nature' narrative, such a critique often involves the simultaneous appropriation and dismissal of women in the Global South, centred in the myth of the Third World Woman (Johnson 2008, 901). This problematic construction not only perpetuates racist narratives about women of colour in both the Global South and the Global North, but also relies on patriarchal interpretations of white women, using women of colour's supposed inferiority to construct white women as civilised, capable mothers. In a postracial context, the mobilisation of 'primitive' cultural practices serves as justification for the withdrawal of adequate funding and support services; if more women are giving birth at home and in standalone midwifery units, the impact of funding crises and personnel shortages is softened. This is particularly true for black women whose alleged 'obstetrical hardiness' (Bridges 2011, 117) has historically led to a lack of adequate care and discriminatory experiences within the health service (Phoenix 1990). That past feminist activism to bring women choice and autonomy has failed to take these experiences into account is evidence of its white, middle-class focus. Black women's status as not quite belonging to the nation and thus further delegitimising their claims on the state result in a particularly racialised disavowal of their maternal care especially given dominant constructions of black mothers as hard workers (Reynolds 1997). Black women's social and economic exclusion is both dismissed and worsened by neoliberal policies and practices which position black women outside the possibilities of 'good' motherhood by failing to acknowledge or address their experiences of racism and sexism. In such a position, both black women's claims on an increasingly punitive welfare state and their capacity for maternal autonomy, shaped by the demands and experiences of white, middle-class feminism, are similarly impossible.

'Natural' birth as essential to public health

By the mid-2000s, the promotion of 'normal' birth was the defining feature of birthing guidance in the UK (Phipps 2014). That 'normal' births are 'cost-effective' (NICE 2014, 197) and have potential long-term health benefits make them an essential part of the new public health model. More than just the prevention of ill health, the contemporary public health model forms part of the neoliberalisation of state policy which identifies good health as an essential government priority and marker of good citizenship (Petersen and Lupton 1996). The prioritising of good health enables the state's entrance into an ever-growing list of different aspects of people's lives and, in this case, uses expert knowledge to promote particular types of birth that have moral implications (Baker 2010).

Contemporary public health discourse defines good health as the 'condition which is least disruptive of production' (Petersen and Lupton 1996, 67). This good health is simultaneously individual and collective as citizens are deemed individually responsible for making 'healthy' choices for the benefit of the wider community. The link between health and good citizenship has particular consequences for women whose good health is directly tied to the reproduction of future citizens (Petersen and Lupton 1996). Pregnant bodies, in particular, are constructed as always already in need of surveillance and possible intervention from medical experts who task women with remaining 'endlessly receptive' (Lee and Jackson 2002, 125) to new advice. Though NICE's guidance is largely directed at NHS healthcare providers, shaping what options they make available to pregnant women before and during labour, it also performs a public health function.

Through this function, NICE guidance produces a certain kind of 'good' motherhood performed by consumer-citizens who will make individualised decisions about healthcare that is best for *their* baby and themselves rather than draw attention to the broader social determinants of the health of children and mothers.[6] The capacity to make (the right) choices is central to this version of 'good' motherhood and thus invokes the neoliberal maternal autonomy described earlier.

Encouraging women to make informed choices about how and where they give birth is a laudable goal. Medical practices that subordinate women in the experience of childbirth reflect broader capitalist, patriarchal ideologies that lead to physical and psychological harm and deny women agency (Rothman 2000). To return choice to women in this arena is a significant victory and is particularly effective when underlined by economic reasoning. However, these choices are not made available in a vacuum. As Crossley points out, the problem with emphasising choice in these circumstances is that choice is governed by the 'irrevocably unequal' social relationships between doctors and patients (Crossley 2007, 559). A woman's choice to have a 'natural' birth is constrained by the doctor's assertion of superior (medical) knowledge and the threat of the potentially fatal consequences of such a choice. Further, that such choices take place in the context of 'limited' budgets and an 'urgent' need to cut costs must be acknowledged. When particular types of birth, especially home births, are conflated with 'good' mothering, the political circumstances that make such advice financially prudent are effaced. Babies' poor outcomes become the result of their mothers' choices rather than a consequence of broader socio-economic realities, thus enabling the withdrawal of state services and programs that might address these structural concerns. Further, drawing a link between a mother's 'economically productive and health-promoting' (Polzer and Power 2016, 16) choices and the health of her baby advances the belief that such a link is definitive, closing off even the possibility of recognising how broader social and economic issues contribute to babies' health and placing additional pressures on women and their care capacities at a socio-economic moment in which caregiving is given little value.

As argued above, my aim is not to dismiss the potential benefit of granting women the opportunity to assert some control over their birthing experiences. Rather, I wish to draw attention to the political context in which such options are made available and the potential dangers they pose to all women, and especially those who are marginalized. The emphasis on more 'choice' for individual users of the NHS has been a particularly effective tool in the neoliberal arsenal, enabling a long-term stealth privatisation strategy towards the NHS by successive governments since the election of Margaret Thatcher in 1979 (Page 2015). Privatisation of the health service disadvantages women (Sexton 2003), both as health workers and as users of the service. Alongside the emphasis on more 'choice' is 'responsibility' in the neoliberal project. Encouraging women to ensure that they have an ideal birth experience for the benefit of bonding is arguably one of the first examples of the transfer of all responsibility for children's optimal development to their mothers. This practice aids in the cultivation of a particular kind of maternal subject, one whose (correct) choices save the state money and enable her to take responsibility for herself and her children, reducing the burden on the state. Limiting choices to those that are fiscally responsible (at least for the state) and cutting services that might otherwise support mothering increasingly undermines the asserted goal of maternal autonomy. In such a context the work of maternal care is easily minimised and usurped by increasingly complex maternal responsibility (Wolf 2011, 67).

Breastfeeding

'Choice' and 'responsibility' are also common themes in British breastfeeding discourse. The World Health Organization (WHO) and the United Nations Children's Emergency Fund's (UNICEF) adoption of the 'breast is best' mantra shapes national responses including the NHS' promotion of breastfeeding since the 2000s (Phipps 2014). Contemporary promotion of breastfeeding is based on evidence that suggests that the practice has far-reaching effects for the health of babies and mothers. The NHS Choices website reports that breastfeeding reduces the rates of infections, diarrhoea, obesity and diabetes in babies and ovarian cancer, postpartum depression and breast cancer in mothers. For both the Sears and the NHS, breastfeeding also plays a crucial role in strengthening the bond between mother and child; both suggest that mothers initiate breastfeeding within an hour of giving birth in order to ensure the beginning of a successful breastfeeding relationship. The Sears (2001) go one step further calling the hormones released during breastfeeding 'attachment hormones' (2001, 53) and arguing that the release of these hormones helps to build the secure attachment AP encourages.

Though there has been growing criticism of the 'breast is best' model (Himmelstein 2014) and even some assertions that the superiority of breastfeeding is overstated (Colen and Ramey 2014; Wolf 2011) my concern here is not with the finer details of the biological benefits of breastfeeding. Nor is it my intention to undermine the potential benefits that might accrue to women and mothers when breastfeeding is recognised as an essential activity that requires support. Instead, my analysis is focused on the justifications used to promote breastfeeding, especially how they coincide with the neoliberalisation of British health policy which, among other effects, leads to the removal of this support for mothers. In particular, I am concerned with the emphasis on cost benefits and breastfeeding's link to 'good' motherhood and how these factors justify the retraction of structural support to the detriment of all mothers, particularly black mothers.

One example of the focus on cost is a report commissioned by UNICEF UK and published in 2012, aptly titled 'Preventing disease and saving resources'. In the foreword, written by Mike Kelly, director of the public health division of NICE, Kelly identifies two challenges facing the NHS: 'the state of public finances and therefore the pressure in real terms on health services funding' and 'the recurring and vexing problem of health inequalities' (2012). Kelly suggests that breastfeeding holds the answer to both these challenges, situating the social problem of austerity and inequity in the bodies of mothers, particularly the 'disadvantaged' who are repeatedly identified as 'at risk' for choosing formula over breast milk. By imbuing the individual act of breastfeeding with this level of significance and emphasising the 'cost savings' (Kelly 2012), NICE and UNICEF UK shift responsibility for easing NHS budget constraints onto the shoulders of mothers thus contributing to the privatisation of child-rearing. This individualised attention also overlooks broader structural realities such as economic inequality, uneven access to healthcare resources, and discrimination in the maternity services that contribute to health inequalities in the first place.

'Deserving' breastfeeders

Nearly all breastfeeding promotion materials recognise a 'socio-economic bias' (Dyson et al. 2006, 18) in the UK's breastfeeding rates. Women with lower than average incomes and fewer school qualifications are among those least likely to initiate and continue breastfeeding until the recommended six months. However, despite this recognition, rather than developing policies that address socio-economic inequality, the state's intense focus on breastfeeding has led to the construction of an idealised version of motherhood that equates breastfeeding with 'good' mothering (Blum 1999). In the climate of 'pressure' on the state's purse, women's capacity to dedicate all energies to the successful rearing of children and be good citizens is measured by this intimate, sometimes painful act. In conjunction with the pressures of intensive mothering, women's failure to breastfeed can be read as a failure to save the state money, an especially dangerous proposition for women already understood as 'undeserving' (Page 2015, 110) such as lone mothers, migrants and racialised women.

For black mothers then, their capacity to feed their infants 'correctly' is a measure not just of 'good' motherhood but also an indication of deservingness; practices that limit black women's use of state resources draw attention away from whether they are and ought to be citizens in the first place. This awkward position may explain why, despite black women's successes[7] in breastfeeding, they continue to be framed as failing breastfeeders, in need of specialised intervention from the state (Ingram et al. 2008). The construction of black motherhood, as a social problem the state needs to solve, contributes to and exacerbates black women's lack of belonging (Phoenix 1990).

Black women's precarious deservingness is couched in broader discourses about British citizenship. Black people's undeserving status was legislatively established by the Thatcher government in 1981. The Nationality Act 'effectively designed citizenship so as to exclude black and Asian populations in the Commonwealth' (Tyler 2010, 63). As Tyler points out, the reaffirming of whiteness as central to ideal British citizenship coincided with Thatcher's neoliberalisation of the British state (2010, 62). In her attempt to articulate a new vision of the state's reduced responsibility to its citizens, Thatcher asserted a particularly racial dimension which reinforced blacks' status as outsiders. Today, Thatcher's neoliberal project is more entrenched than ever, though now articulated through a more 'compassionate' Conservative ideology (Page 2015, 118) that tolerates, for example, lone parents, as long as they 'play by the rules' (129) of economic productivity. Thus low-income mothers are subject to particularly intensive exhortations to breastfeed such as the scheme described above in which their reward for breastfeeding is participation in the 'freedom of the market' (Power 2005, 653).

Nature and work

The 'naturalness' of breastfeeding plays a crucial role in its exalted status. Though the NHS and NICE avoid language that refers to 'nature', it is the logical implication of claims such as the notion that breast milk is 'perfectly designed' for babies (NHS Choices website). The Sears and Sears (2001) are more explicit in their embrace of nature, documenting the various benefits of breastfeeding including serving as a 'natural' form of contraception and stress relief. This emphasis on nature puts all mothers in the precarious position of being understood as 'naturally' capable of appropriately feeding their children but still in need of expert advice and guidance (Apple 1995; Carter 1995; Lee 2014; Murphy 2003). For black mothers, this association with 'nature' evokes historical and ongoing racial oppression that constructs black women as unduly strong and thus responsible for their family and community's problems (Blum 1999; Reynolds 2005, 1), an oppression that is rarely named[8] or addressed in a postracial context.

As Reynolds (1997) argues, black women's 'super strength' is indelibly linked to their capacity to work; and as AP scholars have identified, participation in paid work often represents a potential barrier to breastfeeding (Green and Groves 2008). The struggle to continue breastfeeding once women have returned to work aptly demonstrates the contradiction the concept of intensive mothering identifies as I described earlier; because 'breast is best' women are expected to continue breastfeeding, at least for the first six months of their children's lives and possibly until the age of two, but women also ought to maintain their participation in the paid labour force to ensure they meet the neoliberal criteria of self-sufficiency. For black mothers, the dominance of a 'reductionist discourse on slavery' (Reynolds 1997, 100) has enabled an image of black womanhood fundamentally defined by the capacity for work outside the home (though of course this persists alongside the stereotype of the welfare-dependent black mother). In combination with the undeserving status I outlined above, this can result in black women choosing not to breastfeed (Awoko Higginbottom 2000; Blum 1999) which in turn further compromises their ability to be read as good neoliberal citizens.

This cycle of failed citizenship is not addressed by NHS or NICE policy. Women do not have an explicit legal entitlement to breastfeeding breaks at work, instead employers are 'encouraged' to make such allowances (Maternity Action 2013). The NHS Choices website suggests that employers ought to support breastfeeding because of 'business benefits' such as 'reduced absences' and 'lower recruitment and training costs'. Such encouragement enables individual businesses to 'support' breastfeeding in a manner that least disrupts the overarching goal of economic productivity and puts the onus on mothers to balance work and breastfeeding. Such policies also fail to acknowledge the deleterious effect breastfeeding can have on women's earning potential (Rippeyoung and Noonan 2012), further embodying the intensive mothering contradiction. Through these absences, British health policy individualises mothering and promotes an illusory vision of motherhood within the reach of few women.

When it comes to breastfeeding, the 'choices' are rather limited; breast is the only acceptable option (Andrews and Knaak 2013), and the responsibilities are significant – the power to solve health inequalities and contribute £278 million (Renfrew et al. 2012) to the British economy. That the alleged health benefits of breastfeeding are framed in this way, as reductions to an overtaxed health budget, is a reflection of the widespread acceptance of neoliberal thinking. Women's infant feeding choices are consumer practices and represent consumer-citizens' efforts to take 'greater responsibility' (Page 2015, 145) for not only their own health but for the health of their children and the country's economy. The championing of breastfeeding embodies both the centrality of health in contemporary neoliberal formations of good citizenship and the shift of responsibility for health and well-being from the state to individual mothers. In this way, the state can overlook the continuing effects of racial, classed and gendered structures while simultaneously policing racialised bodies who threaten the survival of the neoliberal state (Kapoor 2013, 1041).

Departures and divergences

The length of time spent breastfeeding represents one point at which AP departs from British public health policy. Though the NHS adheres to the WHO recommendation that children be breastfed into their 'second year and beyond' (NHS Choices website), NICE, UNICEF UK and other British health bodies have concentrated their efforts on improving the rates of breastfeeding in the first six months. Breastfeeding beyond this period tends to generate suspicion and negative attention for mothers (Faircloth 2013) though the Sears and Sears (2001) attempt to remedy this view by emphasising the health benefits of extended breastfeeding (63). The prioritising of extended breastfeeding signals AP's unique and precarious position in contemporary British society; while the belief in the importance of attachment that underpins AP philosophy has largely been endorsed by the state and the wider public (Allen and Duncan Smith 2008; Broer and Pickersgill 2015; Gillies 2012; Lowe, Lee, and Macvarish 2015), there is also apprehension about the 'extreme' (Faircloth 2013) nature of some AP practices. While the NHS never explicitly recommends AP, it is keen to promote skin-to-skin contact, breastfeeding, babywearing and parental self-care and tends to avoid 'baby training' (Sears and Sears 2001, 7), a 'misguided' approach to parenting that requires babies to be 'trained' to fit into adult lives unobtrusively (Sears and Sears 2001, 119). In short, while the techniques associated with AP have been endorsed by the state and global health organisations, the all-encompassing practice of AP itself appears to have had less success. AP's 'extreme' reputation has meant that it is more likely to appear as a subject of ridicule in the media rather than an appropriate and effective form of parenting.

It is precisely this unique position that makes AP worthy of examination. It captures the contradictions and inconsistencies of a neoliberal state that demands mothers' participation in the workforce but withdraws the support many women rely upon to make work outside the home possible. AP's rise in popularity must be read in conversation with the state's endorsement of analogous practices and the increasing tendency to turn towards self-styled parenting 'experts' to inform policy-making (Freeman 2016; Lee 2014). When particular parenting practices are framed as 'choices' that align with neoliberal rationality, the extent to which these choices are made possible or undermined by structural inequality (for example, the building of a birth centre in one area and the cutting of maternity staff in another) is obscured. Further, in its reliance on a nostalgic vision of nature, AP evokes contradictory racialised discourses about 'good' motherhood that homogenize and appropriate women of colour's mothering while also perpetuating a pathologised construction of their motherhood as inferior. AP is but one expression of the convergence of neoliberalism and feminist demands for choice and autonomy; other, more 'structured' forms of child-rearing can also reveal the limits of a marriage between feminism and neoliberalism (Faircloth 2013, 20). The benefits of the state offering women bodily autonomy and celebrating mothers' efforts cannot be ignored. There may be opportunities for women to use these narratives as proof of the need for state support. However, these opportunities are limited by the white, middle-class dominance of childbirth and pro-breastfeeding movements and the co-optation of these movements by neoliberal forces. My intention here is to draw attention to the particular kinds of complementary work performed by both AP and NICE guidance in promoting a vision of good parenting underpinned by certain hegemonic ideas about citizenship and the intersection of race, class and gender.

Conclusion

The vision endorsed by NICE and the Sears combines neoliberal notions of choice and autonomy with conservative constructions of nature and motherhood. Through this combination, parenting practices are measured by their effect on the health budget and wider economy. The argument I raise here is not that women ought to be deprived of birthing and feeding choices; the fight to enable women to exercise choices in these concerns is an important feminist victory especially in how it forces the recognition of women as subjects. However, these victories must be accounted for with attention to the context in which they occur and the particular groups of women they benefit. In this way, it is possible to see how attachment-aligned practices in fact narrow the choices available to women (Craven 2007) and leave little room to organise around demanding better support for child-rearing. This is particularly dangerous for racialised women who, despite being associated with nature, find that their capacity to choose 'well' is already compromised by their marginalised social location.

In a context in which the effects of gendered and racial inequality are disguised as individual failings, AP continues to rely upon an individualist narrative by giving trivial parenting decisions great developmental significance. The construction of AP as a singular, technical solution to the problems wrought by capitalism and patriarchy with little attention to the larger structural issues that govern choice, enables the philosophy to be used to reconcile neoliberalism's central principles of freedom and autonomy with the state's regulatory concern (Murphy 2003), making AP look like freedom while obscuring how the state shapes parenting choices. In its current conceptualisation, attachment parenting placates rather than disrupts neoliberalism and 'resists, but not too much' (Bobel 2008, 121).

Though AP is my focus, it is not the first and will most likely not be the last parenting trend to cohere with neoliberal notions of 'individualised' good parenting. As I've suggested above, the push to promote breastfeeding or 'natural' birth is not unique to AP. Indeed, the tacit promotion of bottle-feeding that began in the early 1900s was couched in a language of national health and maternal civic duty that we might find familiar today (Carter 1995). That there is disjuncture between the appearance of some AP techniques in public policy and the mainstream reception of AP itself reveals the broader project at work; the cultivation of a particular kind of maternal subject who takes full responsibility for her parental choices. Such a subject raises her children on a so-called level playing field free of sexism, racism and class inequities. Thus any demands for material aid are replaced with a focus on individual acts and, most importantly for this article, exhortations to parent more effectively (Gillies 2005).

In this article, I have described how some tenets of AP appear in and are endorsed by British health policy. I argued that these endorsements are shaped by the postmaternal and postracial thinking central to neoliberal ideology; in these policies' emphasis on 'choice' and 'responsibility' they contribute to a self-regulatory model of neoliberal citizenship. Further, this emphasis helps to turn mothering into a private matter that does not require societal support but that the state nevertheless advises while simultaneously constructing an elusive model of motherhood that is increasingly impossible to fulfil, even with access to the racial and economic privileges this model relies upon. Racialised mothers, especially black mothers, are positioned outside the parameters of such a model given their precarious state of belonging. Any attempt to acknowledge or address such a position is thwarted by the notion that such matters as race no longer play a definitive role in people's experiences, if, in fact, they ever did (Kapoor 2013).

Notes

1. See the Sears' (2001) reference to Marcelle Geber's work in Uganda for an example. The use of research in 'traditional' societies is also borne out in attachment theory, see Ainsworth's (1967) *Infancy in Uganda: Infant Care and the Growth of Love*.
2. Though the state is the focus of my article I present my analysis with two important caveats. First, I note that state policy may be carried out by midwives and other healthcare workers in unexpected and sometimes subversive ways, contrary to its purpose (thanks to Robin Hadley for suggesting this point). My intention is not to measure the success of state initiatives but rather their nature. Second, that the state is not the only institution responsible for dispersing these notions of 'good' motherhood (e.g. see Phipps 2014 for a discussion of the role played by the National Childbirth Trust and La Leche League in promoting the particular kinds of maternal practice discussed in this article).
3. While it is clear even in the name of the philosophy that AP builds on the theoretical foundations laid by Bowlby and Ainsworth, the Sears' own description of how they chose the title 'attachment parenting' suggests a rather more strategic approach: 'I realized we needed to change the term to something more positive, so we came up with AP, since the Attachment Theory literature was so well researched and documented' (Sears, Attached at the Heart blog).
4. British public policy tends to adhere to most of the baby Bs with the exception of 'bedding close to baby'. While the phrase is sufficiently vague and capable of capturing a number of sleeping arrangements, the Sears' emphasise bed-sharing as the most appropriate tool to support attachment. NICE guidance discourages bed-sharing but does encourage room-sharing for the first six months of an infant's life. In 2014, NICE reviewed its guidance on co-sleeping and recommended that health workers share 'balanced information' with parents rather than telling them explicitly not to bed-share (Durham University News). A detailed analysis on how this and other AP tools correspond with British policy is beyond the scope of this article.
5. There is a growing body of work examining the confluence of feminism and neoliberalism especially as it contributes to the promotion of a particular kind of 'good' motherhood. See McRobbie (2013) and Phipps (2014) for examples.
6. This is evident even within NICE guidance on caesarean sections. Though the guidance was updated in 2011 to clarify women's right to request a planned caesarean, the recommendations frame such a request as something that needs to be debated to 'ensure the woman has accurate information' about the 'risks and benefits' of caesarean sections. Though my focus in this article is on attachment parenting, I argue that while some parenting choices are valued over the others, much of the work of 'good' parenting ideology is to produce mothers who will accept responsibility for said choices. This is perhaps best demonstrated by the 2016 National Maternity Review that emphasises differences and the need for personalised care.
7. In initiation and duration of breastfeeding but not exclusivity.
8. In the few circumstances in which public discourse does recognise 'racism' it is often characterised as the unfortunate prejudices of rogue individuals rather than a structural concern.

Disclosure statement

No potential conflict of interest was reported by the author.

Funding

This work was supported by the Ontario Trillium Scholarship.

ORCID

Patricia Hamilton http://orcid.org/0000-0003-3040-245X

Notes on contributor

Patricia Hamilton completed her PhD in Women's Studies and Feminist Research at the University of Western Ontario, Canada in 2017. Her PhD thesis examined black mothers' engagements with attachment parenting. Drawing from interviews with black mothers living in Britain and Canada and employing an intersectional feminist theoretical framework, the study explored how black mothers used (and rejected) attachment parenting to assert themselves as good mothers. Her current research interests focus on how race impacts breastfeeding promotion and the intersectional politics of parental leave.

References

Ainsworth, Mary. 1967. *Infancy in Uganda: Infant Care and the Growth of Love*. Baltimore, MA: John Hopkins Press.
Allen, Graham, and Iain Duncan Smith. 2008. *Early Intervention: Good Parents, Great Kids, Better Citizens*. London: Centre for Social Justice and Smith Institute.
Andrews, Therese, and Stephanie Knaak. 2013. "Medicalized Mothering: Experiences with Breastfeeding in Canada and Norway." *The Sociological Review* 61: 88–110. doi:10.1111/1467-954X.12006.
Apple, Rima. 1995. "Constructing Mothers: Scientific Motherhood in the Nineteenth and Twentieth Centuries." *Social History of Medicine* 8 (2): 161–178. doi:10.1093/shm/8.2.161.
Arat-Koc, Sedef. 2006. "Whose Social Reproduction? Transnational Motherhood and Challenges to Feminist Political Economy." In *Social Reproduction: Feminist Political Economy Challenges Neo-Liberalism*, edited by Kate Bezanson and Meg Luxton, 75–92. Montreal: McGill-Queen's University Press.
Arendell, Terry. 2000. "Conceiving and Investigating Motherhood: The Decade's Scholarship." *Journal of Marriage and Family* 62 (4): 1192–1207. doi:10.2307/1566731.
Attachment Parenting International. 2014. "About Us." http://attachmentparenting.org/.
Awoko Higginbottom, Gina M. 2000. "Breast-feeding Experiences of Women of African Heritage in the United Kingdom." *Journal of Transcultural Nursing* 11 (1): 55–63. doi:10.1177/104365960001100109.
Baker, Jen. 2010. "Natural Childbirth is for the Birds." In *Motherhood Philosophy for Everyone – The Birth of Wisdom*, edited by Sheila Lintott, 154–166. Chichester: Wiley-Blackwell.
Bezanson, Kate, and Meg Luxton. 2006. "Introduction: Social Reproduction and Feminist Political Economy." In *Social Reproduction: Feminist Political Economy Challenges Neo-Liberalism*, edited by Kate Bezanson and Meg Luxton, 3–10. Montreal: McGill-Queen's University Press.
Bloch, Katrina, and Tiffany Taylor. 2014. "Welfare Queens and Anchor Babies: A Comparative Study of Stigmatized Mothers in the United States." In *Mothering in the Age of Neoliberalism*, edited by Melinda Vandenbeld Giles, 199–210. Bradford: Demeter Press.
Blum, Linda M. 1999. *At the Breast: Ideologies of Breastfeeding and Motherhood in the Contemporary United States*. Boston, MA: Beacon Press.
Bobel, Chris. 2002. *The Paradox of Natural Mothering*. Philadelphia, PA: Temple University Press.
Bobel, Chris. 2008. "Resisting, But Not Too Much: Interrogating the Paradox of Natural Mothering." In *Mother Knows Best: Talking Back to the "Experts"*, edited by Jessica Nathanson and Laura Camille Tuley, 113–123. Toronto: Demeter Press.
Bretherton, Inge. 1992. "The Origins of Attachment Theory: John Bowlby and Mary Ainsworth." *Developmental Psychology* 28 (5): 759–775. doi:10.1037/0012-1649.28.5.759.

Bridges, Khiara M. 2011. "The 'Primitive Pelvis,' Racial Folklore, and Atavism in Contemporary Forms of Medical Disenfranchisement." Chap. 4 in *Reproducing Race: An Ethnography of Pregnancy as a Site of Racialization*. Berkeley: University of California Press.

Broer, Tineke, and Martyn Pickersgill. 2015. "Targeting Brains, Producing Responsibilities: The Use of Neuroscience within British Social Policy." *Social Science & Medicine* 132: 54–61. doi:10.1016/j.socscimed.2015.03.022.

Brubaker, Sarah Jane. 2007. "Denied, Embracing, and Resisting Medicalization: African American Teen Mothers' Perceptions of Formal Pregnancy and Childbirth Care." *Gender & Society* 21 (4): 528–552. doi:10.1177/0891243207304972.

Bryant, Joanne, Maree Porter, Sally K. Tracy, and Elizabeth A. Sullivan. 2007. "Caesarean Birth: Consumption, Safety, Order, and Good Mothering." *Social Science & Medicine* 65: 1192–1201. doi:10.1016/j.socscimed.2007.05.025.

Bueskens, Petra. 2001. "The Impossibility of 'Natural Parenting' for Modern Mothers: On Social Structure and the Formation of Habit." *Journal of the Association for Research on Mothering* 3 (1): 75–86. https://jarm.journals.yorku.ca/index.php/jarm/article/view/2089/1297.

Cameron, David. 2016. "Prime Minister's Speech on Life Chances." January 11. Accessed 14 April 2016. https://www.gov.uk/government/speeches/prime-ministers-speech-on-life-chances.

Carter, Pam. 1995. *Feminism, Breasts and Breast-Feeding*. London: Macmillan Press.

Colen, Cynthia G., and David M. Ramey. 2014. "Is Breast Truly Best? Estimating the Effects of Breastfeeding on Long-term Child Health and Well-being in the United States Using Sibling Comparisons." *Social Science & Medicine* 109: 55–65. doi:10.1016/j.socscimed.2014.01.027.

Collins, Patricia Hill. 2000. *Black Feminist Thought: Knowledge, Consciousness and the Politics of Empowerment*. New York: Routledge.

Contratto, Susan. 2002. "A Feminist Critique of Attachment Theory and Evolutionary Psychology." In *Rethinking Mental Health and Disorder: Feminist Perspectives*, edited by Mary Ballou and Laura S. Brown, 29–47. New York: The Guilford Press.

Craven, Christa. 2007. "A 'Consumer's Right' to Choose a Midwife: Shifting Meanings for Reproductive Rights under Neoliberalism." *American Anthropologist* 109 (4): 701–712. doi:10.1525/AA.2007.109.4.701.

Crenshaw, Kimberlé. 1989. "Demarginalizing the Intersection of Race and Sex: A Black Feminist Critique of Antidiscrimination Doctrine, Feminist Theory and Antiracist Politics." *University of Chicago Legal Forum* 1989: 139–167. http://chicagounbound.uchicago.edu/uclf/vol1989/iss1/8.

Crossley, Michele. 2007. "Childbirth, Complications and the Illusion of 'Choice': A Case Study." *Feminism & Psychology* 17 (4): 543–563. doi:10.1177/0959353507083103.

Dear-Healey, Sally. 2011. "Attachment Parenting International: Nurturing Generations of Mothers, Children and Families." In *The 21st Century Motherhood Movement: Mothers Speak Out on Why We Need to Change the World and How To Do It*, edited by Andrea O'Reilly, 383–393. Bradford: Demeter Press.

Dill, Bonnie Thorton, and Ruth Enid Zambrana. 2009. *Emerging Intersections: Race, Class, and Gender in Theory, Policy, and Practice*. New Brunswick: Rutgers University Press.

Duggan, Lisa. 2003. *The Twilight of Equality? Neoliberalism, Cultural Politics and the Attack on Democracy*. Boston, MA: Beacon Press.

Duschinsky, Robbie, Monica Greco, and Judith Solomon. 2015. "Wait Up!: Attachment and Sovereign Power." *International Journal of Politics, Culture and Society* 28 (3): 223–242. doi:10.1007/s10767-014-9192-9.

Dyson, Lisa, Mary Renfrew, Alison McFadden, Felicia McCormick, Gill Herbert, and James Thomas. 2006. *Promotion of Breastfeeding Initiation and Duration: Evidence into Practice Briefing*. London: National Institute for Health and Clinical Excellence, July.

Edwards, Rosalind, and Val Gillies. 2011. "Clients or Consumers, Commonplace or Pioneers? Navigating the Contemporary Class Politics of Family, Parenting Skills and Education." *Ethics and Education* 6 (2): 141–154.

Eyer, Diane E. 1992. *Mother-Infant Bonding: A Scientific Fiction*. New Haven, CT: Yale University Press.

Faircloth, Charlotte. 2013. *Militant Lactivism? Attachment Parenting and Intensive Motherhood in the UK and France*. New York: Berghahn Books.

Fawcett Society. 2012. "The Impact of Austerity on Women." March 12. Accessed 15 April 2016. http://www.fawcettsociety.org.uk/the-impact-of-austerity-on-women-19th-march-2012/.

Field, Frank. 2010. *The Foundation Years: Preventing Poor Children Becoming Poor Adults. The Report of the Independent Review on Poverty and Life Chances.* London: Cabinet Office.

Freeman, Hadley. 2016. "Attachment Parenting: The Best Way to Raise a Child – or Maternal Masochism?" *The Guardian*, July 25. https://www.theguardian.com/lifeandstyle/2016/jul/30/attachment-parenting-best-way-raise-child-or-maternal-masochism.

Gillies, Val. 2005. "Raising the 'Meritocracy': Parenting and the Individualization of Social Class." *Sociology* 39 (5): 835–853. doi:10.1177/0038038505058368.

Gillies, Val. 2012. "Personalising Poverty: Parental Determinism and the 'Big Society' Agenda." In *Class Inequality in Austerity Britain: Power, Difference and Suffering*, edited by Will Atkinson, Steven Roberts, and Mike Savage, 90–110. Basingstoke: Palgrave Macmillan UK.

Green, Katherine E., and Melissa M. Groves. 2008. "Attachment Parenting: An Exploration of Demographics and Practices." *Early Child Development and Care* 178 (5): 513–525. doi:10.1080/03004430600851199.

Hall, Stuart. 2011. "The Neoliberal Revolution." *Soundings* 48: 9–28. doi:10.3898/136266211797146828.

Hays, Sharon. 1996. *The Cultural Contradictions of Motherhood.* New Haven, CT: Yale University.

Hays, Sharon. 1998. "The Fallacious Assumptions and Unrealistic Prescriptions of Attachment Theory: A Comment on 'Parents' Socioemotional Investment in Children'." *Journal of Marriage and the Family* 60 (3): 782–790. doi:10.2307/353546.

Himmelstein, Drew. 2014. "It's Time to End the 'Breast is Best' Myth." *Time*, May 15. Accessed 15 April 2016. http://time.com/99746/its-time-to-end-the-breast-is-best-myth/.

HM (Her Majesty's) Treasury. 2010. "Spending Review 2010." Accessed April 15 2016. https://www.gov.uk/government/publications/spending-review-2010.

Ingram, Jenny, Karen Cann, Jennie Peacock, and Barbara Potter. 2008. "Exploring the Barriers to Exclusive Breastfeeding in Black and Minority Ethnic Groups and Young Mothers in the UK." *Maternal & Child Nutrition* 4: 171–180. doi:10.1111/j.1740-8709.2007.00129.x.

Johnson, Candace. 2008. "The Political 'Nature' of Pregnancy and Childbirth." *Canadian Journal of Political Science* 41 (4): 889–913. doi:10.1017/S0008423908081079.

Kandaswamy, Priya. 2008. "State Austerity and the Racial Politics of Same-Sex Marriage in the US." *Sexualities* 11 (6): 706–725. doi:10.1177/1363460708096914.

Kapoor, Nisha. 2013. "The Advancement of Racial Neoliberalism in Britain." *Ethnic and Racial Studies* 36 (6): 1028–1046. doi:10.1080/01419870.2011.629002.

Kelly, Michael. 2012. "Foreword to 'Preventing Disease and Saving Resources: The Potential Contribution of Increasing Breastfeeding Rates in the UK' by Mary J. Renfrew, Subhash Pokhrel, Maria Quigley, Felicia McCormick, Julia Fox-Rushby, Rosemary Dodds, Steven Duffy, Paul Trueman, and Anthony Williams." *UNICEF UK*. Accessed April 15 2016. http://www.unicef.org.uk/BabyFriendly/Resources/General-resources/Preventing-disease-and-saving-resources/.

Kelly, Michael, Antony Morgan, Simon Ellis, Tricia Younger, Jane Huntley, and Catherine Swann. 2010. "Evidence Based Public Health: A Review of the Experience of the National Institute for Health and Clinical Excellence (NICE) of Developing Public Health Guidance in England." *Social Science & Medicine* 71. doi:10.1016/j.socscimed.2010.06.032.

Khan, Omar. 2015. "The 2015 Budget: Effects on Black and Minority Ethnic People." July. Accessed 30 January 2016. http://www.runnymedetrust.org/projects-and-publications/employment-3/budget-2015-impact-on-bme-families.html.

Kukla, Rebecca. 2008. "Measuring Mothering." *International Journal of Feminist Approaches to Bioethics* 1 (1): 67–90. https://muse.jhu.edu/.

Larner, Wendy. 2000. "Neo-liberalism: Policy, Ideology, Governmentality." *Studies in Political Economy* 63: 5–25. http://resolver.scholarsportal.info.proxy1.lib.uwo.ca/resolve/07078552/v63inone/nfp_npig.xml.

Lee, Ellie. 2014. "Experts and Parenting Culture." In *Parenting Culture Studies*, edited by Ellie Lee, Jennie Bristow, Charlotte Faircloth, and Jan Macvarish, 51–75. Basingstoke: Palgrave Macmillan.

Lee, Ellie, and Emily Jackson. 2002. "The Pregnant Body." In *Real Bodies: A Sociological Introduction*, edited by Mary Evans and Ellie Lee, 115–132. Basingstoke: Palgrave.

Lentin, Alana, and Gavan Titley. 2011. *The Crises of Multiculturalism: Racism in a Neoliberal Age*. London: Zed Books.

Liss, Miriam, and Mindy J. Erchull. 2012. "Feminism and Attachment Parenting: Attitudes, Stereotypes and Misconceptions." *Sex Roles* 67: 131–142. doi:10.1007/s11199-012-0173-z.

Lowe, Pam, Ellie Lee, and Jan Macvarish. 2015. "Biologising Parenting: Neuroscience Discourse, English Social and Public Health Policy and Understandings of the Child." *Sociology of Health & Illness* 37 (2): 198–211. doi:10.1111/1467-9566.12223.

Maternity Action. 2013. "Autumn Statement – Cumulative Impact on Cuts on New Mothers." Accessed April 15 2016. http://www.maternityaction.org.uk/wp/2013/11/autumn-statement-cumulative-impact-on-cuts-on-new-mothers/.

McRobbie, Angela. 2013. "Feminism, the Family and the New 'Mediated' Maternalism." *New Formations* 80: 119–137. doi:10.3898/newF.80/81.07.2013.

Murphy, Elizabeth. 2003. "Expertise and Forms of Knowledge in the Government of Families." *The Sociological Review* 51 (4): 433–462. doi:10.1111/j.1467-954X.2003.00430.x.

NICE (National Institute for Health and Care Excellence). 2014. "Intrapartum Care for Healthy Women and Babies." Accessed April 15 2016. https://www.nice.org.uk/guidance/cg190.

NICE (National Institute for Health and Care Excellence). 2015. "More Choice and Fewer Interventions, NICE Sets Out Priorities for Straightforward Births." December 10. Accessed 15 April 2016. https://www.nice.org.uk/news/press-and-media/more-choice-and-fewer-interventions-nice-sets-out-priorities-for-straightforward-births.

Orloff, Ann S. 2006. "From Maternalism to 'Employment for All': State Policies to Promote Women's Employment Across the Affluent Democracies." In *The State After Statism: New State Activities in the Age of Liberalization*, edited by Jonah D. Levy, 230–268. Cambridge, MA: Harvard University Press.

Page, Robert M. 2015. *Clear Blue Water? The Conservative Party and the Welfare State Since 1940*. Bristol: Policy Press.

Peck, Jamie, Nik Theodore, and Neil Brenner. 2009. "Postneoliberalism and its Malcontents." *Antipode* 41 (S1): 94–116. doi:10.1111/j.1467-8330.2009.00718.x.

Petersen, Alan R., and Deborah Lupton. 1996. *The New Public Health: Health and Self in the Age of Risk*. London: Sage.

Phipps, Alison. 2014. *The Politics of the Body: Gender in a Neoliberal and Neoconservative Age*. Cambridge: Polity Press.

Phoenix, Ann. 1990. "Black Women and the Maternity Services." In *The Politics of Maternity Care*, edited by Jo Garcia, Robert Kilpatrick, and Martin Richards, 274–299. Oxford: Clarendon Press.

Polzer, Jessica, and Elaine Power. 2016. "Introduction: The Governance of Health in Neoliberal Societies." In *Neoliberal Governance and Health: Duties, Risks and Vulnerabilities*, edited by Jessica Polzer and Elaine Power, 3–42. Montreal: McGill-Queen's University Press.

Power, Elaine M. 2005. "The Unfreedom of Being Other: Canadian Lone Mothers' Experiences of Poverty and 'Life on the Cheque'." *Sociology* 39 (4): 643–660. doi:10.1177/0038038505056023.

Reich, Jennifer A. 2014. "Neoliberal Mothering and Vaccine Refusal: Imagined Gated Communities and the Privilege of Choice." *Gender & Society* 28 (5): 679–704. doi:10.1177/0891243214532711.

Renfrew, Mary J., Subhash Pokhrel, Maria Quigley, Felicia McCormick, Julia Fox-Rushby, Rosemary Dodds, Steven Duffy, Paul Trueman, and Anthony Williams. 2012. "Preventing Disease and Saving Resources: The Potential Contribution of Increasing Breastfeeding Rates in the UK." *UNICEF UK*. Accessed April 15 2016. http://www.unicef.org.uk/BabyFriendly/Resources/General-resources/Preventing-disease-and-saving-resources/.

Reynolds, Tracey. 1997. "(Mis)representing the Black (Super)woman." In *Black British Feminism: A Reader*, edited by Heidi Safia Mirza, 97–112. London: Routledge.

Reynolds, Tracey. 2005. *Caribbean Mothers: Identity and Experience in the UK*. London: Tufnell Press.

Rippeyoung, Phyllis L. F., and Mary C. Noonan. 2012. "Is Breastfeeding Truly Cost Free? Income Consequences of Breastfeeding for Women." *American Sociological Review* 77 (2): 244–267. doi:10.1177/0003122411435477.

Roberts, Dorothy. 1997. "Unshackling Black Motherhood." *Michigan Law Review* 95 (4): 938–964. http://www.jstor.org/stable/1290050.

Roberts, David J., and Minelle Mahtani. 2010. "Neoliberalizing Race, Racing Neoliberalism: Placing 'Race' in Neoliberal Discourses." *Antipode* 42 (2): 248–257. doi:10.1111/j.1467-8330.2009.00747.x.

Rothman, Barbara Katz. 2000. *Recreating Motherhood*. New Brunswick: Rutgers University Press.

Samerski, Silja. 2009. "Genetic Counseling and the Fiction of Choice: Taught Self- Determination as a New Technique of Social Engineering." *Signs* 34 (4): 735–761. http://www.jstor.org/stable/10.1086/597142

Sears, William, and Martha Sears. 2001. *The Attachment Parenting Book: A Commonsense Guide to Understanding and Nurturing Your Baby*. New York: Little, Brown.

Sexton, Sarah. 2003. "GATS, Privatisation and Health." *The Corner House*, May 11. http://www.thecornerhouse.org.uk/resource/gats-privatisation-and-health.

Spence, Lester K. 2012. "The Neoliberal Turn in Black Politics." *Souls: A Critical Journal of Black Politics, Culture and Society* 14 (3–4): 139–159. doi:10.1080/10999949.2012.763682.

Stephens, Julie. 2011. *Confronting Postmaternal Thinking: Feminism, Memory, and Care*. New York: Columbia University Press.

Tyler, Imogen. 2010. "Designed to Fail: A Biopolitics of British Citizenship." *Citizenship Studies* 14 (1): 61–74. doi:10.1080/13621020903466357.

Vandenbeld Giles, Melinda. 2014. "Introduction: An Alternative Mother-Centred Economic Paradigm." In *Mothering in the Age of Neoliberalism*, edited by Melinda Vandenbeld Giles, 1–30. Bradford: Demeter Press.

Wacquant, Loïc. 2012. "Three Steps to a Historical Anthropology of Actually Existing Neoliberalism." *Social Anthropology* 20 (1): 66–79. doi:10.1111/j.1469- 8676.2011.00189.x.

Wolf, Joan B. 2011. *Is Breast Best? Taking on the Breastfeeding Experts and the New High Stakes of Motherhood*. New York: New York University Press.

A Vision for Postmaternalism: Institutionalising Fathers' Engagement with Care

Junko Yamashita

ABSTRACT
Social policy development under neo-liberal logic glorifies paid work in the market over relationships involving care, nurture and dependency. Under neo-liberal conditions, the social policy framework in a large number of welfare states has moved towards the norm of the adult worker model. The prevalence of this model, which signalled a 'farewell to maternalism', has had the consequence that supporting mothers' care-giving roles are dismissed in state policy-making. Such neo-liberal logic leads to the creation of an apparent cultural anxiety about caregiving and nurturing. Julie Stephens [2011. *Confronting Postmaternal Thinking: Feminism, Memory and Care*. New York: Columbia University Press] calls this 'postmaternal' thinking. Drawing on feminist critiques of neo-liberal developments in social policy, this article provides a divergent and even slightly positive interpretation of postmaternalism that does not abandon care and nurture. This is evident in the recent development of parental leave policies that institutionally encourage men to become involved with caring. I argue that a 'farewell to maternalism' in social policy is therefore not too problematic. Parental leave policy – particularly with institutionalised incentives for men to take up parental leave – is creating a transformative space for men to experience the maternal thinking that confronts the cultural logic of what Stephens conceptualises as postmaternal thinking.

Introduction

The concept of 'postmaternity' has recently been theorised by feminist scholars such as Julie Stephens (2011). It is part of a critique of the changing cultural, economic and political conditions experienced through the influential neo-liberal cultural logic which gives prominence to a rational and autonomous self. As Stephens (2011) argues, under neo-liberal conditions, social policy in a large part of Europe and North America has moved towards the norms of the adult worker model (Lewis and Giullari 2005). In this model, it is assumed that all adults whether male or female, parents or otherwise, should enter the labour market. The roots of this shift are multifaceted and can be traced firstly through the claims of those in the second wave of women's liberation for labour market participation and access to equal work and pay, and secondly in neo-liberal ideals of market individualism, liberal freedom and small government. However, the underpinning premise of neo-liberal logic that envisages all individuals as autonomous selves is only made possible by disregarding the complexity of care responsibilities and ignoring the fact that, inevitably, we all need to be cared for and to varying degrees during different life stages. The prevalence of the adult worker model, which signalled a 'farewell to maternalism' (Orloff 2009), has had the consequence that 'maternalist ideology has long departed from state policy decision making' (Stephens 2011, 20). Stephens (2011) goes on to identify how neo-liberal logic leads to the creation of an apparent cultural anxiety about caregiving, nurturing and human dependency. She calls this 'postmaternal thinking'.

Stephens' perception of postmaternal thinking emerged from understandings of social policy, the discourse surrounding care and the process of cultural forgetting that has accompanied the repudiation of the maternal in Australia and the U.S. This research leads her to revisit Ruddick (1995) on the concept of maternal thinking. Maternal thinking is defined as a type of reasoning created and developed through the daily practice of continuous effort in building sustainable relationships with unpredictable and, as yet, unimagined difference (Ruddick 1995, 134). Stephens' response to the question Ruddick (1995, 194) poses as to 'why the complex modes of thought and action that constitute maternal thinking' have been forgotten or overlooked in social policy and beyond appears in the text *Confronting Postmaternal Thinking: Feminism, Memory and Care*. In this book, it is Stephens' conviction that the way to challenge gender-neutral neo-liberal policies which disregard human dependency and vulnerability is to cast off a feminism based on 'gender neutrality under the guise of equality' and instead 'reinvigorate the strands of feminism that are attuned to gender difference' (Stephens 2011, 137). She argues that the task for feminism is to actively remember maternal thinking as the paradigm for an alternative model of social and political life (142). It is claimed that the intersection between feminism, environmentalism and peace politics can therefore be portrayed as an alternative feminist politics (143).

This article investigates a different interpretation of postmaternalism to that of Stephens', as it is evident in parental leave policy in various countries such as Iceland, Sweden, South Korea and Canada (Québec) that men are being institutionally encouraged to become involved with caring. This policy extends the opportunity for men to engage in maternal practice and to acquire maternal thinking. I argue that a 'farewell to maternalism' is acceptable, because maternalist policy is too problematic. It restricts the opportunity to be engaged with maternal practice and thinking to women alone and excludes men.

The article starts by examining the literature on feminist social policy scholarship which shows a divergent, and perhaps even a slightly positive interpretation of postmaternalism. I adopt the concept of postmaternalism for an investigation of social policies that extend opportunities and obligation for men to become engaged with care. After sharing Stephens' attention to the theoretical and methodological significance that Ruddick (1995) ascribes to her concept of maternal thinking, I examine recent policy development in the area of parental leave. I argue that parental leave policy which includes incentives to encourage fathers to take it up serves the function of institutionalising men's experience of maternal practice. Thus, this aspect of parental leave policy allows us to envisage a postmaternalism that does not abandon care, nature and human dependency.

Welfare states, gender and responsibility for care: feminist social policy scholarship

In this section, I aim to expound Stephens (2011) engagement with the feminist critique of neo-liberal developments in social policy. I re-examine the literature on welfare states' interventions to citizen's engagement with both paid and unpaid care work, as well as the gendered balance between both types of work. By incorporating the significant contributions made by feminist scholars on welfare states and gender, this article aims to discuss a different vision of postmaternalism that is imagined by feminist welfare states scholarship to challenge neo-liberal logic in policy development. I argue that the universal care model proposed by Fraser (1994) is normatively desirable, but suggest that The dual-earner/dual-caregiver model (Gornick and Meyers 2008) is a more pragmatic model which aims to shift the focus of social policy into the domestic sphere and enhance men's participation in caring.

Referring mainly to Orloff's work, Stephens (2011) positively acknowledges the feminist critique of social policy development under neo-liberal influence that glorifies paid work in the market over relationships involving care, nurture and dependency. The policy shifts since the 1990s throughout the developed world, and in particular in English-speaking countries, has held the dominant neo-liberal view that recognition and support should only flow to those who are economically active (Stephens 2011). She argues that the current dominance of 'degendered social policy' which expects all citizens to be paid workers undervalues caregiving, as social rewards are given to paid labour, but not to unpaid caregiving. Eligibility for social security benefit has been crucially connected to the employment status of claimants in the historical development of welfare states, and this welfare–market nexus has been the central feature of the welfare state since its establishment. Despite the fundamental and universal importance of care, the responsibility for providing care and the necessity of receiving care have not been sufficiently recognised and rewarded during the development of welfare states (Yamashita 2014).

Welfare states, which are systems of social provision, distribution and regulation, and the gender relations within them, have been the foci of considerable feminist research. Ungerson (1983), one of the pioneering feminist social policy scholars, addresses the significance of policy analysis in understanding the influence of welfare systems on women's life as follows:

> Of course, research into the impact of ideology on people's lives inevitably leads to questions about how ideology and behaviour interact ... behaviour is subject to such a range of determinants and constraints. But ... the way in which the structure of state benefits and the allocation of state resources actually determines the way people behave, more directly tackles the issues of material effects. (Ungerson 1983, 45)

As Ungerson argues, the arrangement of welfare has a decisive influence in enhancing or reducing gender equality. Social policies recognise and offer institutional support to some models of caring and family organisation while sanctioning others. Feminists have explored how the social and cultural categories of gender come to be understood, constructed and transformed through the institutions, practices and policies of welfare states. Analysis of how welfare states are gendered has stressed the linkages between specific gendered divisions of labour, models of family life and social policy configurations (e.g. Jenson 1997; Leitner 2003; Lewis 1992; Orloff 1996, 2009; Sainsbury 1996). Care work, especially unpaid care work, has been central to many feminist understandings of gender and welfare (e.g. Daly 2002; Daly and Jane 2000; Finch and Groves 1983; Land 1978; Lewis 1992; Pfau-Effinger and Geissler 2005; Ungerson 1983).

It is beyond the scope of this article to fully engage with the respected body of feminist welfare state scholarship. The focus of this article is to expand Stephens' (2011) discussion on the feminist research that questions the prevailing adult worker model under neo-liberal logics of gender-neutrality in the public sphere. I argue that this feminist research proposes different versions of postmaternalism which have the potential to offer alternatives to the kind of postmaternalism that Stephens critiques.

Fraser (1994) puts forward three feminist visions of a post-industrial welfare state; a universal breadwinner model, a caregiver parity model and a universal caregiver model. She argues that welfare systems were in crisis as the male breadwinner model was crumbling. It was then suggested feminists could engage in 'systematic reconstructive thinking about welfare states' (1994, 593) and she asked if a new gender order should replace the family wage thus informing 'an emancipatory vision'. The universal breadwinner model aims to achieve gender equality by promoting female employment and requiring care support services to be designed to 'free' women from the caring responsibilities that create obstacles to women's full engagement with 'paid' work. Fraser (1994) importantly argues that if this model is to succeed, it must redress the widespread lack of valorisation of care work, as well as skills and jobs coded as feminine, and it must remunerate such jobs with breadwinner-level pay.

If the model's success depends on these conditions, the universal breadwinner model is not likely to become 'an emancipatory vision'. This is because it accepts the primacy of the public sphere for individual empowerment, flourishing and identity, and as a primary site for gender equality. It also views caregiving as a 'problem' to be solved through the commodification of care, enabled by increased availability of child and elderly care.

It is thus understood that the adult worker model, which is the dominant and neo-liberal model (Lewis and Giullari 2005; Stephens 2011), is an inevitable and modified version of the universal breadwinner model. None of the welfare states implemented effective policy to redress the undervaluation of care work, skills and jobs coded as feminine. In other words, the adult worker model promoted 'equality' in terms of workforce participation and encouraged women to enter the labour market in steadily increasing proportions, but it did so without valorising and remunerating care and other skills and jobs associated with femininity.

As Lewis and Giullari (2005) point out, there is evidence that policy-making in most European welfare states has been moving towards an adult worker model (or dual adult worker model in their terminology). The model is prevalent throughout the developed world beyond Europe and in countries such as Australia, Canada, the U.S. (Orloff 2006), South Korea and Japan (e.g. Lee and Seung-ho 2014), but in each country there are notable differences in its implementation. For instance, the U.S. approach is to increase women's labour market participation through the market expansion of care services, accompanied by less gender discrimination in the labour market. By contrast, Sweden's approach focuses on public care support for women to enable their participation in the labour market, but which is gender discriminated and segregated (Orloff 2009). In other countries, such as Spain, Italy and Japan, the adult worker model has not been accompanied by the expansion of public child care support services nor the reduction of the gender gap in the labour market. Rather, it has been supported informally by extended family networks or privately financed 'employment' of documented and undocumented migrant workers (Pfau-Effinger and Geissler 2005).

These countries are identified as having 'familialism' in their social policy framework, where caregiving is privatised in the public sphere. According to Esping-Andersen (2009), familialism is a concept where the family assumes the bulk of welfare responsibility towards its family members, in terms of both income distribution and care provision. He argues that familialistic social policy is 'anathema' to family formation (Esping-Andersen 2009). Welfare states that have taken a familialistic approach to the provision of care but still encourage women to participate in the labour market are now witnessing a dramatic decline in fertility rates. This phenomena indicate that the alignment between the neo-liberal logic and familialistic social policy may lead women to have less children, which can be identified as an outcome of postmaternalism.

The second vision of Fraser's (1994) three feminist visions of a post-industrial welfare state is a caregiver parity model which aims to enhance gender equality principally by supporting informal care work. It requires care work to be regarded and remunerated as other paid employment (Fraser 1994). Examples of relevant policy programs are carer/caregiver allowance, parental leave and carer leave. In addition to these measures, there can be exemptions in social security contributions and taxation. If the caregiver parity model is to be successful in promoting gender equality, the allowances must be sufficiently generous and comparable to the equivalent rate of a breadwinner wage. The caregiver parity model problematises income inequality and the lack of recognition for care work; however, it does not view the gendered distribution of labour as problematic. As a result, it often involves little incentive for men to take up care allowances or parental leave. In addition, for both the universal worker/adult worker model and the caregiver parity model, paid employment represents the general norm.

Stephens (2011, 19) emphasises that by perceiving women in the same way as men, neo-liberal policy intersects with feminist demands for freedom and autonomy. This intersection between neo-liberal policy and feminist demands has had a significant cost for women. It could be posited that, even with less neo-liberal influence, support for the universal breadwinner model is an almost inevitable means for feminist promotion of gender equality in welfare state politics. This is because the main foundational functions and aims of the welfare state were to tackle the contingent risks for citizens facing exclusion from the labour market. Therefore, entitlement to social security benefits is based on labour market participation or engagement in paid work. For instance, Esping-Andersen's (1990) welfare regime theory developed and adopted the analytical concept of 'de-commodification' with which the extent to which people could sustain their own living outside of the labour market was measured. In response to Esping-Anderson's theory of the welfare regime, feminist scholars argue that women labour needs to be commodified first in order to be decommodified, so that women can also have as equal an entitlement as that of men to social security programs. As expressed in such a claim, women's participation to the labour market was pursued by feminist scholars as the primary agenda in order to achieve equality of access to welfare state benefits and services.

At the same time though, as Stephens frequently points out, a significant strand of feminism was never built on the assumed equivalence between workforce participation and emancipation (Stephens 2011, 22). Also, feminist scholars not only supported women's participation in the labour market, but also supported men's participation in domestic and unpaid work. Stratigaki's (2004) analysis provides an interesting account of 'the cooptation of gender equality policy' that occurred within the European Union (EU) policy-making process. Stratigaki sheds light on the changes in the meaning of gender equality in EU acts, changes which happened in order to create compatibility with prevailing political and economic priorities in the EU. She reveals a shift in the meaning of the concept of the 'reconciliation of working and family life', as it gradually changed from an objective with feminist potential (sharing care and domestic work between women and men) to a market-oriented objective; 'encouraging flexible forms of employment' for women to manage both paid and unpaid work.

As illustrated by the discussion above, the primacy of paid work is dominant in both the universal breadwinner model/adult worker model and the caregiver parity model. Neither of these models challenges the assumption of an autonomous, independent worker as the model citizen envisaged by neo-liberalism. The ideal universal breadwinner model encompasses the provision of sufficient services for women to fully participate in paid employment on par with men. The caregiver parity model seeks to recast unpaid care work in the mould of paid work. Both models are concerned with the redistribution of what has conventionally been viewed as the domain of men's work, that is, paid employment, and the reconceptualisation of care work and other non-economic activities to resemble paid work. The dominant concern of policies in relation to enhancing gender equality has been to support (sometimes force) women to participate in paid work, or to recognise unpaid care work with the monetary equivalence and value of paid work. However, the remaining gender inequality in the labour market and the 'double shift' women endure in 'reconciling work and family life' indicate that focusing only on increasing women's participation in the labour market cannot achieve gender equality. In order to achieve gender equality, the redistribution of what is considered as primarily women's work, namely care work, is required. According to Fraser (1994, 611), the key to achieving gender justice in a post-industrial welfare state, then, is to 'make women's current life-patterns the norm for everyone'. Her work, however, falls short in considering what policy can institutionally encourage such change in men's behaviour. This article aims to explore this question by examining policy evidence related to parental leave. The next section investigates the vision Fraser (1994) proposes, the universal carer model.

The dual-earner and dual-caregiver model: a different version of postmaternalism

In the universal carer model, all citizens are assumed to be participants in both paid and unpaid work, and employment systems and welfare systems need to be reconstructed in order to support both men and women in carrying out this dual responsibility. She argues that the universal caregiver model would liberate citizenship from its androcentric roots by necessitating many men to become more like most women. The universal caregiver model would dismantle 'the opposition between breadwinning and caregiving' and 'integrate activities that are currently separated from one another, eliminating their gender coding' (Fraser 1994, 611). Kershaw (2006) also points out that the need to reconfigure social institutions to induce far more men to take additional responsibility for caregiving is the principle theme in feminist citizenship research.

The idea that the reorganisation of paid work, unpaid work and welfare requires influencing men's behaviour to encourage them to participate in care and domestic work underpins other scholars' research into gender justice (e.g. Cass 1994; Esping-Andersen 2009; Kershaw 2006; Orloff 2009). For instance, Orloff (2006, 2009) also deems the universal carer model, a theoretically desirable direction, allowing social policy to contribute to the enhancement of gender equality. After examining the prevalence of the adult worker model, which signals a farewell to maternalism, she argues that the universal care model is a utopian idea but the ultimate solution to the problems of reconciling employment, care and women's economic dependence (Orloff 2009).

Yet, the universal caregiver model is concerned with a certain part of care that would never be commodified, and assumes that care would be provided as a non-market activity. It would thus necessitate changing workplaces to accommodate caregiving, and more significantly would call upon income security systems to insure that people can take time to care and have access to care services. In this sense, it is argued that the introduction of a basic income will build a social security system for realising the universal caregiver model (McKay 2007; Rubery 2015; Yamamori 2009). Providing an income to all its members on an individual basis, without means testing or the requirement to be part of the labour market, a basic income offers every citizen access to a guaranteed income, regardless of marital or employment status. Levitas (2013) emphasises that a basic income at an adequate level for a decent existence is the only basis for effective validation of, and adequate recompense for care work, voluntary work and other non-market activities.

Nevertheless, whether a basic income would enhance the recognition of care and unpaid work and encourage the sharing of this type of labour between men and women is a central question for feminist scholars considering the implications of a basic income for gender equality. I have argued that a basic income itself is not sufficient to reduce unequal gender divisions of labour since a basic income does nothing to destabilise this inequality (Yamashita 2014). The universal caregiver model is normatively desirable, as a basic income will, to some extent, untangle the links between welfare and labour and enhance the recognition and valorisation of a wider variety of unpaid activities (Yamashita 2014). It would promote women's economic independence regardless of their labour market participation (Alstott 2004). With all these theoretical potentials, the universal care model supported by basic income legislation can be a powerful proposal for addressing neo-liberal logic that gives prominence to an autonomous self and disregards caregiving and human dependency. There is, however, a shared understanding that a basic income needs to be part of a raft of other measures in the redistribution of care and unpaid work between women and men if the gendered distribution of paid and unpaid work is to be redressed (e.g. Pateman 2004; Robeyns 2008; Yamashita 2014). In addition, the universal carer model supported by Basic Income legislation has not yet been introduced in any welfare state. As Orloff (2009) comments, the universal carer model is the ultimate 'but possibly utopian' solution, and identifying the way forward is not equivalent to meeting the political resources required to undertake the journey.

The model that envisages men and women contributing 'equally' to paid employment and domestic work is also referred to as a dual-earner dual-caregiver model (e.g. Crompton

1999; Gornick and Meyers 2008). The universal carer models and dual earner and dual caregiver models are treated as the same concept (Dearing 2016; Gornick and Meyers 2008), but they are different in their thinking of what gives income security to citizens. As named, the dual-earner and caregiver model envision a social and economic outcome in which men and women engage 'systematically' in both paid work and in unpaid caregiving (Gornick and Meyers 2008). In addition, it also assumes that the state would support both parental and non-parental care for children, providing access to quality care across families with different means (Crompton 1999). Gornick and Meyers (2008, 324) suggest three areas of policy that help parents share 'equally in the costs and benefits of earning and caring': paid family leave granting parents the right to take time off to care for children, regulation of working time enabling parents to reduce and reallocate employment hours for caring, and early childhood education and care, all of which would be publicly subsidised and of a high standard of quality. The dual-earner caregiver model is gaining some policy attention through the implementation of parental leave policies which designates a time period of leave for fathers who engage in caring.

I argue that the dual earner and dual caregiver model is not comparable with the universal carer model as it venerates labour market participation for women and men. Rather, the dual-earner caregiver model combines the adult worker model with the care parity model which aims to regard and remunerate caregiving as equivalent to other paid employment. Thus, this model allies with social policy under the neo-liberal influence that upholds the primacy of labour market participation. Accordingly, there is accumulating evidence of policy implementation that supports a dual-earner caregiver model. The dual-earner caregiver model, then, reflects a key feature of postmaternal thinking.

The dual-earner and caregiver model, however, proposes a different version of postmaternalism in which maternal practice is not limited only to women. This model often encompasses a type of parental leave policy that institutionally encourages men to become engaged with caring and thus to acquire maternal thinking. The proceeding discussion will investigate such policy developments after revisiting Ruddick's concepts of 'maternal thinking', as these highlight the significance of policy which can influence men's involvement with caregiving.

Do men do maternal thinking?

The reorganisation of paid work, unpaid work and welfare requires influencing men's behaviour; care must become an obligation of men's citizenship because the disregard in which most men hold care work is coupled with the added risk of economic insecurity and dependence that many women encounter. In addition to this point, I would argue, care must become an obligation of men's citizenship because men are excluded from engaging in maternal practices, thus missing opportunities to learn maternal thinking. In other words, Ruddick's (1989) concept of 'maternal thinking' offers additional justification for the desirability of men to be engaged with the early stages of caring for children. In this section, a brief discussion of maternal thinking is first offered. I highlight the societal meaning and significance of maternal thinking, as well as the profound importance of both men and women experiencing maternal practice. This sustains the point that the dual-earner and caregiver model/universal carer model is the vision that the welfare state should aim to achieve.

In order to understand the significance of maternal thinking, it is salient to understand how central and complex the question of 'femininity' is in feminist thought.

> That dilemma can be summarised as follows: if there is to be feminism at all, we must rely on a feminine 'voice' and a feminine 'reality' that can be identified as such as correlated with the lives of actual women; and yet at the same time all accounts of the feminine seem to reset the trap of rigid gender identities, deny the real differences between women (white, heterosexual women are repeatedly reminded of this danger by women of colour and by lesbians) and reflect the history of oppression and discrimination rather than an ideal or an ethical positioning to the Other to which we can aspire (Cornell 1999, 3).

In other words, a dilemma always exists as to whether to deny 'femininity' and to strive for a universal existence, or to eschew universality. Maternal thinking does not fall into this dichotomy. It is an attempt to identify the social meaning of mothering, and to universalise what is considered a 'feminine reality'. As Stephens (2011) points out, the theoretical problem with essentialism haunts any discussion of mothering. The primary focus of the second-wave feminists has been one long struggle against essentialism, whether this be biological, cultural or ideological (Stephens 2011, 10). By theorising mothering as a form of 'practice-based reasoning', Ruddick manages to construct the concept without falling into the trap of essentialism.

In her book, *Maternal Thinking; Towards a Politics of Peace*, Ruddick addressed her philosophical interests as follows:

> Or, more daringly, were there alternative ideals of reason that might derive from women's work and experiences, ideals more appropriate to responsibility and love? (Ruddick 1989, 9)

Ruddick went back to study Wittgenstein, Winch, and Habermas and found that 'all thinking arises from and is shaped by the practices in which people engage'. Then she posed a question that had never been properly asked; 'what then is a women's practice?' (Ruddick 1989, 9). Ruddick thus reflected on how mothering had never been considered as a rational activity. She aimed to 'articulate distinct ways of thinking about the world; for example, about control, vulnerability, "nature", storytelling, and attentive love' (Ruddick 1989, 12). By doing so, she revealed alternative ideals of reason different from those associated with impersonal, detached and objective judgment.

According to Ruddick, maternal practice is constituted by love, nurturance and training. Each practice aims to meet the demand for preservation, growth and the social acceptability of the lives of children. Those who commit to maternal practice continuously try to respond to these demands which arise from a child's birth, however, cannot predict the consequence or influence of their own practice to children 'Whatever you do, is somebody going to get hurt? Love may make these questions painful; it does not provide the answer. Mother must *think*' (Ruddick 1989, 23). In such relationships with children, mothers reflect on their practice and think what needs to be done.

> Some mothers struggle to create non-violent ways of living with and among children. They school themselves to renounce violent strategies of control and to resist the violence of others despite provocation, exhaustion, and multiple temptations to assault and passivity. Second – and as part of the struggle towards non-violence – some mothers strive to create welcoming responses to bodily life despite the disturbing wilfulness, difference, frailty and neediness of the vulnerable bodily beings in their charge (Ruddick 1989, xix).

Okano (2012, 213) argues that, by describing the tensions and struggles mothers experience in responding to demands from children, Ruddick resists idealising motherhood but identifies thought emerging between mothers and their children as an 'ideal more appropriate to responsibility and love'. Importantly, it is maternal practice that creates a different way of seeing, knowing and acting. As a form of practice-based reasoning, maternal thinking is not confined only to mothers, but it is an ideal that can be realised to varying degrees by women and men (Stephens 2011). As DiQuinzio (2009, 120) argues, maternal thinking also indicates that 'mothering is an individually and socially significant practice in which both men and women can and should practice'. In this way, it undermines essentialist maternalist claims that all women and only women should be mothers. Women acquire maternal thinking through engaging with maternal practice. Maternal thinking is not ascribed to mothers. This means that men can become 'mothers' through engaging with maternal practice. If Ruddick's concept of maternal thinking as practice-based reasoning and thinking is to be valued as a public form of reflection, the significance of encouraging men to become involved in the practice is apparent.

Maternal practice is historically considered to be part of a woman's role and is deeply embedded in the construction of gender. Moreover, as Fraser (1994) addresses, the construction of breadwinning and caregiving as separate roles, coded masculine and feminine respectively, is a principal undergirding of the current gender order. Thus, it is difficult to imagine that the change of men taking a greater part in maternal practice will occur without institutional arrangements and force. In the next section, I will return to the discussion of social policy scholarship and examine how social policy can best support men in engaging with caring.

Parental leave policy and men's engagement with maternal thinking

The implementation of a 'father's quota' that reserves some portion of leave for each parent has become the 'most popular' gender equality policy (Dearing 2016), especially in the Nordic countries (Gíslason 2007). The trend is also recently observed beyond the Nordic countries, such as the U.K. and South Korea (Kim 2015). For instance in Sweden, parental leave policy development has focused on promoting men's use of leave with the intention of encouraging men to take more responsibility for their children, as well as freeing women's time for participating in the labour market (Almqvist and Duvander 2014; Haas and Philip Hwang 2008). The data which revealed the gender division in parental leave take up, rather than women's economic participation rate, became one of the most cited indicators of gender equality in Sweden (Almqvist and Duvander 2014). Iceland has also made a radical progress in the development of its parental leave policy during the last two decades. The law on parental leave in 2000 provides fathers and mothers with equal rights to three months non-transferable leave, equipping Icelandic fathers with the longest non-transferable period of parental leave in the world (Arnalds, Eydal and Gíslason 2013).

South Korea is another interesting example that implemented 'daddy's month' to encourage fathers to take parental leave in 2015 (revised in 2016). In the case that one parent (usually the mother) takes parental leave first and then the other parent (usually the father) takes parental leave, the allowance for the first three months of leave for the second parent is 100 per cent of prior earnings with a ceiling of KRW1,500,000 (€1152). Its take-up rate has been steadily increasing.

There is a growing body of literature examining whether fathers taking leave influence the division of care between parents. Paternal leave use has been related to later increased father–child engagement and more equal sharing of childcare and domestic work (Almqvist and Duvander 2014; Arnalds, Eydal, and Gíslason 2013; Haas and Philip Hwang 2008; Kotsadam and Finseraas 2011; Rehel 2014). For instance, Haas and Philip Hwang (2008) found that men who took parental leave also reported taking more childcare responsibility and providing more hours of childcare involvement, as well as experiencing higher satisfaction with child contact. Although just taking leave is 'not significant enough a departure from traditional gendered expectations' (Haas and Philip Hwang 2008, 99), the number of days of leave taken had a significant and positive impact on fathers' participation in child care and fathers' relations with children. Similar findings that fathers' leave promotes involvement in childcare and housework is presented based on analysis of Norwegian survey data (Kotsadam and Finseraas 2011) and also based on survey data with Icelandic fathers (Arnalds, Eydal, and Gíslason 2013). Kim (2015) discusses the changes in attitudes to caring and family relationships among fathers who took parental leave in South Korea and argues that parental policy can be the key to institutionally changing men's behaviour. The research so far provides evidence that paternal leave matters in increasing men's sharing of childcare.

The shared interest among these studies is to explore whether social policy can be an instrument for changing the 'traditional' division of labour for childcare that was once strongly supported by the male breadwinner model that modern welfare regimes have all subscribed to varying degrees. To this end, Hook's (2006) extensive study of time user surveys from 20 countries found that the policy context especially affects fathers' unpaid domestic work, childcare and their availability for taking leave. Interestingly, her work also revealed that lengthy parental leave taken by mothers decreases a father's unpaid work time by reinforcing women's role as caregiver during a critical period of change in the division of unpaid domestic labour. Evidence that highlights the importance of state-level policy in facilitating men's experience of taking leave is also provided by Rehel (2014), based on strategic qualitative research on comparing the experience of fathers in three different policy contexts in Montreal, Toronto and Chicago. She argues that when the transition to parenthood is structured for fathers in ways comparable to mothers, fathers come to think about and enact parenting in ways that are similar to mothers (Rehel 2014).

Men's capacity for 'mothering' is also much demonstrated by the existing research (e.g. Doucet 2009; Ranson 2015). For example, in the U.K., there exists an increased recognition of a father's changing roles: in comparison to traditional ideals, the 'new' father is more intimate, more nurturing and seeks an active role in childcare (Dermott and Millar 2015; Featherstone 2009). Based on the analysis of fathers in Canada, the UK, the US and Australia, Ranson (2015) explores the transformative experience of men who do the work more often associated with a mother, namely caring for babies and young children. They became deeply attached to the children in their caring practice, and committed to engaged involvement in family life (Ranson 2015).

In sum, there seems to be sufficient evidence that policy is crucial in motivating men to take parental leave, and that the experience of taking parental leave positively influences a father's relations with his children. The taking of paternal leave also enhances their contribution to sharing child care and domestic labour. Referring to Ruddick (1995), Rehel (2014, 111) addresses this point:

The opportunity to experience the transition to parenthood freed of the demands and constraints of work provides fathers the space to develop a sense of responsibility that is often positioned as a core element of mothering.

Haas and Philip Hwang (2008, 86) go further to point out that it is institutional policy and practice that lead to a lack of opportunity for men to be involved in nurturing activities, as well as cultural discourses that emphasise the importance of maternal care. Kershaw (2006) argues that fathers desire more involvement in caring for their children, but are thwarted due to financial rewards of sticking to traditional gender roles, and by socialised patriarchal attitudes to labour division. It is deemed that men are not participating in unpaid care work, not because they are lazy or 'bad' parents, but because they are reasonable people who are taking advantage of what social policy offers them (Kershaw 2006).

Kershaw (2006) considers policy options under the neo-liberal Canadian context to support the 'universal caregiver model' that Fraser (1994) envisages, and recommends a caregiving analogue to workfare that would use policy more aggressively to influence men's choices between employment and care. His argument supports the state authority to impose citizenry care obligation in order to universalise care responsibility for men. Kershaw (2006, 356) states that the only way to defend against 'the deleterious dynamic', in which 'the failure to oblige all to partake in some caregiving perpetuates added vulnerability for those who do', is for 'welfare contractualism to embrace some care activities as a civic duty that binds men as much as women and that is enforced on a par with emergent employment and job search obligations as well as taxation'. He conceptualises this as *carefair*. As Fraser (1994, 612) pointed out, in this carefair, the key is to develop policies that discourage free-riding of unpaid care. Such policy includes some economic sanctions on those who do not take part in caregiving such as postponed eligibility for a full public pension and the loss of leave benefits.

Parental leave can be considered degendered policy, as it can ignore the materiality of embodied motherhood that is acutely marked for women after they have given birth, as critiqued by Stephens (2011). However, parental leave policy can be constructed in a way to acknowledge embodied motherhood and at the same time encourage men to engage in caring. For instance, Blofield and Martínez Franzoni (2015) suggest a way to distinguish policy that recognises 'embodied motherhood' as well as redressing the gender gap in the involvement with caring, from one that recognises and rewards care as a female responsibility without seeking to reduce the gender gap per se. They categorise the former as maternalist floor policy, and the latter as maternalist policy. Maternalist policies recognise the importance of caregiving but these make it solely or primarily women's responsibility (Blofield and Martínez Franzoni 2015, 47). Such policy is based on maternalism that 'exalts women's capacity to mother and extends to society as a whole the values they attached to that role; care, nurturance, and morality' (Michel 2012). Thus, maternal policies have the effect of constraining maternal practice only to women.

On the other hand, maternalist floor policy acknowledges the role of women in giving birth and breast feeding by providing maternity leave that helps women to recover from giving birth and to establish routines and bonds with the new born[1]. However, 'generous maternity leave beyond this period of time, or a tax incentive or a cash transfer for stay-at-home mothers can be considered maternalist' (Blofield and Martínez Franzoni 2015, 47). As mentioned earlier, maternalist policy decreases fathers' unpaid work time (Hook 2006). Maternalist policy would hinder a society to establish either the universal caregiver model or the universal breadwinner model. Maternalism embedded in a maternalist policy would therefore obstruct the enhancement of gender equality in both paid and unpaid work. For instance, Miura (2014) provides an insightful discussion of how strong maternalism hinders Japanese society in increasing both female labour participation and the fertility rate, and leads women not to form a family.

I would argue that maternalist floor policy is not degendered policy if embodied motherhood is addressed through maternity leave strategies which, for example, in the case of the EU, create a minimum standard for maternal health and welfare. Maternalist floor policy is realised in parental policy in which each parent can take parental leave after the mother takes maternal leave.

Conclusion: parental leave, maternalism and maternal thinking

A remaining question is whether or not the development of a parental leave policy which places incentives for fathers to take up leave is a sign of a 'farewell to maternalism'. Stephens (2011, 41) highlights that far from witnessing the expansion of maternal forms of subjectivity to men and to the wider society, as Ruddick so persuasively advocated, there has been a contraction of the value of care and nurturance in the public sphere. She then refers to Orloff's (2009) statement that maternalism at the policy level has been well and truly dismissed. It seems that even though Stephens (2011) examines the different nature of the concepts of maternalism and maternal thinking, her discussion implies that she considers the 'farewell to maternalism' as almost equivalent to a denial of care and nurture. However, as the preceding discussion reveals, a farewell to maternalism does not directly indicate a contraction of the value of care and nurturance. I would argue that this 'farewell to maternalism' is not the core problem, as maternalism limits the opportunity to get engaged with maternal practice and thinking only to women. In this sense, a farewell to maternalism even offers a positive feminist vision of postmaternalism.

I consider that a careful discussion regarding maternalism and maternal thinking must be required to understand what gender equality policy aims to achieve. I argue that it is the policy discourse surrounding parental leave, in particular, institutionalised incentives for father to take up the leave that creates a space to disseminate opportunities for men to experience maternal practice, which will allow the realisation of maternal thinking. Policy encouraging men's involvement with care is not only aimed at realising gender equality both in the public and domestic sphere, but it aspires to an alternative social formation by supporting men and allowing them to experience maternal practice and thinking. According to Ruddick (1995, 131), a defining task of caregiver's work is to maintain mutually helpful connections with another person whose separateness they create and respect. Thus, caregivers are continuously involved with issues of connection, separation, development, change and the limits of control. As a form of practice-based reasoning, maternal thinking is a type of reasoning developed through the daily practice of continuous effort in building sustainable relationships with 'unpredictable and, as yet, unimagined difference' (Ruddick 1995, 134). Therefore, maternal thinking is a way of respecting and connecting with different and separated others.

At the policy level, the dual earner and dual caregiver model can create a transformative space for men to experience the maternal thinking that confronts the cultural logic of what Stephens conceptualises as postmaternal thinking. Thus, when incentives or sanctions for motivating men to take parental leave are well integrated into parental leave policy, postmaternalism could in fact concede a glimmer of hope.

Note

1. Blofield and Martínez Franzoni (2015) refer to the ILO agreement 183 that defines maternity leave of 14 weeks.

Acknowledgements

I am grateful to Maud Perrier and Maria Fannin, the special issue editors, and two anonymous referees for giving detailed and constructive comments on this manuscript.

Disclosure statement

No potential conflict of interest was reported by the author.

Notes on contributor

Junko Yamashita is Senior Lecturer at the School of Sociology, Politics and International Studies, University of Bristol, UK. Her expertise is in comparative analysis of East Asian and European Social policy, especially in relation to care and gender.

References

Almqvist, Anna-Lena, and Ann-Zofie Duvander. 2014. "Changes in Gender Equality? Swedish Fathers' Parental Leave, Division of Childcare and Housework." *Journal of Family Studies* 20 (1): 19–27.
Alstott, Anne. 2004. *No Exit: What Parents Owe Their Children and What Society Owes Parents*. Oxford: Oxford University Press.
Arnalds, Ásdís A., Guðný Björk Eydal, and Ingólfur V. Gíslason. 2013. "Equal Rights to Paid Parental Leave and Caring Fathers – The Case of Iceland." *Icelandic Review of Politics and Administration* 9 (2): 323–344.
Blofield, Merike, and Juliana Martínez Franzoni. 2015. "Maternalism, Co-responsibility, and Social Equity, a Typology of Work–Family Policies." *Social Politics* 22 (1): 38–59.
Cass, Bettina. 1994. "Citizenship, Work and Welfare: The Dilemma of Australian Women." *Social Politics* 1 (1): 106–124.
Cornell, Drucilla. 1999. *Beyond Accommodation: Ethical Feminism, Deconstruction, and the Law*. Lanham, MD: Rowman & Littlefield.
Crompton, Rosemary, ed. 1999. *Restructuring Gender Relations and Employment: The Decline of the Male Breadwinner*. Oxford: Oxford University Press.
Daly, Mary. 2002. "Care as a Good for Social Policy." *Journal of Social Policy* 31 (2): 251–270.
Daly, Mary, and Jane, Lewis. 2000. "The Concept of Social Care and the Analysis of Contemporary Welfare States." *The British Journal of Sociology* 51 (2): 281–298.

Dearing, Helene. 2016. "Gender Equality in the Division of Work: How to Assess European Leave Policies Regarding their Compliance with an Ideal Leave Model." *Journal of European Social Policy* 26 (3): 234–247.

Dermott, Esther, and Tina Millar. 2015. "More than the Sum of Its Parts? Contemporary Fatherhood Policy, Practice and Discourse." *Families, Relationships and Societies* 4 (2): 185–195.

DiQuinzio, Patrice. 2009. "Mothering Without Norms? Empirical Realities and Normative Conceptions of Mothering." In *Maternal Thinking: Philosophy, Politics, Practice*, edited by Andrea O'Reilly, 104–120. Toronto: Demeter Press.

Doucet, Andrea. 2009. "Dad and Baby in the First Year: Gendered Responsibilities and Embodiment." *Annals of the American Academy of Political and Social Science* 624: 78–98.

Esping-Andersen, Gøsta. 1990. *The Three Worlds of Welfare Capitalism*. Cambridge: Polity Press.

Esping-Andersen, Gøsta. 2009. *Incomplete Revolution: Adapting Welfare States to Women's New Roles*. Cambridge: Polity Press.

Featherstone, Brid. 2009. *Contemporary Fathering: Theory, Policy, and Practice*. Bristol: Policy Press.

Finch, Janet, and Dulcie Groves, eds. 1983. *A Labour of Love: Women, Work and Caring*. London: Routledge and Kegan Paul.

Fraser, Nancy. 1994. "After the Family Wage: Gender Equity and the Welfare State." *Political Theory* 22 (4): 591–618.

Gíslason, Ingólfur V. 2007. *Parental Leave in Iceland. Bringing the Fathers In: Developments in the Wake of New Legislation in 2000*. Akureyri: Jafnréttisstofa.

Gornick, Janet C., and Marcia K. Meyers. 2008. "Creating Gender Egalitarian Societies: An Agenda for Reform." *Politics & Society* 36 (3): 313–349.

Haas, Linda, and C. Philip Hwang. 2008. "The Impact of Taking Parental Leave on Fathers' Participation in Childcare and Relationships with Children: Lessons from Sweden." *Community, Work & Family* 11 (1): 85–104.

Hook, J. L. 2006. "Care in Context: Men's Unpaid Work in 20 Countries, 1965–2003." *American Sociological Review* 71 (4): 639–660.

Jenson, Jane. 1997. "Who Cares? Gender and Welfare Regimes." *Social Politics* 4 (2): 182–187.

Kershaw, Paul. 2006. "Carefair: Choice, Duty, and the, Distribution of Care." *Social Politics* 13 (3): 341–371.

Kim, Jin Wook. 2015. "Parental Leave and Korean Fathers: Bringing Fathers Back to Their Families?" Paper presented at the 13th East Asian Social Policy research conference, South Korea, July1-2.

Kotsadam, Andreas, and Henning Finseraas. 2011. "The State Intervenes in the Battle of the Sexes: Causal Effects of Paternity Leave." *Social Science Research* 40 (6): 1611–1622.

Land, Hilary. 1978. "Who Cares for the Family?." *Journal of Social Policy* 7 (3): 257–284.

Lee, Sophia Seung-yoon, and Seung-ho, Baek. 2014. "Why the Social Investment Approach Is Not Enough – The Female Labour Market and Family Policy in the Republic of Korea." *Social Policy & Administration* 48 (6): 686–703.

Leitner, Sigrid. 2003. "Varieties of familialism: The Caring Function of the Family in Comparative Perspective." *European Societies* 5 (4): 353–375.

Levitas, Ruth. 2013. *Utopia as Method: The Imaginary Reconstitution of Society*. London: Palgrave Macmillan.

Lewis, Jane. 1992. "Gender and the Development of Welfare Regimes." *Journal of European Social Policy* 2 (3): 159–173.

Lewis, Jane, and Susy Giullari. 2005. "The Adult Worker Model Family, Gender Equality and Care: The Search for New Policy Principles and the Possibilities and Problems of a Capabilities Approach." *Economy and Society* 34 (1): 76–104.

McKay, Ailsa. 2007. "Why a Citizens' Basic Income? A Question of Gender Equality or Gender Bias." *Work Employment and Society* 21 (2): 337–348.

Michel, Sonya. 2012. "Maternalism and Beyond." In *Maternalism Reconsidered*, edited by Marian van der Klein, Rebecca Jo Plant, Nichole Sanders, and Lori R. Weintrob, 22–37. New York: Berghahn Books.

Miura, Mari. 2014. "Shinjiyushugi teki Bosei: 'Kosei no Katsuyaku' Seisaku no Mujyun [Neoliberal Motherhood: Contradictions of Women's Empowerment Policy in Japan]." *Jenda Kenkyu [Gender Studies]* 18: 53–68.

Okano, Yayo. 2012. *Feminism no Seijigaku: Kea no Rinri wo Global Syakai he* [Politics of Feminism: Ethics of Care Towards Global Society]. Tokyo: Misuzu Shobo.

Orloff, Ann. 1996. "Gender in the Welfare State." *Annual Review of Sociology* 22 (1): 51–78.

Orloff, Ann. 2006. "From Maternalism to 'Employment for All': State Policies to Promote Women's Employment Across Affluent Democracies." In *The State After Statism; New State Activities in the Age of Liberalisation*, edited by D. Levey Jonah, 230–268. Cambridge Massachusetts: Harvard University Press.

Orloff, Ann. 2009. "Gendering the Comparative Analysis of Welfare States: An Unfinished Agenda." *Sociological Theory* 27 (3): 317–343.

Pateman, Carole. 2004. "'Democratizing Citizenship: Some Advantages of a Basic Income'." *Politics & Society* 32 (1): 89–105.

Pfau-Effinger, Birgit, and Birgit Geissler, eds. 2005. *Care and Social Integration in European Societies*. Bristol: Polity Press.

Ranson, Gillian. 2015. *Fathering, Masculinity and the Embodiment of Care*. Basingstoke: Palgrave Macmillan.

Rehel, Erin. M. 2014. "When Dad Stays Home Too: Paternity Leave, Gender, and Parenting." *Gender & Society* 28 (1): 110–132.

Robeyns, Ingrid. 2008. "Introduction: Revisiting the Feminism and Basic Income Debate." *Basic Income Studies* 3 (3): 1–6.

Rubery, Jill. 2015. "Regulating for Gender Equality: A Policy Framework to the Universal Caregiver Vision." *Social Politics* 22 (4): 513–538.

Ruddick, Sarah. [1989] 1995. *Maternal Thinking: Towards a Politics of Pease*. Boston, MA: Beacon.

Sainsbury, Diane. 1996. *Gender, Equality and Welfare State*. Cambridge: Cambridge University Press.

Stephens, Julie. 2011. *Confronting Postmaternal Thinking: Feminism, Memory and Care*. New York: Columbia University Press.

Stratigaki, Maria. 2004. "The Cooptation of Gender Concepts in EU Policies: The Case of 'Reconciliation of Work and Family'." *Social Politics* 11 (1): 30–56.

Ungerson, Clare. 1983. "Why Do Women Care?" In *A Labour of Love: Women, Work and Caring*, edited by Janet Finch and Dulcie Groves, 31–50. London: Routledge and Kegan Paul.

Yamamori, Toru. 2009. *Be-sikku Inkamu Nyūmon; Mujyōkenkyūfu no kihon shotokan wo kangaeru* [Introduction to Basic Income: Examining Basic Income as Universal Benefit]. Tokyo: Kobunsya.

Yamashita, Junko. 2014. "The Impact of Basic Income on the Gendered Division of Paid Care Work." In *Basic Income in Japan: Prospects for a Radical Idea in a Transforming Welfare State*, edited by Yannick Vanderborght and Toru Yamamori, 117–131. New York: Routledge.

Belly Casts and Placenta Pills: Refiguring Postmaternal Entrepreneurialism

Maud Perrier and Maria Fannin

ABSTRACT
This article takes at its starting point the idea that maternalism and entrepreneurialism are necessarily antithetical as Julie Stephens argues in *Confronting Postmaternal Thinking: Feminism, Memory, and Care* [2012. New York: Columbia University Press]. Building on scholarship which shows how motherhood has become commercialised and commodified in contemporary culture, we extend this field by investigating how mothers who are providers of services to other mothers and pregnant women are negotiating neoliberalism and entrepreneurialism. Through an empirical investigation of birth and parenting entrepreneurs – including hypnobirthing classes and placenta pill businesses – in Bristol, UK we argue that our self-employed participants were building community and care economies within neoliberal modes of self-production, thus suggesting a more complex and ambivalent relationship between entrepreneurialism and postmaternalism. We suggest that the experiences of women entrepreneurs or 'mumpreneurs' offer insights into how the spaces of work might be, counter to Stephens' characterisation, places of negotiation and struggle for the politics of feminism, rather than sites of 'anti-maternalism' or the 'forgetting' of maternalism. Moreover, our participants' accounts were strongly shaped by feminist ethics of care thus challenging the representation of such services as therapeutic postfeminist technologies of self-work.

Introduction

Stephens (2011) argues in her book, *Confronting Postmaternal Thinking: Feminism, Memory and Care*, that we live in 'postmaternal' times. In her view, postmaternal thinking disavows the importance of mothering and dependency as legitimate concerns for public policy-making. To be postmaternal is both to be free of the obligations and dependencies associated with mothering, as well as to render illegible the demand for public policies that specifically support women as mothers. Stephens seeks to show how maternalism, as both an embodied materiality as well as a gendered approach to policy-making, has diminished in value and political authority. The decline of the post-Second World War welfare state is also a 'degendering' of policy initiatives, maintained by the 'normative idea of self as both genderless and autonomous' and embodied in the abstract figure of the worker or the citizen-subject (Stephens 2011, 22). Feminist movements have also been transformed through this period. Accusations of essentialism continue to make discussions of pregnancy and mothering difficult to navigate, in effect obscuring a critical aspect of the gendered dimension of embodiment from critical discussion. Political activism, and in particular feminist activism, Stephens suggests, no longer calls for the recognition of states of 'interdependency'. Furthermore, as Stephens demonstrates in her reading of contemporary writers' narratives of their feminist mothers, feminism's second wave is characterised in cultural memory as the rejection and overcoming of the maternal condition.

For Stephens, the disappearance of policies aimed at women as mothers is part of a broader devaluation of the state's maternalist role of caring for its citizens and subjects in favour of entitlements linked to women's formal participation in the labour market, for example, in the establishment of welfare-to-work programs. Stephens characterises work by drawing on the figure of the professional career woman either with no caring responsibilities or whose corporate work is facilitated by technologies such as the breast-pump. Stephens (2011, 26) thus aligns work and being an employee as anti-maternal: 'In the popular imagination second-wave feminism is still "linked with the glorification of market work and the devaluing of family work"' (as quoted by Williams 2000). She cites this popular imaginary of the relationship of second-wave feminism to work to argue that such characterisations presume an alliance between paid work and feminist goals for liberation that obscure 'maternal forms of selfhood' and the extension of the ethics and practices of mothering into wider social and political spheres (Stephens 2011, 35). Yet by setting up the memory of a 'degendered' feminism as pro-market work and against the maternal, what gets obscured are the complex ways in which women make claims not only as mothers but as mother workers. This risks ignoring the dependencies that also characterise relationships at work, and the presence of maternal identities, practices and bodies in workplaces.

This article takes at its starting point the complex relations between maternalism and entrepreneurialism, as a way of generating dialogue with Stephens' characterisation of contemporary political economies and cultures of postmaternalism. We explore this through a discussion of interviews with women whose working lives embody the in-between spaces of work and care that Stephens' suggests are less visible in contemporary public cultures. Stephens argues that what is needed to redress the devaluation of the maternal in the contemporary period is a 'regendering' of the public sphere in which a maternalist ethics of care for vulnerable others, including the vulnerability of the environment and the embodied transformations that accompany mothering, are recognised as the basis for a potentially more affirmative political culture. We consider how the relations of care that Stephens suggests are crucial for regendering public cultures might be reread into the workplace. The experiences of women entrepreneurs or 'mumpreneurs' who ambivalently inhabit the spaces of work and care offer insights into how the spaces of work might be, counter to Stephens' characterisation, places of negotiation and struggle for the politics of feminism, rather than sites of 'anti-maternalism' or the 'forgetting' of maternalism.

We consider Stephens' argument for regendering the public sphere by examining the relationship between neoliberalising imperatives to regard the 'entrepreneur' as the model worker against the backdrop of intensive and commercialised mothering (Duberley and Carrigan 2013). We draw on interviews with women providing services to mothers in Bristol, UK to consider how self-employed women negotiate neoliberal imperatives to become 'entrepreneurial' subjects. Women seek to negotiate work and care in different ways, and we argue that these negotiations are themselves sites of ethico-political struggles. The work of care for the women we interviewed is intimately bound up with concepts of mothering, not only in terms of the relationship between a mother and her child but also through the kinds of 'public' instantiations of mothering that Stephens suggests have disappeared. These include efforts to create communities, to recognise interdependencies, to work for reasons other than purely market-driven competition and to engender caring for self and others in one's own work. These ways of navigating the 'postmaternal' condition of neoliberal economies and cultures suggests the building of alternative spaces within neoliberal modes of self-production, an effort contemporary theorists of capitalism suggest needs more critical attention (Gibson-Graham and Roelvink 2010; McRobbie 2013).

This article focuses on interviews carried out with seven women in 2016 in Bristol who advertise their services on parenting websites, noticeboards in community centres as well as through word-of-mouth. They offer a range of complementary therapies, including hypnobirthing, pregnancy yoga, doula services, postnatal fitness training, alternative therapies, creative workshops and other forms of 'care' work for pregnant women and mothers. Our study thus addresses an empirical gap in the literature on the care sector that tends to focus on childcare and elderly care. For almost all of the women we interviewed, their primary form of paid labour was self-employment. One also worked in the National Health Service (NHS) as a midwife. Contact was made by email or phone and one or both of the researchers carried out interviews. All of the interviews were recorded and transcribed and pseudonyms assigned to research participants. Six of the women interviewed were also mothers and ranged in age from early 30s to early 50s. Some of the interviews were carried out while women's children were present, including one of the interviewer's daughter. Five of our participants had a child under three years of age at the time of the interview and two were still on maternity leave. Most of our participants' journeys towards motherhood were intimately connected with the development of their business. Their businesses were either motivated by their new experience as mothers or developed in anticipation of becoming pregnant. One participant did not have children but explicitly talked about how she imagined herself as a mother.

All but one of our participants lived with a partner at the time of the interview and those households relied on other sources of income from that of their business, either through their other employment (such as one interviewee, Claire, who was a part-time NHS midwife) or their partner's employment. The only exception was Abbie, whose hypnobirthing business was run jointly by herself and her partner and the sole source of income for their household. One participant, Ellen, did not have a partner when she started her business as a personal trainer but did receive some financial support from her parents; her current partner works and contributes to their household expenses. Five of our participants had transitioned to becoming self-employed in the last 5–10 years following a period of re-training and had occupied jobs in Sustainability and Arts Management, Investment Banking, the charity sector, and as teachers and press officers (see Table 1). The alternative maternal economies they were building through their self-employment were

Table 1. Participants' paid work activities.

Pseudonyms	Description of activities
Sofia	Yoga teacher, massage therapist, birthing community organiser
Abbie	Yoga teacher, hypnobirthing
Rachel	Personal trainer, postnatal training
Ellen	Personal trainer, postnatal training
Claire	Pregnancy yoga teacher, midwife
Helen	Shiatsu practitioner and placenta encapsulation
Natasha	Creative workshop facilitator and photographer

facilitated to some extent by a male breadwinner household model. Several participants discussed that the more modest household income incurred by them choosing this type of self-employment was a joint decision with their partners.

The aim of our interviews was to gain a better understanding of the experiences and views of women involved in what we identify in this article as birth and parenting economies and cultures in Bristol. We are interested in better understanding the intersection of mothers' self-employment with their involvement in the particular 'maternal economies' oriented around pregnancy, childbirth and early infancy. We asked women about the origins and motivations of their work and about the challenges they faced, their personal experiences as well as their views of the kinds of services available to parents and families in the Bristol area. We also asked questions about the everyday geographies of their spaces of work, whether they were home-based, involved aspects of social media or other digital technologies, and whether they took place within a particular area within the city. We were interested in the extent to which women, if they were mothers, identified with the literature or discourse of the 'mumpreneur' and whether they had made use of any business-orientated training or support available for self-employed workers or entrepreneurs. We suggest the mumpreneur who combines caring work with entrepreneurial activities or self-employment offers one way to explore the relationship between public cultures of the 'maternal' and neo-liberal imperatives to become an 'entrepreneur of the self'. Our analysis thus presents a more ambivalent and complex relationship between entrepreneurialism and postmaternalism.

Maternal economies and postfeminist mumpreneurs

This article contributes to three interconnected debates about transformations to contemporary motherhood: the conceptualisation of the commodification of motherhood, the study of mumpreneurs and care businesses, and debates about the difference between 'self-work' and 'self-care' in the postfeminism literature. Scholars interested in the economic dimensions of maternity have pointed to the growth of classes, services and products associated with pregnancy, birth and parenting as evidence of how contemporary cultures of motherhood in the UK and elsewhere are increasingly commodified and commercialised. Pregnancy, in this light, constructs mothers as singular kinds of consumers (Hewitson 2014; O'Donohoe et al. 2014; Tyler 2011). The products and services listed on Bristol social media parenting sites do seem to invite women to participate in 'consuming motherhood' (Taylor, Layne, and Wozniak 2004). Negra (2009, 7) discusses this increasing fetishisation of the maternal within popular culture as a 'master narrative' of postfeminism. She argues that 'retreatism' – or the 'pull back of affluent women to perfected domesticity' – falsely 'presents the habits, interests and desires of the wealthy as universal' (Negra 2009,

9) thereby reinforcing classed exclusions. These consumption practices are part of the broader cultural ideals in which middle-class women are viewed as the ideal mothers: able to devote significant amounts of time to their children's educational and personal success and to practice 'intensive' parenting, involving both emotional and financial commitments to parenting well.

Research in this field also notes the emergence of the 'Yummy Mummy' as a cultural phenomenon that tightly knits maternity with consumption, as the good mother is represented as an intensely acquisitive and corporate consumer subject (Littler 2013). Yummy Mummies are described as affluent:

> older mothers, who have established a successful career before embarking on a family [...] influenced by the celebrity mother culture [and] willing to spend significant money on themselves, as well as insisting on the highest quality goods for their family. (Allen and Osgood 2009, 5)

As Littler notes (2013) the figure of the Yummy Mummy has an ambiguous relationship to the stay at home mother: while in some of the novels she analysed working in the public sphere is simply abandoned, in others the former career woman goes back to work part-time or from home. In this figure, a very specific configuration of motherhood (occupied by white, heterosexual, middle-class women) is being celebrated as a desirable identity, one that embodies female choice, autonomy, consumerism and aesthetic perfection (Allen and Osgood 2009). These observations of the contemporary cultural and economic presumptions surrounding middle-class parenting are reflected in local birth and parenting cultures and economies in Bristol.[1] Consuming such an array of products and services aimed at pregnant women and new mothers requires access to financial resources and presents motherhood as a singular experience to be documented, memorialised and experienced as a time to invest heavily in the cultivation of one's child's cognitive and sensory abilities.

In this article, however, we focus less on the representations of aspirational motherhood found in these consumption spaces, and more on the narratives of women providing these products and services. Their work as 'entrepreneurs' in the space of consuming motherhood, as we will demonstrate below, points to important tensions in the formation of neoliberal subject positions like the 'Yummy Mummy' and their alternatives. Our examination of the activities of the maternal and birth entrepreneurs we interviewed illustrates how they both participate in the increasing commodification of the maternal experience but sometimes challenge it by seeking to build alternative maternal economies. We ask, to what extent does mothers buying 'care' from other women result in a different kind of commodification of mothering and birth? Do they constitute attempts to make up for the familial knowledge and support that urban middle-class women often lack (Davis 2008)? 'Markets' and other spaces of consumption around mothering are increasingly differentiated, as we discuss below. Our research demonstrates how scholars need to stay attuned to the ways in which consuming motherhood encompasses both purchasing care and taking part in community building.

McRobbie (2015) notes that invoking the ability to follow one's passion and work flexibly may also hide processes of exploitation, in which self-employment acts as a form of labour marginalisation and is part of the feminisation of labour. Indeed, there is a burgeoning field of research on mumpreneurs which identifies the growth of small businesses by mothers as evidence not just of women trying to find work that fits their caring responsibilities but as underpinned by transformations and constraints of the labour market for working mothers:

> The move from conventional employment to this new situation ... is of course a move to precariousness consistent with the general thesis of the feminization of work. The larger narrative of neoliberalism here is that of creeping privatization, exclusion and the personalization of responsibility for dealing with circumstances – retirement, caring responsibilities, unemployment and under-earning – which formerly warranted support from a welfare state. (Taylor 2015, 185)

The decrease in forms of conventional employment that are less compatible with caring and the emergence of new forms of flexible, 'family-friendly' work also represents the emergence of new forms of precarity, where working for yourself results in exclusion and low status on the margins of the neoliberal economy (Wilson and Yochim 2015). The literature on self-employed care workers suggests that this growing sector of women's employment presents difficult employment conditions, such as low pay and concerns over one's health (Anderson and Hughes 2010).

The literature on 'mumpreneurs' also highlights how one's identity and knowledge as a mother is central to some women's entrepreneurial work: mumpreneur businesses [tend] to offer a product or service that is associated with family and motherhood. Rather than providing flexibility around the running of the distinct domains of work and home, the doing of maternal entrepreneurial femininity represents the establishment of an explicit link between motherhood and entrepreneurial activities (Duberley and Carrigan 2013; Ekinsmyth 2011; Lewis 2010; Nel, Maritz, and Thongprovati 2010). Thus the mumpreneur's focus is on what will not only fill a market gap but also connect to women's traditional caring responsibilities of looking after home and children (Lewis 2014a, 120). This figure can also be read through a postfeminist lens: 'maternal entrepreneurial femininity explicitly and visibly incorporates both masculine and feminine aspirations and is held out to women as something which is "progressive but also consummately and reassuringly feminine"' (McRobbie 2009, 57 as quoted in Lewis 2014b, 1856). The literature on mumpreneurs highlights that women are forging new ways of doing business by following a business model that does not necessarily prioritise profit and are motivated by the desire to help others and contribute to their community (Nel, Maritz, and Thongprovati 2010). Mumpreneurs have been described as creating a subculture of female entrepreneurship in unconventional economic spaces including family and community (Ekinsmyth 2011).

Our study contributes to these discussions based on a distinct subset of 'mumpreneurs' who provide care for pregnant women birthing and new mothers, rather than products or services for their children. Our discussion of our participants as self-employed care workers also contributes to moving the debate about care work beyond the established assumption of hostile worlds – where markets contaminate and erode care (England 2005; Zelizer 2005) and where care is coopted by market forces. Moreover, research on 'care entrepreneurs' (Gallagher 2014) identifies important tensions in combining care work with entrepreneurialism. The constitution of idealised entrepreneurial subjects, who are seen as capable of operating in a competitive environment, allows little space for the 'messiness' of the relational work of care.

Our final contribution concerns how we can characterise the type of care work performed by our interviewees for others and to what extent it represents 'self-work'. Gill and Scharff have argued that women are positioned as the ideal neoliberal subjects: 'To a much greater extent than men, women are required to work on and transform the self, to regulate every aspect of their conduct, and to present all their actions as freely chosen' (2011, 9). This injunction to transform themselves becomes particularly visible with regard to the management of the body and sexuality, but also in the language of empowerment, aspiration and self-expression in the world of work and motherhood (Gill and Scharff 2011). We are interested in adding nuance to this discussion by drawing attention to how popular cultural invitations for mothers to 'pamper themselves' and to be 'body confident' contrasts with our participants' attempts to equip women with knowledge about their bodies and time for self-care which may be more consistent with a feminist politics of mothering critical of neoliberalism's empowerment rhetoric. We show how for those providing such 'technologies of transformation' to maternal subjects, taking up neoliberal subjectivity is not necessarily equated with depoliticisation, the repudiation of vulnerability and dependency and the internalisation of competition, but rather is characterised by a feminist ethic of care.

'But how do you measure success?': narrating self-employment

In this section, we discuss how women described becoming self-employed, their orientations to the 'figure' of the entrepreneur or mumpreneur in their own work, and the efforts they took to generate income from their work. Their perspectives resonate with much of the critical literature on women entrepreneurs and 'mumpreneurs'. Women may describe the motivation to become self-employed in terms consonant with notions of self-fulfilment, passion and a calling towards more meaningful work, but struggle with the precarious nature of self-employment, the financial uncertainty and dependence on partners or others for support, and the tension between their work and caring for children (Ekinsmyth 2011; Lewis 2010). Reflecting on the difficulties of being self-employed, Helen, who works as an alternative therapist, doula and placenta encapsulator, said:

> I've been self-employed since 2002 I think. No, 2003, since I qualified. I would say it's definitely difficult to make a living out of it. Yes, the first 10 years when I was only doing that, just treatments and teaching, I was struggling to make ends meet. Now I find the placenta pays well and so that helps me in terms of feeling a bit more secure. Yes, I would say it's mainly whether you're going to make enough money for everything.

Other women spoke about the uncertainty of whether their business would survive when they first began, and of relying on a partner's income or redundancy pay from their previous job to support the initial period of self-employment.

> Well, I did it really gradually because my partner had a full-time job at the time. I started the business just before I gave birth to my first child. That was quite a challenging time but because I ran my classes from home, to start off with, there weren't really many costs involved. It's something that I'd built up gradually. I didn't put on loads of classes at once and built it up as we went along. (Abbie)

Claire also described working part-time in order to spend more time with her children, sharing childcare with her partner, also self-employed, and making do with less: 'very minimal camping holidays and a moderate life'.

Women approached the label and identity of entrepreneur with circumspection, and often dis-identified with the identity of entrepreneur or mumpreneur. For example, Helen said 'I don't use that term "entrepreneur," but yes, I'm definitely self-employed. Yes, I feel I've got my own business. Yes, I don't use that word though. It feels a bit grand … or a bit business-like'. When asked whether she had heard of or participated in any activities organised for 'mumpreneurs', Abbie replied:

> I've heard of it. I'm familiar with it. I guess it's what I would be classified as but it's not necessary what I think of myself as. These days women are looking for more diverse and flexible ways to combine looking after kids and working, but I think it's definitely a fine line and it's not necessarily the easy option that people may think it is. Just things like going on holiday. Who takes care of all the booking and the enquiries that are coming in every day? Things like that. So I know quite a lot of women who've gone into their own businesses, and they've said it's not necessarily given them the lifestyle balance that they were looking for.

This distancing from the identity of mumpreneur also took the form of comparisons between their work and others who were more 'entrepreneurial'. Abbie continued:

> Abbie: I also know lots of women entrepreneurs, who've taken it to a much greater level than me. They're much more motivated by business success, but because I wanted to be at home a lot with the kids that's always been the …
> Interviewer: the balance?
> Abbie: Yes. So I think every woman is different. They have their own set of goals or values in life. They arrange their lives accordingly to that.

The majority of our participants when asked about the future of their business responded that they wanted to 'keep things ticking over' so that they could carry on earning enough and caring for their family rather than prioritising expansion and growth. Helen struggled to find the right balance between her earnings and offering services to other women:

> Again, we were talking about, as a mum, providing those kind of services, it's too much now because it's taking too much of my time. Because of that it's hard to give discounts because then I feel I'm giving everything and I've got nothing left for myself, and so you don't want to do that either. I think as a therapist you need to be able to give from a place that is comfortable and sustainable …. I used to do that. I used to give discounts to people, but then I would just literally barely earn anything.

Interestingly their accounts highlight how the cost and availability of childcare and the lack of adequate maternity pay are particularly challenging as self-employed workers in small businesses. They lack the provision women who work in bigger organisations benefit from, organisations some of them left hoping for more freedom.

Our participants both identified and dis-identified from the label mum/entrepreneur suggesting an ambivalent relationship with a particular type of business identity, especially its explicit gendering. Few felt comfortable with a predominantly profit-driven model of business and instead wanted to make enough money to live on, and to develop their work in relationship to other values:

> I am always amazed that I have been self-employed for such a long time because I am the most … I am a very organised person, I have to say, I have done a lot. Before I used to do lots of PA [personal assistant] work for other people so I am good at admin stuff but I am definitely no good with money in terms of financial stuff. And doing my tax return is always a big mission every year and marketing is horrible, I am just terrible. So I am always amazed in how,

you know, because I have been so busy how it has happened. I guess people say that when you put your heart into what you are doing, you receive a lot back. So that is probably from a yogi place – an honest yogi place of being – that I have I have run my business. But I definitely don't feel I am an entrepreneur. (Sofia)

While Claire described her orientation towards her work as 'bumbling around' and herself as 'not a businesswoman particularly', she also spoke eloquently of how her work as a yoga teacher 'is about *sangha*, is about community. It's about building community'. It is a form of work that cannot be easily described as profit-motivated, but it is work that seeks to generate value, and not only for the worker herself. Claire continues:

> I think it's really important bringing people into their bodies. I really like the practical aspect of *asana*. I really like trying to build communities. There's nothing better than if I've taught a yoga class and then all the women are chatting at the end or I bump into them in the street a couple of days later. The same with the antenatal classes that we teach, or I facilitate. I don't feel like people learn that much particularly. I just like people getting together.

Generating a different kind of value and questioning what constitutes the success of her business was something that Natasha described in response to whether she identifies as an entrepreneur:

> No, not at all. No. No, that's for someone who makes money, I don't make any bloody money. Maybe when I've made some money maybe I'll start thinking of myself like that. No, no. Like I said, I've got a glorified hobby. I've got a good idea and, yes, it would take a lot more to get it to the point where it's a successful business, but how do you measure success? (Natasha)

These accounts highlight dimensions of the existing literature on self-employed women and 'mumpreneurs': some of the women we interviewed might be described as 'under-employed' given their pursuit of part-time rather than full-time self-employment. They also drew on gendered narratives of 'women's work' as a 'glorified hobby' and appeared to 'choose' not to take their work to the next level. But these narratives also challenge dominant ideas of what constitutes economic value and suggest efforts by women to participate in the growth of alternative economies, economies that value *community* and question conventional measures of success. Such a model of self-employed subjectivity is rarely reflected in current entrepreneurial research that positions women as failed or reluctant entrepreneurial subjects (Ahl and Marlow 2012).

Inextricable from these narratives that recount the lack of job security involved in becoming self-employed, especially at the start, were accounts of living their passion and helping others, as we discuss in more detail in the next section. Similar to the young entrepreneurs in the Berlin fashion industry McRobbie (2013) discusses in her work on new social enterprises, the women we interviewed sought to navigate the 'self-employment bureaucracy' to generate support for each other's work and to find ways to put other values and other 'ways of being' into practice. Our participants attempted to create a maternalist culture in their work, a project that was both hindered and facilitated by their self-employed status.

(Post)maternal community economies

Most of our participants saw 'community building' and bringing women together to share experiences in a culture where motherhood is isolating as an important part of their work.

Here we find Angela McRobbie's idea of 'radical social enterprise' and J.K. Gibson-Graham's diverse economies framework helpful to make sense of how women combined employment with their ethico-political motivations. In McRobbie's discussion of immaterial labour and the growing numbers of women becoming small-scale creative entrepreneurs, she proposes a renewal of radical social enterprise, co-operatives and collectives that would reconnect creative labour to its radical roots which she locates as directly linked to social movements of the late 1960s and 1970s. She writes:

> I argue for a more historically informed perspective which pays attention to the micro-activities of earlier generations of feminists who were at the forefront of combining forms of job creation with political activity (e.g. women's book stores and publishing, youth-work or *'madchenarbeit'*, child care and *kinderladen*) under the auspices of what would now be called 'social enterprise'. (McRobbie 2011, 60)

For McRobbie these are not just examples of women combining work (and motherhood) with activism but of the possibility of establishing a radical politics of the workplace within the culture of the small enterprise: 'The women who set up these kinds of ventures were multi-taskers *avant la lettre*; they also inhabited the long-hours culture and were more than passionately attached to their work' (2011, 76).

Interestingly, for some of the women we spoke with this is not a practice located in the past where the connection between women's work and feminist activism needs reviving, but rather very much part of the contemporary life/work configuration of this generation of women in their mid-30s to early 50s. This highlights the significant continuities between their community building practices and the feminist tradition of consciousness raising groups of the 1970s and beyond. Our participants wanted to build a community of women that could support each other through the transition to motherhood and they articulated this desire as one of the main motivations for their work. As Sofia, a pregnancy yoga teacher, describes:

> There has been lots of tears, there has been lots of laughter and problems that arise – especially in the last trimester women can get a bit stressed if they are over the due date. So the fear of being induced and the fear ... And we just bring it all in and this way we create a community. And as I said my intention was to create a community of women that was the most important thing for me more than like anything else. I wanted all the women could create a network and then support each other.

Moreover for a few of our practitioners community was also mentioned in relation to building a professional community of birth and postnatal workers that could support one another. This was enabled by a childbirth group Sofia established in 2013 in Bristol. Here she describes how the group works both as a space for women to share birth stories but also as an opportunity for other self-employed postnatal workers to network and meet potential clients:

> We decided to set up a free group for Bristol. And it has been amazing, like, really incredible. So the group is free – we only ask for donations to cover the cost of the rental room because we don't get it for free and to buy teas and stuff. And every month there is a topic that have [inaudible] to all the groups but we can change it. Topics can be like place of birth, it can be the first hour after birth. It can be options in birth, having or not having a doula – all of these kind of stuff ... And it is all about really giving women options – women and men because this group is lovely because loads of them bring their partners which is really nice

because apart from the NCT [National Childbirth Trust] courses there are no other courses they can go to – well, unless they pay obviously for hypnobirthing, you know, things like that. And, yes, so for me it has been a way obviously to create a bigger community of the birthing community in Bristol. So my own connections and networking. Also to be able to offer to my students – okay you want to encapsulate your placenta. My friend Helen does this or my friend Rebekah does this. Or, do you want an independent midwife? Emily is a consultant … So the [group] for me has been this. And also obviously now that I have had my son, it has also helped me so much to hear all these stories. It has been amazing. Because when we think about positive birth, lots of people think a straightforward two hour laboured birth but it is not. We have had incredible powerful stories of women being in 72 hours and still finding the power and positivity. And wanting to come and share their story.

Sofia's account of her involvement in setting up this group in a gentrified alternative neighbourhood of the city may not reflect the dominant birth and maternal culture but it offers insights into how neoliberal entrepreneurial subjectivities overlap and cohabit with 'earlier' forms of women's health activism, including consciousness raising about natural birth. The more openly entrepreneurial or business-minded of our participants whose work centred on fitness or creativity said they did not have enough time for networking or that the networking they did through a local mumpreneur group was not always successful, in any case the kind of community building they did was more about women getting together to share information and resources. This suggests that the link between women's reproductive health and feminist activism has partly facilitated the growth of more radical social enterprises. Interestingly the lack of maternity leave McRobbie (2011) identifies as a significant deficiency in creative workers' work rights was also an issue highlighted by some of our participants; they would receive only statutory maternity pay during their maternity leave and have to organise cover for their classes/services during their absence from work to ensure they would not lose their base of clients when they returned from leave.

Community building was not just restricted to their employment and these participants mentioned communal childcare either through childcare swaps or co-ops as one of the ways in which they managed to 'afford' to work:

> The older I get the more I think actually human beings are supposed to be part of extended-family network. We're not supposed to be in these little isolated pods on our own. That's the other thing that you do when you're a working mummy, is you make friendships with other mummies. When I was on my days off I'd be like Julie Andrews. (Laughter) I'd have about five kids with me because I was returning childcare favours. In fact the girl who's coming to stay, she's a single mum as well. I had her son three days a week. I used to cycle home with him on the back of my bike from primary school. I believe in communal parenting as well. I say to people, 'Please tell off my children if they're misbehaving. That's fine. Don't pussyfoot about. Just get on with it'. I suppose, yes, you make extended family networks, don't you? (Claire)

Community economies connected our participants' professional and personal lives, so that their professional relationships were not entirely separate from their home lives and that of their children's. Some women who perceived the problem of affordable childcare as a political rather than an individual problem used some form of communal childcare. The fact that a lot of their work happened in their own homes (two participants had a therapy room at home) also facilitated such alternative arrangements.

The women we spoke to enacted a social enterprise ethos for their business through their insistence on the affordability of their service and their attempts to reach a more diverse demographic than the middle-class women who constitute their main clientele. Participants did this in different ways either by providing discounted services on requests (Abbie, Helen), seeking government funding to run pregnancy yoga classes (Claire) in disaffected parts of the city or becoming involved in charitable work with mothers who suffer from postnatal depression (Natasha). This was often mentioned in response to our question about who their typical clients were. The socio-economic inequalities amongst mothers and the cost of their services was something they critically reflected on although what was considered affordable varied considerably. Claire spoke of offering lower-cost services:

> I don't mind doing things for not very much, but I don't like doing things for nothing. I don't get paid very much to teach pregnancy yoga. I get a flat rate for a local yoga studio. I'm in service. I've got a life of service. That's what I do.

In their efforts to organise alternative approaches to economic sustainability, the women we interviewed used the language of 'creating community', signalling ways that their work is not motivated solely by increasing the market share of their businesses. Their working lives are also organised around caring responsibilities – caring for members of their families or with an ethos of care for their clients – and rather than viewing this as a failure to live up to neoliberal ideals of self-sufficiency and the exhortation to become autonomous subjects of markets, we interpret their work as an effort to generate other non-capitalist or alternative economies. Indeed, efforts to build community through work and the combination of unpaid housework with socially responsible enterprise can be generatively understood as instances of alternatives to capitalist economic practice within what J.K. Gibson-Graham have called a 'diverse economies' framework.

From this perspective, women's efforts to combine paid work with a broader ethos of community building and care are not add-ons or marginal to neoliberal capitalism, but become distinctive sites of ethical struggles (Gibson-Graham 2008). The postmaternal community economies described in this section suggest that women's ongoing efforts to balance an ethos of community building, unpaid care work, paid self-employment as well as non-market childcare swaps are both symptomatic of the decline of the welfare state's provisions for social support *as well as* experiments in forging different ways of living. The radical social enterprises being forged here were similar to the ones McRobbie describes as belonging to London in the 1970s (2011) or to contemporary Berlin fashion designers (2013). We suggest that the connections between feminist activism and health/body work also facilitated such an explicitly community-based form of enterprise. The community building which was at the heart of our participants' work illustrates how an analysis of postmaternal thinking needs to include the tight connections between women's paid labour, their activism and how they care for their families within the same space, rather than characterising work and care as located in separate spaces.

Self-care, self-work

Our research illustrates how our participants are creating spaces for women to self-care, acquire reproductive bodily knowledge and receive care from other women. Our participants explicitly stated that this was because mothers often lack time and resources as carers themselves. Self-care featured through different practices and vocabularies including physical exercise, spiritual balance/energy, creativity or being connected to one's body. While such practices of self-care could be read as symptomatic of therapeutic cultures where care of the self is a requirement of the neoliberal citizen, in our interviews the imperative to 'self-care' was often described by practitioners as a place of education, connection and new knowledge rather than the premise of an ideal autonomous citizen healed through self-work as heralded by Rose (1989).

There were important distinctions in the type of self-care provided and its aims: some explicitly encouraged women to gather together and build communities as a form of support, others had a more individualistic vision of how self-care would be empowering (this was more the case for the postnatal fitness and hypnobirthing businesses). This is similar to Nash's (2012) analysis of Australian pregnancy fitness classes, which highlighted their role in the surveillance and discipline of women's pregnant bodies amidst moral panic about maternal obesity. We suggest here, contra Stephens, that this form of maternal support is neglected in her argument which focuses on maternal and elderly care. We interpret our participants' accounts of their work as connected to a long feminist genealogy of women providing care for other women, both in the sense of emotional support and of equipping women with knowledge about their bodies, especially their reproductive capacities (Boston Women's Health Collective 1973). At the same time, therapeutic cultures themselves are entangled with postfeminism as self-regulation and self-work are key characteristics of the new sexual contract (Gill 2008; McRobbie 2009).

Our participants enacted a version of self-care that acknowledged the importance of resources such as time, support from a practitioner and knowledge about one's body. This suggests an important distinction between self-help and self-care, as this type of self-care does not just reproduce the dominant psychological discourse that 'one should work on oneself' but recognises that care involves a set of material resources and relationships. Beyond educating women about their bodies, a strong motivation for our participants was to teach women how to care for themselves in the sense of having time either for physical exercise, relaxation or creative pursuits. One pregnancy yoga teacher who describes her work as 'mothering for the mothers' highlights this:

> Well we get these two weeks where you have your husband or partner at home and maybe if you are lucky you get some help like my mum came for two weeks and it was amazing. But it is not just that it is not about me, it is about wanting *to re-educate women to self-care*. You need self-care because only by taking care of yourself can you take care of a child. And all I see most of the – even the groups they are for babies. It is all about babies. We need to look after the mothers – I think – a bit more and especially after the birth. (Sofia)

Here Sofia is articulating the difficulties mothers have in feeling entitled to self-care. Interestingly she makes the link that women need to care for themselves so they can take care of their children, thus invoking a maternalist rationale for self-care. Similarly Natasha talks about running creative workshops with women as a way to provide caring spaces of respite from the intensity of motherhood:

> A lot of women just say they just wanted to be creative. They just wanted to do something that was either for themselves, or, B, they just wanted to actually just get creative and have some time for themselves. Even with a little nurturing, is the word that comes most out of the

feedback. Nurturing and lots of people just saying inspiring. I don't think they mean that I'm inspiring, I think they just mean like they feel inspired to be creative. They're like there, in this role that we're in, which is hard bloody slog being a mum, and actually it's kind of like, 'Oh, look there's something over here and I can possibly achieve this thing, possibly, whilst I'm breastfeeding. Whilst I'm being a mum'.

Self-knowledge was a significant way in which our participants described the motivations for their work. They wanted to equip women with knowledge about their bodies – including how to prepare for birth and how to recover postnatally. For all but one of our participants self-care was connected to taking care of one's body, including the necessity to be patient with regard to postnatal recovery. Indeed some of our participants played an active role in mitigating the dominant cultural imperative many postnatal women feel to return quickly to a pre-pregnancy body by sharing their knowledge:

> I think, you know, as I said so many, yes, so many mums say, 'Well I wish I knew'. And, 'I wish I'd known this beforehand'. So many don't know that really you should give it six weeks and you really should wait. If you have got any pelvic floor issues just don't put it under any more pressure ... I think, 'Have your little baby. Enjoy the first six weeks of your baby and then start thinking'. C-sections they are still mending for six months and to try and get through to them, 'You're still mending within. Everything is still changing whether you've had a C section or not everything is still going in'. So that is really an interesting side is the whole psychological – I need to get my body back. I just want to get my tummy. And I just say, 'You will not be back to how you ever were. You will always have that little slight post-natal tummy, little skin'. And it is, 'Oh my God, how long?' And that is always the question. How long will it take for my tummy to come back? And my split abs to come back? (Rachel)

Articulating the impossibility of getting one's pre-pregnancy body back shows how practitioners criticised the dominant representation of post-pregnancy bodies that quickly spring back into shape.

The way our participants emphasised having time to receive care illustrates the importance of recognising the resources women need to self-care. For one of our participants, a Shiatsu therapist, self-care is also about receiving care and support from other women, including its embodied aspect:

> I'm sure you know that just to have the space for yourself, as a gift to yourself and not to have the baby with you demanding your attention, so that you have this space, even if it's just for an hour. You've got 100% just for yourself. (Laughter). You don't need to think about your partner, your kid and all of that. The main job of a therapist is to listen and just to provide that space where, they feel cared for, they feel listened to in a non-judgemental way. Then to be touched and to be helped like that. I want to find a way to be strong enough to do that because it's amazing. Also, Shiatsu, I think it's one of these rare treatments that actually help you recharge your batteries. It's not just about helping you to relax. It's much more than that. (Helen)

While helping mothers regain their energy can be seen as a typical example of mothers being required to perform more self-work, the place of the therapist in guiding this process suggests a type of care that requires both time and bodily connection, as well as empathy.

The way our participants discussed self-care jars with other feminist engagements with how neoliberalism works on women's bodies. Specifically, Gill and Orgad (2015, 340) describe how what they call 'the feminist technology of confidence' demands that women constantly self-regulate to work on their bodies and selves and 'is (ostensibly) about self-love, not self-hate, self-assurance not insecurity, building the self, not self-harm, positive image not self-criticism'. Using evidence from advertising and self-help manuals such as *Lean In* they argue that confidence culture is a distinctive expression of neoliberal and postfeminist culture that encourages women to turn inwards to solve external problems. Interestingly the idea of confidence itself was altogether absent from our interviewees' accounts, and instead the 'old-fashioned' vocabularies of care permeated their accounts. Some of our interviewees are performing a different kind of body and soul work from the ones discussed by Gill and others, suggesting that an exploration of postfeminist subjectivities needs to deploy a wider range of methodologies. Indeed much of the critical literature on this topic is dominated by analyses of self-help manuals, makeover television shows (Ringrose and Walkerdine 2008) and psychic labour (Salmenniemi and Adamson 2015) as archetypal representations of postfeminist neoliberal culture, yet our conversations with postmaternal entrepreneurs suggest a more complex entanglement between care and self-work.

Our participants were acutely aware of how the self-care they advocated required material resources (time, cost of the service, practical knowledge): they challenged the idea that women already have the resources within themselves to feel well and acquire self-belief. This suggests that discourses of 'feminist self-care' significantly shaped these practices and work subjectivities. The growth and intensification of experts on emotion such as therapists, psychologists and human resource professionals who draw upon a range of 'technologies' of emotion so that therapeutic ways of thinking have now moved out of the counselling room into new social arenas such as the workplace (Swan 2008) is reflected in their accounts. However, the type of self-care provided by our participants foregrounded the physical self and emphasised connections. We argue that these particular 'technologies of self-care' were less individualising than suggested by some of the literature that sees such therapies as forms of self-work.

Contrasting with the uplifting stories of caring for other women our participants shared as motivation for their work, a few of our participants mentioned their own lack of self-care. They saw this deficit as the cost of taking care of others or trying to work too much with combining caring responsibilities, which often resulted in exhaustion.

> I wouldn't recommend what I did, personally, to other people. No because I just don't think it gives you, especially because I started it just before my first child was born, the opportunity to really relax with your child and look after yourself. So when he was sleeping, instead of me just sleeping or relaxing, I was on the computer answering people's emails and things. Then in the evening when he went to bed, instead of relaxing, I was out teaching. So it got to the point where I was looking after all these other women and I wasn't really looking after myself. (Abbie)

> As a mum like you, I just know that we are knackered. We need support. Women/mothers are amazing and nothing would happen in the world (Laughter) without mothers. We need to value them and we need to look after them. I think my main passion will be to focus on just helping mothers regain their energy and everything that they need in order to feel strong. Yes, but then it's hard because I'm knackered myself. It's like trying to go back to work in order to help other women, but actually I need it too. (Helen)

Whereas Abbie looks back on the first few years of her business with some degree of regret over both her own health and having enough time with her child, Helen later describes needing the services of other therapists to help her feel strong and make up for this 'care deficit'. This suggests that there were significant costs to being self-employed and a mother, and often the imperfect solution to exhaustion was simply to work less. Importantly even though some of our participants saw the structural problem of the lack of affordable childcare as one of the reasons for their lack of self-care and exhaustion, they seldom mentioned this when we asked them about resources that would support their businesses. In *Confronting Postmaternal Thinking* Stephens points to both ecofeminism and feminist ethic of care traditions as resources for *regendering* feminism. Similarly, the women we interviewed also drew on ecofeminist ideas and principles in their work to reconnect women to their bodies. However whereas Stephens sees the femivores from *Radical Homemakers: Reclaiming Domesticity from a Consumer Culture* (Hayes 2010) who abandon careers in urban environments to work on the land with their families as a form of imperfect resistance to postmaternal thinking, our participants are attempting to make maternalism central to creating economically sustainable work within consumer culture.

Conclusion

We argue that Stephens' depiction of postmaternal thinking needs to take account of what happens inside mothers' working and caring lives. We suggest that we need to connect Stephens' analysis of the widespread cultural hostility to care and dependency to how maternal values appear in women's work, both in terms of the work they do and how they combine it with their caring responsibilities and ethico-political projects. The way our participants combined paid work with community activism, sharing childcare and caring for others can be seen as enactments of the feminist project of radically transforming the work and care conundrum. The way our participants' spaces of work and care and their identities as mothers and care workers were inextricable from one another demands a more complex analysis of postmaternal economies. This echoes Adkins and Dever's (2014) call for feminists to think of new categories that can better capture women's reconfigured waged and unwaged labour under the post-Fordist sexual contract. Moreover, the activities of nurturing others and community building in which the self-employed women we interviewed took part can also be read as public appearances of the feminist ethic of care which Stephens argues has disappeared. Given the niche sector we studied and the small number of our informants, we offer a starting point for questioning the extent to which women's experiences of work can be characterised as anti-maternal. The hostility to care and nurturance Stephens describes was absent from the maternal community economies and entrepreneurs we met but may still be part of other sectors of the labour market from which these women sought to escape. We see their attempt to combine socially productive paid work, unpaid childcare and making an economically sustainable living as challenging the entrepreneur as ideal neoliberal worker especially given the centrality of care and feminist/feminine knowledge in their accounts. These ways of navigating the 'postmaternal' condition of neoliberal economies and cultures suggests the building of alternative spaces within neoliberal modes of self-production. However, it is significant that our participants building of community maternal economies was partly facilitated by their partner's or their own additional sources of income, suggesting that their location within (heterosexual) nuclear families plays an important role in their access to both not-for-profit community building and varying degrees of insecure self-employment. Our findings echo other studies of mumpreneurs that highlights their preference for a business model motivated by the desire to help others and contribute to their community (Nel, Maritz, and Thongprovati 2010) and the development of a sub-culture of female entrepreneurship in unconventional economic spaces. We need more research into how entrepreneurialism, the maternal and the economic realm are intertwined and tools to analyse how categories like 'work' and 'care' are dissolving.

Our work also suggests that the ways in which Stephens identifies examples of challenges to postmaternal thinking by focusing on certain types of activism is limiting and confines her understanding of maternal politics to a narrow definition of the spaces of politics. The examples of Code Pink, the Motherhood Project and Mumsnet discussed as evidence of a reconfigured maternalism assume that women's individual and collective ethico-political decisions with regard to work and care do not count as forms of maternal activism. Such a definition misses the myriad ways in which not only our participants but mothers in general negotiate work and care in ways which often challenge the prioritising of autonomy over dependency. We found evidence of the neo-maternal activism Stephens discusses in the efforts by women to generate new relationships between work and care and to bring maternalism into their paid work. Thus our article is also a call to expand definitions of maternal feminist politics to include such negotiations and creative responses to postmaternalism.

Beyond this methodological contribution, our work adds nuance to how we can understand the imperative for women to become entrepreneurs of the self: for our participants feminist ideals and ways of working are not necessarily subsumed by the neoliberal project of the self and its accompanying technologies. The community building and body/care education central to their professional sense of self were less forms of neoliberal 'self-work' than enactments of an alternative ethos of 'mothering for mothers'. For these women the building of alternative spaces within neoliberal modes of self-production takes place within the commercialisation of birth and mothering but cannot be fully captured by the logics of commodification of these practices. The development of such alternative community economies was facilitated by their location within women's health and maternal cultures that have been and continue to be profoundly critical of autonomy as an ideal, for as Tyler (2011, 31) observes, 'there is something about the maternal, understood as a relation between subjects, that troubles neoliberalism'.

Note

1. In Bristol, mothering and pregnancy have generated a local economy and culture that is reflected in the wide range of services and products available for pregnant women and new mothers. The Bristol forums for two popular online parenting networks, Netmums and Mumsnet, include notice boards and advertisements for a range of classes, products, therapies and other services aimed at pregnant women and new mothers. These include hypnobirthing, antenatal classes, pregnancy and newborn photography studios, placenta encapsulation services, baby swim classes, sensory classes, mother and baby yoga, prepared baby food companies and women's fitness classes. The services being marketed to pregnant women and new mothers offer enrichment, leisure and health related activities. They offer ways to fill the time of maternity leave and avoid isolation for women who may be temporarily out of the workplace; in the process re-making early motherhood into an experience to be consumed.

Disclosure statement

No potential conflict of interest was reported by the authors.

Notes on contributors

Maud Perrier is Senior Lecturer in Sociology at the University of Bristol, UK. She has written about class and contemporary motherhood and the relationship between neoliberalism, work, care and feminisms. She is currently researching women food social entrepreneurs in Sydney, Australia with Elaine Swan. She has published in *Sociology, Sociological Review, Sociological Research Online, Continuum: Journal of Media and Cultural Studies, Humanities, Gender and Education* and *Feminist Formations*.

Maria Fannin is Reader in Human Geography in the School of Geographical Sciences at the University of Bristol, UK. Her research focuses on the social and economic dimensions of health, medicine and technology, particularly in relation to reproduction and women's health. She is currently researching the multiple forms of value attached to human placental tissue in the biosciences, medicine and alternative health practices. Her work has appeared in *Body & Society, Feminist Theory* and *New Genetics & Society*.

ORCID

Maud Perrier ⓘ http://orcid.org/0000-0001-8531-5092
Maria Fannin ⓘ http://orcid.org/0000-0002-8922-2499

References

Adkins, Lisa, and Maryanne Dever. 2014. "Gender and Labour in New Times: An Introduction." *Australian Feminist Studies* 29 (79): 1–11.
Ahl, Helen, and Susan Marlow. 2012. "Exploring the Dynamics of Gender, Feminism and Entrepreneurship: Advancing Debate to Escape a Dead End?" *Organization* 9 (5): 543–562.
Allen, Kim, and Jayne Osgood. 2009. "Young Women Negotiating Maternal Subjectivities: The Significance of Social Class." *Studies in the Maternal* 1 (2): 1–17.
Anderson, Nickela, and Karen D. Hughes. 2010. "The Business of Caring: Women's Self-employment and the Marketization of Care." *Gender, Work & Organization* 17 (4): 381–405.
Boston Women's Health Collective. 1973. *Our Bodies, Ourselves*. New York: Simon & Schuster.
Davis, Kelly. 2008. "'Here's Your Baby, On You Go': Kinship and Expert Advice Amongst Mothers in Scotland." Unpublished PhD Thesis, University of Edinburgh.
Duberley, Joanne, and Marylyn Carrigan. 2013. "The Career Identities of 'Mumpreneurs': Women's Experiences of Combining Enterprise and Motherhood." *International Small Business Journal* 31: 629–651.
Ekinsmyth, Carol. 2011. "Challenging the Boundaries of Entrepreneurship: The Spatialities and Practices of UK 'Mumpreneurs'." *Geoforum* 42 (1): 104–114.
England, Paula. 2005. "Emerging Theories of Care Work." *Annual Review of Sociology* 31: 381–99.
Gallagher, Aisling. 2014. "The 'Caring Entrepreneur'? Childcare Policy and Private Provision in an Enterprising Age." *Environment and Planning A* 46 (5): 1108–1123.

Gibson-Graham, J. K. 2008. "Diverse Economies: Performative Practices for 'Other Worlds'." *Progress in Human Geography* 32 (5): 613–632.

Gibson-Graham, J. K., and Gerda Roelvink. 2010. "The Nitty Gritty of Creating Alternative Economies." *Social Alternatives* 30 (1): 29–33.

Gill, Rosalind. 2008. "Culture and Subjectivity in Neoliberal and Postfeminist Times." *Subjectivity* 25 (1): 432–445.

Gill, Rosalind, and Shani Orgad. 2015. "The Confidence Cult(ure)." *Australian Feminist Studies* 30 (86): 324–344.

Gill, Rosalind, and Christina Scharff, eds. 2011. *New Femininities: Postfeminism, Neoliberalism and Subjectivity*. Basingstoke: Palgrave.

Hayes, Shannon. 2010. *Radical Homemakers: Reclaiming Domesticity from Consumer Culture*. Richmondville, NY: Left to Write Press.

Hewitson, Gillian. 2014. "The Commodified Womb and Neoliberal Families." *Review of Radical Political Economics* 46 (4): 489–495.

Lewis, Patricia. 2010. "Mumpreneurs: Revealing the Post-Feminist Entrepreneur." In *Revealing and Concealing Gender: Issues of Visibility in Organizations*, edited by Patricia Lewis and Ruth Simpson, 124–138. Basingstoke: Palgrave Macmillan.

Lewis, Patricia. 2014a. "Feminism, Post-Feminism and Emerging Femininities in Entrepreneurship." In *The Oxford Handbook of Gender in Organizations*, edited by Savita Kumra, Ruth Simpson, and Ronald J. Burke, 107–129. Oxford: Oxford University Press.

Lewis, Patricia. 2014b. "Postfeminism, Femininities and Organization Studies: Exploring a New Agenda." *Organization Studies* 35 (12): 1845–1866.

Littler, Jo. 2013. "The Rise of the "Yummy Mummy": Popular Conservatism and the Neoliberal Maternal in Contemporary British Culture." *Communication, Culture & Critique* 6 (2): 227–43.

McRobbie, Angela. 2009. *The Aftermath of Feminism: Gender. Culture and Social Change*. London: Sage.

McRobbie, Angela. 2011. "Reflections on Feminism, Immaterial Labour and the Post-Fordist Regime." *New Formations* 70 (17): 60–76.

McRobbie, Angela. 2013. ""Fashion Matters Berlin: City-Spaces, Women's Working Lives, New Social Entreprise?" *Cultural Studies* 27 (6): 982–1010.

McRobbie, Angela. 2015. "Is Passionate Work a Neoliberal Delusion?" *Transformations*. https://www.opendemocracy.net/transformation/angela-mcrobbie/is-passionate-work-neoliberal-delusion.

Nash, Meredith. 2012. "'Working Out' for Two: Performances of 'Fitness' and Femininity in Australian Prenatal Aerobics Classes." *Gender, Place & Culture* 19 (4): 449–471.

Negra, Diane. 2009. *What a Girl Wants?: Fantasizing the Reclamation of Self in Postfeminism*. Abingdon: Routledge.

Nel, Pieter, Alex Maritz, and O. Thongprovati. 2010. "Motherhood and Entrepreneurship: The Mumpreneur Phenomenon." *International Journal of Organizational Innovation* 3: 6–34.

O'Donohoe, Stephanie, Margaret Hogg, Pauline Maclaran, Lydia Martens, and Lorna Stevens, eds. 2014. *Motherhood Markets and Consumption: The Making of Mothers in Contemporary Western Culture*. Abingdon: Routledge.

Ringrose, Jessica, and Valerie Walkerdine. 2008. "Regulating the Abject: The TV Make-over as Site of Neo-Liberal Reinvention Toward Bourgeois Femininity." *Feminist Media Studies* 8 (3): 227–246.

Rose, Nikolas. 1989. *Governing the Soul: The Shaping of the Private Self*. London: Free Associations Book.

Salmenniemi, Suvi, and Maria Adamson. 2015. "New Heroines of Labour: Domesticating Post-feminism and Neoliberal Capitalism in Russia." *Sociology* 49 (1): 88–105.

Stephens, Julie. 2011. *Confronting Postmaternal Thinking: Feminism, Memory, and Care*. New York: Columbia University Press.

Swan, Elaine. 2008. "You Make Me Feel Like A Woman: Therapeutic Cultures and the Contagion of Femininity." *Gender, Work and Organization* 15 (1): 88–107.

Taylor, Stephanie. 2015. "A New Mystique? Working for Yourself in the Neoliberal Economy." *The Sociological Review* 63 (S1): 174–187. doi:10.1111/1467-954X.12248.

Taylor, Janelle S., Linda L. Layne, and Danielle F. Wozniak, eds. 2004. *Consuming Motherhood*. New Brunswick: Rutgers University Press.

Tyler, Imogen. 2011. "Pregnant Beauty: Maternal Femininities under Neoliberalism." In *New Femininities: Postfeminism, Neoliberalism and Identity*, edited by Rosalind Gill and Christina Scharff, 21–36. Basingstoke: Palgrave Macmillan.

Williams, Joan. 2000. *Unbending Gender: Why Family and Work Conflict and What to Do About It*. New York: Oxford University Press.

Wilson, Julie Ann, and Emily Chivers Yochim. 2015. "Mothering Through Precarity: Becoming Mamapreneurial." *Cultural Studies* 29 (5–6): 669–686.

Zelizer, Viviana A. 2005. *The Purchase of Intimacy*. Princeton, NJ: Princeton University Press.

Embodied Care and Planet Earth: Ecofeminism, Maternalism and Postmaternalism

Mary Phillips

ABSTRACT
The article engages with Julie Stephens (2011) book, *Confronting Postmaternal Thinking*, which argues for a 'regendered' feminism to counter the current postmaternal and neoliberalist focus on paid work to the detriment of relationships of care. Stephens points to ecofeminism as illustrative of a potentially new form of maternalism which could achieve this. While broadly agreeing with Stephens's diagnosis of neoliberalism as amplifying the impoverishment of relations within natural and societal worlds, I contest her construal of ecofeminism and care ethics to maternalism. Instead, I propose a concept of embodied care that speaks to the ecofeminist imperative to support a radical restructuring of social and political institutions such that they focus on more-than-human flourishing. This is not to argue for a form of regendered maternalism, but neither does it seek to cast maternalism as something to be transcended. Rather, an approach to care that foregrounds connectivity and entangled materialisations provides an ethical resource to confront the dead hand of neoliberalism and a starting place from which to re-figure the postmaternal through a radical and liberatory focus on embodied relatedness.

Introduction

Contesting the social and ecological crises amplified by neoliberalism's focus on atomistic individualism requires ethical resources that empower us to imagine and act on alternatives. In her 2011 book, *Confronting Postmaternal Thinking*, Julie Stephens offers a diagnosis of the problem and a potential solution. Stephens defines the postmaternal as a current sense of antagonism associated with 'maternal' values such as nurture, care, protection and dependency and the ways in which such ideals, which Stephens associates with practices of mothering, are disavowed in the public sphere and conflicted in the private. She points to what she regards as an 'increasingly widespread cultural unease, if not hostility, toward certain expressions of the maternal and maternalist political perspectives in general' (Stephens 2011, ix). Stephens argues that postmaternalism colludes with neoliberalist processes which celebrate the self-identical, autonomous and self-sufficient individual and which are disquieted by notions regarding vulnerability or emotional connectedness.

For Stephens, those versions of feminism that strove to achieve gender-neutrality in the name of equality not only failed to challenge neoliberal policies, but were implicated in a neoliberalist focus on paid work to the detriment of relationships of care.[1] Thus Stephens argues for a 'regendered' feminism that takes up and revalues notions of care and nurturing and points to ecofeminism as a potential way forward. Ecofeminism has been developed in response to the ways in which 'woman', other subordinated groups (e.g. the aged, differently abled, ethnic minorities) and 'nature' are conceptually linked in Western thought, such that processes of inferiorization have been mutually reinforcing. Ecofeminist philosophy has sought to instate care as a means of engaging publics and individuals with the ecological and social challenges with which we are faced, and as a social, political and moral resource from which to motivate action. This paper, however, was born out of a sense of frustration, not with Stephens's confrontation with postmaternalism as an expression of neoliberalism, but the way in which she portrays ecofeminist philosophy and activism as illustrative of a new form of maternalism which could provide a means to point to and correct what she perceives as the limitations of a degendered feminism.

Indeed, there is much to agree with in Stephens's linked critiques of neoliberalism and postmaternalism. It is increasingly evident from programs of austerity and the retreat of the welfare state that humans, whether mothers or not, are valued only if they are economically productive, self-sufficient, self-responsible and entrepreneurial. The withdrawal of state support for those with caring responsibilities, the poor, the sick, children or the aged – all those who are unproductive – is justified by claims that such support produces unaffordable and morally questionable dependencies. The provision of caring and nurturing services is seen as the responsibility of the individual and available through the operation of the market through processes of commodification and marketisation that continue to under-value its contribution.

Similar trends of marketisation, the maximisation of economic utility and a focus on individual responsibility are evident in neoliberalist treatments of nature also. Castree (2008) argues that ever greater areas of the natural world are falling subject to neoliberal practices. Some of these practices make claims to the effective conservation of the natural environment through privatisation and marketisation, through seeking opportunities for growth by developing new, 'greener', products or technologies or through making win-win eco-efficiencies (see also Murphy 2000). Nature, it is claimed, will thus be preserved by integrating environmental issues within current business and economic priorities. Castree (2008) also points out that many neoliberal measures and policies are undertaken that have no ecological motivations but are simply about the biophysical world being used as a means to the end of capital accumulation and that such policies can seek actively to degrade natural resources to generate profit and disregard environmental or social consequences. Seyfang (2005), meanwhile, argues that the discourses of sustainability and environment often adopted by governments and also by some environmental NGOs place an onus on the individual citizen to change their lifestyle by, for example, conserving energy, consuming less and recycling more or reducing car use (see also Dobson 2009; MacGregor 2014; Shove and Walker 2010) in a movement that mirrors that of a state retreat from the public provision of welfare and a focus on the self-sufficient citizen and sovereign consumer. However, ecological degradation, a reduction of 52% in global wildlife populations between 1970 and 2010 that can only be described as a genocide of animal life (World Wildlife Fund 2014) as well as the threats posed by climate change continue apace. Neoliberalising processes amplify the impoverishment of our relations within natural and societal worlds, and we are led to ignore more-than-human interconnections and interdependencies. As a result, we are tearing apart the fabric of the planet.

To challenge neoliberal thinking, but contra Stephens, I propose a concept of care that expresses embodied compassion and emotions that encompass, but are not reduced to, maternalism and which takes account of more-than-human connectivities. The term 'more-than-human' has become currency across disciplines and in a plethora of debates around the ontological and epistemological status of 'nature' wherein a central focus is placed on materiality, the 'thingness' of things and the matter of matter (e.g. Barad 2003; Whatmore 1999, 2002, 2004). Probyn (2014) suggests that this is related to increasing anxiety at the impacts of human activity which have become so far-reaching that our current age is said to be a new era; the Anthropocene. This is allied to a growing awareness of the interconnectivity and complexity of all lives and life forms. At the same time, Gibson-Graham (2011) points to the exciting possibilities opened up by re-thinking forms of belonging and subjectivities; from being part of a larger planetary family suggesting an affect of love and ethic of care, to our constitution as co-beings in a 'a vital pluriverse, suggesting an affect of uncertain excitement and an ethic of attuning ourselves more closely to the powers, capacities and dynamism' of our co-habiting companions (Gibson-Graham 2011, 3). My use of 'more-than-human' thus draws on Probyn's recognition of the need to capture 'the diverse and shifting relationships between and among humans and the many different aspects of the non-human' (2014, 593). It recognises 'the essential role of the nonhuman in the human' (Bennett 2010, 152) and it attests to Haraway's recognition that our materiality is entangled with that of our co-beings:

> I love the fact that human genomes can be found in only about 90 percent of all the cells that occupy the mundane space I call my body; the other 10 percent of the cells are filled with the genomes of bacteria, fungi, protists, and such, some of which play in a symphony necessary to my being alive at all, and some of which are hitching a ride and doing the rest of me, of us, no harm. I am vastly outnumbered by my tiny companions; better put, I become an adult human being in company with these tiny messmates. To be one is always to *become with* many. (Haraway 2008, 3–4, emphasis in original)

The concept of care I propose is politicised and speaks to the ecofeminist imperative to support a transformative agenda that campaigns for a radical restructuring of social and political institutions focused on more-than-human flourishing. This foregrounds an anti-anthropocentric concern to displace 'the hubris of humanism so as to admit others into the calculus of the world' (Braun 2004, 273). I therefore position ecofeminist care not as a form of 'regendered maternalism' (Stephens 2011) but neither does it seek to cast maternalism as something to be transcended. I suggest that this is how the postmaternal could be reconfigured; as a way of reconceptualising relationships that does not rely on 'feminine' maternal models but which stresses a 'feminist' approach to connection, embodiment and emotion that is equally valued in both personal and political spheres. Borgerson (2007) sees the difference thus: feminine ethics is centred on essentialising, trait-based ethical positions associated with women's 'natural' propensities. Feminist ethics 'calls attention to relationships, responsibility and experience and their cultural, historical and psychological contexts' (Borgerson 2007, 479) such that these concerns exceed women's oppressions and encompass all who are impacted by exclusionary or subordinating processes and practices. Thus an ecofeminist notion of embodied care is developed as a social and political as well as individual practice necessary to bring about radical changes in our relationships in a more-than-human world.

I develop my argument as follows. First, I outline the main imperatives of ecofeminism which include a challenge to the excessive claims made for rationality as the ground for disembodied and transcendent universal truths. Neoliberalism has, as I will show, amplified the tendency for the subject to be cast as a rationally self-optimising, atomised individual and this has resulted in a disengagement with relational and embodied aspects of being. I then turn to Stephens's call for maternalism, and care ethics, to be regendered; a development which she can discern in contemporary ecofeminism. This is important not only because it is a misconstrual of much ecofeminist work, but because allying ecofeminism and care ethics to maternalism is, as I shall demonstrate, a high risk and limiting strategy. Having set the context, I then come to the main contribution of the paper which is to develop an ecofeminist concept of embodied, care sensitive ethics and practices in which 'mothering' is not transcended but neither does it ground itself in maternalism expressed as practices of mothering. Caring is instead expressed as a recognition of our entangled materialities, the ways in which the matter of the more-than-human is interconnected, and about 'responsibility and accountability for the lively relationalities of becoming of which we are a part' (Barad 2007, 393). This provides an ethical resource to confront the dead hand of neoliberalism and a starting place from which to re-figure the postmaternal through a radical and liberatory focus on embodied care.

Ecofeminism, neoliberalism and maternalism

Before turning to how ecofeminism can engage with notions of care that emphasis embodiment rather than maternalism, it is worth delineating the elements that broadly comprise an ecofeminist philosophy. I will then outline how neoliberalism has amplified the privileging of rationality over emotion that ecofeminism in general, and ecofeminist care ethics in particular, seeks to challenge.

Ecofeminism emerged in the late 1970s building on women's experiences of direct action; in particular, protesting the use of nuclear technologies in energy generation and weapons. It was also a response to what was perceived as a masculine bias in existing environmental philosophies and activist groups. Covering a range of issues, such as toxic waste, deforestation, reproductive rights and technologies and animal liberation, ecofeminism has always combined activism and philosophy, developing ecological and social theory in a range of disciplines over the social sciences and humanities.[2] Ecofeminists largely reject a reformist or incrementalist approach that assumes that any changes in policy and lifestyle required to address mounting environmental and social problems can be achieved within present socio-economic structures (Hopwood, Mellor, and O'Brien 2005). Instead, it upholds a transformative agenda that will bring about more radical change and to this end, has initiated and supported social and political action that involves those outside the centres of power.

Ecofeminism has been described as a patchwork quilt (Warren 2000) that encompasses a range of issues and views (Cuomo 2002), but common to all is the argument that systemic injustices such as colonialism, racism, sexism and the subordination of nature are interwoven and cross-cutting (Cudworth 2005; Glazebrook 2005; Plumwood 1993; Warren 2000). Striving for new connectivities of care, responsibility and justice therefore has to be extended to natural and social realms as they are bound in the same systems of oppression and cannot be addressed in an atomistic way (Lahar 1991). These injustices are grounded in 'patriarchal logic' (Plumwood 1993) expressed through sets of interrelated and hierarchical dualisms, such as mind/body, reason/nature, reason/emotion, masculine/feminine or human/nature, that support a 'culturally exalted hegemonic ideal' of masculinity (Kheel 2008, 3). The privileging of the first terms in these dualisms expresses what can be regarded as authentically human/masculine and this is defined as superior and in opposition to the natural, physical or biological realm. Idealised masculinity qua humanity transcends this realm, while women, nature and all else that do not conform are 'othered' to confirm and justify their subordination. Thus a genuinely human self is one that is essentially rational, disembodied and sharply differentiated from that which is associated with, for example, emotions, bodies and nature which are construed as inferior and given instrumental value only (Phillips 2015).

For ecofeminists, the privileging of rationality within these systems of oppression has led to the suppression of ecocentric perspectives and values and has resulted in a patriarchal culture which 'looks but doesn't see, acts but doesn't feel, thinks but doesn't know' (Kheel 1993, 257). Instead rationality 'has liquidated itself as an agency of ethical, moral and religious insight' (Horkheimer [1947] 1974, 18). Plumwood has termed the ecological crisis with which we are faced a 'crisis of rationality, morality and imagination' (Plumwood 2002, 98) and points to:

> ... the familiar view of reason and emotion as sharply separated and opposed, and of 'desire,' caring, and love as merely 'personal' and 'particular' as opposed to the universality and impartiality of understanding and of 'feminine' emotions as essentially unreliable, untrustworthy, and morally irrelevant, an inferior domain to be dominated by a superior, disinterested (and of course masculine) reason. (Plumwood 1991, 5)

Ecofeminism thus provides a jumping-off point for re-envisioning relations within the more-than-human in a way that values care, emotion and embodiment.

The rationality to which Plumwood refers has been amplified through processes of neoliberalism that currently dominate economic and political thinking. Neoliberalism is a complex and often contradictory set of practices, best described as sets of processes of neoliberalisation that vary through time and geography rather than a fixed ideology (Larner 2003). However, broadly speaking, the neoliberal agenda argues that the interests of society are best served by the individual maximisation of self-interest, which is most effectively achieved through the operation of the market and devolution of regulatory authority. The role of the state is focused on ensuring that prevailing conditions are conducive for deregulation, the expansion of markets and the privatisation of assets (Dowling and Harvie 2014). The moral qualities of subjects, presumed to pursue personal material advantage ad infinitum, are based on their ability to rationally assess the costs and benefits of proposed acts such that there is a congruence between a responsible and moral individual and an economic-rational actor. This choice of action is 'an expression of free will on the basis of a self-determined decision, the consequences of the action are borne by the subject alone, who is also solely responsible for them' (Lemke 2001, 201). The criterion of economic efficiency resulting in economic prosperity thus becomes closely linked with personal and moral well-being and with individual freedom. It is this focus on individualism and the pursuit of individual advantage, where the needs of other living beings are disregarded, that an embodied ethics of care seeks to counter.

Moreover, such a focus produces the ideal and idealised individual as a disembodied and disengaged subject 'free and rational to the extent that he [sic] has fully distinguished himself from the natural and social worlds' such that 'the subject withdraws from his own body, which he is able to look on as an object' (Taylor 1995, 7). As a result, and particularly in the Global North, humans have become emotionally and physically distanced from the ways in which our[3] actions impact on nature, on ourselves and on other humans, an alienation that Claire Colebrook links to the lack of 'panic, [or] any apparent, affective comportment that would indicate that anyone really feels or fears [the threat of climate change]' (Colebrook 2011, 53). The ecofeminist project challenges dualistic thinking that privileges rationality and rational ways of knowing in order to redress the physical, emotional and moral alienation and disconnection from nature that are its outcome.

For Stephens (2011), a means must be found to resist neoliberalist and postmaternal thinking. She argues that a feminist maternalism can be reconceptualised through combining maternalism and egalitarianism, by resisting the privatisation of motherhood and by mobilising non-violent activism and an expressive politics that draws on heightened gendered symbols of motherhood or female sexuality. This is underpinned by Sara Ruddick's notion of maternal thinking; a form of moral attentiveness and reasoning judgement that develops from the practices of mothering expressed as the loving relationship between two unequal partners. Stephens believes that resistance is already growing evidenced by the increasing numbers of maternal advocacy groups, particularly those operating through social media. These range from, for example, Mumsnet in the United Kingdom, who offer a platform for shared parenting advice and policy formulation around family issues, to CODEPINK, an anti-war coalition of mothers in the United States. She acknowledges the tensions apparent in such groups' recognition and communication of the value of motherhood which often fail to challenge dominant cultural understandings around family, work and the values promoted by the market. Indeed, she notes that motherhood can be celebrated as an identity decoupled from the everyday care of babies and children. I would argue that Stephens's critiques of such online campaigners and activists do not go far enough as many have a poor record of, for example, challenging cuts to welfare that affect poor women and the 'othering' of single mothers in stark contrast to the glamorisation of celebrity mothers in the popular media (Littler 2013; McRobbie 2013).

In the final chapter of her book, Stephens turns to ecofeminism and ecofeminist activism, where she sees possibilities for meaningful engagement with a reinvigorated 'feminist maternalism' (Stephens 2011, 143). She sees ecofeminist work on care ethics as a theoretically informed re-gendering through examining the intersections between feminism, environmentalism and peace politics. She refers briefly to the work of Carol Gilligan, Nel Noddings and Jean Tronto (among others) but seemingly without much appreciation of the very different approaches taken by such scholars. Tronto, for example, eschews linkages between maternalism and care. She also points to Gloria Orenstein's idea of 'the femivore', where an ethic of care for children and the environment is expressed through a focus on home and community (raising chickens, making jam and growing organic vegetables) in acts of shared resistance to consumer capitalism. She recognises the 'uncomfortable ideological associations that hark back to the gender politics of the 1950s' (Stephens 2011, 139) that such ideas might raise but contrasts this with the pressures on mothers to return to work after childbirth that are captured through images of corporate-sponsored breast pumping. However, while Orenstein is recognised as an ecofeminist scholar (see Sturgeon 1997 for an overview and critique of her work), the link to ecofeminism more broadly is not well made and indeed, a construal of ecofeminist care ethics as grounded in maternalism, whether reinvigorated or not, is a mis-reading of ecofeminist work. Leading ecofeminist thought around care such as the work of Curtin (1991), Gaard (1993), Kheel (1993), Plumwood (1993) or Warren (2000) does not refer to 'mothering as a paradigm of political and social care' (Stephens 2011, 141). Niamh Moore, whose work Stephens cites in support of her claim that it is time for feminism to move beyond the impasse created by accusations of essentialism, rejects the disavowal of maternalism or motherhood as incompatible with feminist activism but equally resists the reduction of ecofeminism to maternalism. Moore found no evidence that maternalist discourses were dominant among the peace camp activists she studied but instead sees such camps as 'sites of struggle over the meaning of woman and the practice of eco/feminist politics, where the meanings of woman, and eco/feminism, are not just reified but are also refigured' (Moore 2008, 294). Other ecofeminist thinkers explicitly warn against linking ecofeminism with maternalism. For example, ecofeminist political theorist Sherilyn MacGregor calls for a *'properly political* ecofeminism' that eschews 'rhetorics rooted in fixed and privatized feminized identities that are themselves depoliticised (for example maternalism)' (2014, 630, emphasis in original. See also MacGregor 2006). Thus, while Stephens could perhaps argue that ecofeminism resists a purported directive to 'leave motherhood behind' as ecofeminism does not seek to exclude any group that is oppressed by patriarchal structures, it is difficult to claim that it builds its program on a maternalist platform.

The history of ecofeminism offers one explanation as to why some ecofeminists might wish to avoid an association with maternalism, howsoever it could be reconfigured. From the turn of the century, ecofeminist voices became relatively muted, and according to some (e.g. Moore 2008; Sturgeon 1997; Thompson 2006; Twine 1997), silenced by accusations of essentialism, often originating from other feminists. Critics claimed that ecofeminism celebrated a special affinity between women and nature based in biologically determined and embodied experiences of, for example, childbirth or menstruation. Care and nurturing were, therefore, 'womanly' values expressive of what was disparagingly termed a form of motherhood environmentalism (Thompson 2006, 506; Sandilands 1999). This, it was argued, was supportive of and colluded with patriarchal ideas where the association of the maternal, the polluting body and the emotional with women provides the explanation for inherent female inferiority. Similarly dismissive claims were made against ecofeminist explorations of human/animal relations while ecofeminist versions of earth-based spirituality were labelled as goddess-worship (see Gaard 2011 for a full discussion). Moreover, critics claimed that such positions ignored the complexity of women's experiences which are mediated by intersections of class, ethnicity, sexuality or able-bodiness and that ecofeminism was a white women's movement that ignored women of colour. Gaard (2011) has comprehensively rebutted such claims, as have Sturgeon (1997) and Moore (2008, 2015), who argue that ecofeminisms are situated in multiple forms of action and theory that contest relations of power and that much of this criticism was unfair, decontextualised and inaccurate. However, the ferocity of the attacks on ecofeminism warns that identification with a program based in celebrating maternalism is not without risk. As we shall see, approaches to morality based in care have attracted similar critique and it could be strategically unwise, as well as theoretically limiting, for ecofeminism to be identified with a 'new' maternalism. An ecofeminism that makes strong links to relationship and embodiment, however, does provide the ethical and political grounds for resisting the icy grip of neoliberalism and its postmaternal handmaiden.

Care, embodiment and the natural world

I will first outline the general principles of care ethics on which ecofeminists have drawn to develop ways of being in the world that are specifically situated in our relationships both human and more-than-human. I then develop this further as an ecofeminist ethics that values emotion and embodiment and which provides a springboard for action but which is not grounded in maternalism.

An ethics of care begins from an understanding of human interaction such that people are constantly enmeshed in relationships and not seen primarily as rational actors pursuing their own goals and maximising their own interests. Indeed personhood is relational, a becoming-in-the-world-with-others (Price and Shildrick 2002) which is focused on 'a capacity to reshape and cultivate new relations, not to ever more closely resemble the unencumbered abstract rational self of liberal political and moral theories' (Held 2006, 14). While there are different nuances in how care can be defined, I am drawn to Hamington's definition which stresses the embodied dimension to care:

> Care denotes an approach to personal and social morality that shifts ethical considerations to context, relationships and affective knowledge in a manner that can be fully understood only if care's embodied dimension is recognized. Care is committed to the flourishing and growth of individuals yet acknowledges our interconnectedness and interdependence. (Hamington 2004, 3)

This is an ethics that values interdependencies and caring relations that connect persons to one another. It describes a process of making judgements based in context and real, lived experiences and in the constellation of relationships and institutions in which caring is positioned. It recognises specific relations of dependency, responsibility and interconnection as well as respecting the difference and independence of the other.

As a practice it is evident that care underpins human life. All humans and most life forms require care or give care at some point over their lifespans. Care thus flows through everyday experience and effort and energy is necessary to form and maintain caring relationships such that care is an ongoing process. An ability to care, to experience sympathy, to demonstrate understanding and sensitivity to a situation and to the fate of particular and general others through dynamic, imaginative responses to context and situation is regarded as the hallmark of moral capacity. Qualities such as empathetic responsiveness, emotion, appropriate trust, solidarity and shared concern are to be encouraged and developed rather than rejected as potentially threatening (Held 2006).

For Tronto:

> On the most general level, we suggest that caring be viewed as a *species activity that includes everything that we do to maintain, continue, and repair our 'world'* so that we can live in it as well

as possible. That world includes our bodies, our selves, and our environment, all of which we seek to interweave in a complex, life-sustaining web. (1993, 103, emphasis in original)

Tronto's delineation of the world as a web of relationships resonates with the ecocentric perspectives that inform ecofeminism. Ecocentrism espouses a view of the world as ' … an intrinsically dynamic, interrelated web of relations [with] no absolutely discrete entities and no absolute dividing lines between the living and the nonliving, the animate and the inanimate, or the human and the nonhuman' (Eckersley 1992, 49). All elements within nature are interconnected and all should be respected because they have intrinsic value. As a holist philosophy that emphasises respect for the inherent value of individual beings as well as the totality of ecological processes and which is sensitive to the relationships that sustain life (Plumwood 1993), it is appropriate that ecofeminism has drawn on the moral significance of care. For ecofeminism, caring is grounded in an ability to see connections to others who are different from us, perhaps indifferent to us and not necessarily equal or not equal and is underpinned by a focus on:

> values typically unnoticed, underplayed, or misrepresented in traditional ethics (e.g. values of care, love, friendship, and appropriate trust). These are values that presuppose that our relationships to others are central to an understanding of who we are. (Warren 2000, 100)

Care is grounded in a practical morality that sees the self not as atomised nor as self-optimising, but as positioned in a web of caring relationships more fulfilling than the narrow pursuit of self-interest. Ecofeminist philosopher Warren (2000) argues that care, and the ability to empathise through care, is a moral emotion essential to ethical motivation, deliberation and practice. Ethical action should be located in 'care-sensitive' ethics in which such sensitivity determines how principles such as duty, utility or justice can provide guidance for action. Appropriate principles are those which take into account the extent to which 'care practices' are reflected, created and maintained in a given context. Care practices are those that maintain, promote or enhance the flourishing of relevant parties. Practices that cause unnecessary and avoidable harm to selves and relevant others such as the destruction of the stability, diversity and sustainability of first people's cultures or natural ecosystems such as rainforests, oceans or deserts are not care practices and neither are those that oppress or exploit others or violate their civil rights. Any claim that humans are separate from nature is refuted; humans are biophysical members of an ecological community and, at the same time, different, in some respects, from other members of that community. The attention to relationships and community does not erase difference, but respectfully acknowledges it (Warren 2000).

What is currently largely missing from ecofeminist care ethics is an explicit attention to the embodied aspects of care and I have argued elsewhere that ecofeminism needs to embrace the body (Phillips 2015) to challenge the ways that nature and emotionality are cast and to begin to reimagine and revalue them. An acceptance of the organic materiality of human bodies, as beings who are part of the natural world, can overcome our estrangement from nature and remind us that our future and well-being is inherently entwined with that of the planet. Hamington points out how the body and embodied experience, learning and imagination combine to develop understandings of interconnection, engagement and relations with others and thus we are empowered to develop care practices (Hamington 2004). The potential for an ethics grounded in care to motivate and inspire political action resides in a capacity for feeling pain at the distress of others and responding imaginatively. Care and compassion enable us to visualise the suffering caused by injustice and to consider how best to ameliorate that. In this way, care is not confined within an impersonal straightjacket of logic and rationality, and neither is it reduced to maternality, but involves 'a complex weaving of imaginative processes with embodied practices' (Hamington 2004, 5). This includes the interplay between mind and body that produces the embodied experiences which enable individuals to develop empathy and the understanding of the other that is often not a product of conscious thought, but which originates in the body. We are moved to act morally through a personal and embodied caring.

Thus attention to the visceral, embodied aspects of care is an imperative so that the current alienation between most of those living in the Global North and the biophysical world can be overcome. A recognition that 'the fleshy, damp immediacy of our own embodied existences' (Neimanis and Walker 2014, 559) is deeply bound up with the impacts of human activity on the planet help to connect the imaginary and the corporeal as entwined in 'a common space, a conjoined time [and] a mutual worlding' (Neimanis and Walker 2014, 560). A re-discovery of our 'earthian' place means becoming aware of and accepting our fleshiness and the frailties of that flesh, as well as recognising the vulnerability of nature. Perception is thus shifted to acknowledge the substantial interconnections between human corporeality and the more-than-human world. As Alaimo (2008, 238) points out, 'human corporeality in all its material fleshiness is inseparable from "nature" or "environment"' such that embracing the vulnerability of the body is a recognition of precarious, corporeal openness to the material world where the human is not in nature but of nature. Thus we need to reaffirm the visceral sensations and emotions experienced through our bodies to begin to develop the kind of affective, caring engagement with and embodied knowledge of nature and thus of ourselves that might lead us to respond more appropriately to the ecological threats with which humanity is faced.

Embodied experiences combine with a caring imagination to create points of departure for developing responsive interconnections that inform action. For example, I might have a favourite walk through a particular piece of woodland. My relationship with the woodland ecology of animals, trees and plants is formed through corporeal and sensual encounters. I know the different colours of the wood as they change through the seasons, hear the birdsong and rustling of small animals and smell the wood's damp, leafy perfume. I have been captivated by the patterns made by sunlight through leaves, or the bark of a gnarled tree or the discovery of fungus nibbled by a mouse. The breeze has touched my skin too as it ruffles the tree canopy. This is a form of knowing and meaning creation that extends beyond the rational and involves a responsive, emotional engagement with nature which values what 'cannot be fully articulated according to the demands of objectivity … knowledge guided by and responsive to the physical environment in which it is practiced' (Glazebrook 2005, 80). It is a corporeal and affective knowing in and through the body which goes beyond the propositional knowledge generated by gathering facts and information and a means of learning that challenges the excessive claims to universal truths of knowledge grounded in rationality which is disembodied and transcendent (see also Alaimo 2008, 2009). This embodied and situated knowledge can be gained from direct experience of 'concrete others' (Benhabib 1992, 164) which facilitates our understanding of at least some of the other's needs, and, at the same time, underlines the nature of our differences (Porter 2006). The wood with whom I have a relationship is not an abstract entity that is interchangeable with any other, but has a material presence that develops connection through sympathetic identification. Such experiences build situated knowledge and reasons to care, but they also facilitate making connections between the well-being and flourishing of the particular, including the self, as intimately intertwined with the well-being and flourishing of the general (Curtin 1991; Gaard 1993; Plumwood 1993; Warren 2000). To care about and understand the particular environmental, social and economic struggles of humans and other life forms we must recognise and have some level of understanding of those issues as features of contemporary social structures. To care about and understand such structural features, we must recognise how they exist in particular lives and experiences.

One day, I hear that the woodland is threatened by a road-building program which will tear down the trees and replace them with a highway. The environmental campaigner George Monbiot has written that we care about the living world because we love it. Acknowledging this love can inspire and empower us, and can allow us to engage the imagination as well as the intellect in ways that appeals to self-interest or to cold rationality cannot (Monbiot 2015). Thus it is out of love that I will act to try to protect the wood and resist the developers, not out of a rational calculation of the costs and benefits that might accrue to me or to my community. To inform that resistance, I will learn more about the political and economic systems within which road-building is more important than the preservation of natural space. When I hear of other threats to the natural environment, even though they might be places which I have never visited, I will remember how I felt – the trace of those feelings will resonate within my body – and I can imagine how those affected, human and other life forms, will be impacted. Experiencing loss, anger and sadness myself allows me to develop empathy: the response to the other that combines embodied and other forms of knowledge with emotion to enable me to understand the situation of the other. Our capacity to care thus extends beyond our personal experiences to an ability to respond to difference, and to visualise what the other, given their specificity, is undergoing. This pre-supposes a sense of shared vulnerability to suffering and an ability to respond to the other's pain (Alaimo 2009). Equally, we demonstrate the equal worth of the other by furthering their flourishing. The actions required of us to promote such flourishing can only be discerned by careful attention to and respect for the other's needs and we should make room in ourselves to be moved by the experiences of the other and not just because the other's pain resonates with our own (Porter 2006). In this way, embodied care is not reduced to individual bodily experience but works together with the imagination to allow us to overcome the limitations of individual physical existence and reach out to the other over time, space and difference (Hamington 2004). We can extend care to those with whom we have no direct personal relationship and who are in circumstances that perhaps we have not experienced ourselves but who are part of the web of interconnections in which we are situated; orangutans threatened by forest fires in Indonesia, the plight of refugees fleeing war or other deprivations or the circumstances of bonded labourers. As Hamington (2004) points out, it is through our imagination that we are moved to care even for fictional characters in books, plays or films and indeed, the imaginative and emotional shifts stimulated by engagement with narrative, whether fictional or based in 'reality', develops and increases the capacity for care (Manning 1992). The concretisation of the other also therefore emerges from indirect experience such as through the news or other media and through the vicarious experiences produced through engagement with the arts whether that be fiction, poetry or visual art (Gayá and Phillips 2015; Phillips 2014, 2015). We cannot possibly have full access to the experience of even proximate others, let alone to distant others where that distance is between human and other life forms, but while these accounts often anthropomorphise the actualities of the more-than-human, they challenge us to engage with difference, to see the familiar from a radical perspective and provide an additional means for encountering and reflecting on the experiences of the other. It is this empathetic act of imagination that allows a move from the personal and known to the wider world and to the unknown as we have to consider how to act in new situations or when faced with unknown others. Both our direct and indirect encounters with the other combine embodied feeling and caring imagination stimulated by active engagement and listening so that we hear and respond to the plight of distant others. Indeed, for Hamington (2004), it is part of our moral responsibility to seek out experiences that develop embodied understanding and connection with the other. This is a wider, more inclusive, vision on which to build care ethics than a narrow appeal to maternalism.

As noted earlier in this paper, I pointed to the critiques levelled at ecofeminism in which it was claimed that it was an essentialist form of environmentalism that made particular claims for women's innate connection to the earth. Similar minefields are strewn around concepts of care grounded in the relationship between mothers and children which makes any appeal to maternalism a high-risk strategy for ecofeminism. The early work of care ethicists such as Gilligan (1982) and Noddings (1984) was interpreted as positioning care as an essentially female practice and disposition because women are more likely to experience care-giving activities and therefore have a greater understanding of and empathy for practices of care. Noddings, in particular, argued that women's orientation to care was shaped by the loving and emotional bonds developed through maternal experience which challenged the concept of a rational, disembodied and detached self. This work was widely criticised for promoting an essentialist view of women, for ignoring the cultural specificities of 'mothering', for failing to take account of the hierarchical nature of mother/child relations and more generally for 'reaffirming a dichotomy between those who care and those cared for' (Beasley and Bacchi 2005, 59). In her later work, Gilligan (1995) herself was clear that care should not be labelled a 'feminine' ethic to be associated with essentialised female traits such as passivity, irrationality and, importantly from the perspective of care, a desire to nurture at the expense of the self. Gilligan asserts that 'selflessness or self-sacrifice is built into the very definition of care when caring is premised on an opposition between relationships and self-development' such that an ethic identified with putative feminine traits in a patriarchal order would posit relationships that are fundamentally unequal (Gilligan 1995, 122). A one-sided preoccupation with the flourishing of others is thus deeply problematic particularly when it is premised on the prior assumption that women are 'naturally' able and willing to sacrifice their own needs and development in the interests of others.

It is also the case that caring is usually a socially stratified activity in Western society where the work of care is not only gendered but also raced and classed such that it falls on those who have the least power and voice. Indeed, more recently, it has come to be understood not as a distinctively or exclusively feminine perspective, but as a potential orientation emerging from political or social subordination which includes gender, but also encompasses race, class and other categories (Simola 2010; Skeggs 2014; Tronto

1987). This has been described in positive terms as a strategy of solidarity that helps relatively excluded groups cope with vulnerability and as reflecting a vision for a more compassionate society that might emerge in those groups because of their experiences of oppression. However, care ethics has been critiqued for ignoring such power assymetries, a concern amplified by Noddings's assertion that becoming better at caring for oneself can be morally justified as it leads to better caring for others. For Hoagland (1991), care could become a one-way-traffic that is fraught with the potential for personal and political danger as it could be used to maintain current divisions of labour; feminist scholarship, for example, has pointed to the 'tyranny of maternity' generated by the repetitive and exhausting daily round of housework and childcare and the ways in which this burden still falls disproportionately on women (McRobbie 2013; Wood and Janice 2006). The emphasis placed on the importance of relationships has therefore prompted some critics to express concern that women and other marginalised groups may be led to prioritise the other at the expense of the self; thus supporting oppressive social constraints placed on women's behaviour in particular.

The counter to such critiques enlarges the focus of care beyond the individual and beyond maternalism as a necessary move to bring about the social and political changes required to reinvigorate more-than-human relationships and to ensure the flourishing of life on this planet. An ecofeminist, embodied ethics of care such as I have outlined points to the potentially liberatory and radical aspects of relatedness and does not ground its argument in a reification of women's 'maternal' propensity to care. It is liberatory because it is available to men and to women, enabling and empowering all those who are excluded from hegemonic masculinity's construction of the ideal to flourish as a self in relationship. It is radical because, as Curtin (1991) points out, caring must be understood and developed as integral to a wider political agenda which challenges the atomisation of the individual amplified by neoliberalism. Caring thus focuses on a relational sense of self that is nonabusive and nonexploitative, that embraces but does not subsume the difference of the other and which extends care to contexts in the public sphere where it is currently deemed inappropriate. More importantly, it is radical also because it starts to address the challenge of how can we live differently, of finding 'a way of belonging differently in the world' (Gibson-Graham 2011, 1) that opens up possibilities for re-imagining humanity in ways that are exciting and, more pragmatically, necessary in order to survive at all.

Conceptualising the self as part of a wider web of interconnected selves reduces the risk of falling into a paternalistic trap where there is an asymmetrical relationship between those who are vulnerable, dependent and in need of care, and those who deliver it (Hughes et al. 2005), or conversely, that giving care necessarily involves the privileging of the other over the self. This dualistic concept of care has been supported by assumptions that care relationships are exclusively dyadic such as that of mother and child espoused by maternalist thinking. However, Tronto points out that such assumptions are inaccurate and a distortion of care because, to follow the same example, mothers do not provide care alone but childrearing is situated in a complex set of social relationships that includes the wider family, neighbours, health and education services and other carers. Moreover, Tronto argues that the particular bond between mothers and children and its representation as the primary relationship of life is a social construction and one that is relatively recent (Tronto 2013). The capacity to see the self as vulnerable and to recognise that those who receive care and those who give care are the same people undercuts the processes whereby care recipients are viewed as other and, for Tronto, 'forces us to recognize the limits of market life as the metaphor for all human actions' (151).

So a recognition of the embodiment and vulnerability that is shared by the more-than-human moves the focus of care away from a primary engagement with those deemed to be needy or dependent, such as the maternal relation to a child, to the interdependence of all beings on the planet. It casts care as a process which requires work, but without expecting reciprocation, and which takes place in the intersections between more-than-humans. It foregrounds the interconnections between caring as a set of values and caring as a set of material and embodied practices rather than as a 'thing' which is bestowed by one party on another. Moreover, this process of active caring does not background emotion but emphasises the importance of feeling that is also embodied, and the need to reflect on convictions and feelings. It is thus also distinguished from forms of postmaternity that are antagonistic to embodied experience and emotional connectedness. Active and embodied caring encourage an understanding of self and humanity as part of nature such that we can 'dare to care' (Warren 2000, 212); an essential precursor to political action which could challenge the dominance of neoliberalism. Thus an appeal to maternalism is neither necessary nor desirable in order to emphasise the importance of a caring that is and should be embodied through emotional attachments to animals, landscapes or ecosystems which increase awareness of interdependence and foster action and which signify the need to make nature present in the conscious life of the Global North.

Concluding thoughts

A greater emotional and embodied connectivity with nature, a recognition of our vulnerability and an embracing of the importance of care is part of a more positive imaginary of an ecology of self in relationship with the more-than-human which contrasts with what Ghassan Hage (cited in Beasley and Bacchi 2005) argues is the perception that states and other institutions care for increasingly smaller groups of their 'stakeholders' and see nature only as a resource. The resulting insecurity, hyper-competition and scapegoating of 'others' that results is socially destructive such that it becomes increasingly difficult to care for each other or for the environment (Beasley and Bacchi 2005). An ecofeminist approach to embodied care is thus a resource to inform political action that can challenge the dominant neoliberalist discourses and practices that are damaging our planet and threatens more-than-human futures. This account of care suggests an alternative to the neoliberalist assumption of an autonomous, atomised and self-optimising individual though a focus on elements such as relationship, emotion and intersubjectivity that neoliberalism and its postmaternal derivatives disregards. The combination of embodied elements of care with affective knowledge fosters compassionate connection that motivates action. Action, experience and understanding are held together in a fluid but self-reinforcing relationship where a philosophy of care and connectedness informs and is informed by action. For Joan Tronto:

> Care is a way of framing political issues that makes their impact, and concern with human [and more-than-human] lives, direct and immediate. Within the care framework, political issues can make sense and connect to each other. Under these conditions, political involvement increases dramatically (Tronto 1993, 177)

But to build societies grounded in care will require a reconception of the human self in mutualistic terms – 'a self-in-relationship with nature, formed not in the drive for mastery and control of the other but in a balance of mutual transformation and negotiation' (Plumwood 2006, 142). This is based in self-knowledge and an ability to distinguish self-interests from those of others, and a willingness to pay attention to the independence of the other. This is a relationship built on foundations of respect, care and love as we strive to replace more instrumental and mechanistic models that have not served thus far to mitigate disastrous outcomes for the more-than-human. Ecofeminist care could refigure the postmaternal, not by specifically pointing to the relationships between mothers and children as exemplars of care and neither by 'leaving motherhood behind' but by building on care for particular others to enhance wider and more generalised concerns and for feeling and understanding the relationships between particular commitments and losses and those of more distant others.

Finally, I hope I have demonstrated that an appeal to maternalism is limiting. An embodied conception of care, grounded in ecofeminist principles, such as I have outlined provides more vibrant, exciting and radical inspiration that is sorely needed if humanity is to reconfigure its place within the world.

Notes

1. Whether 'equality feminism' is complicit in neoliberalist processes is a debate beyond the scope of this article. However, see McRobbie (2008), Fraser (2009) and in particular McRobbie (2013) for an interesting discussion on 'new maternity'.
2. For a history of ecofeminism, see Sturgeon (1997) and Moore (2015).
3. I include myself as a being who dwells in the geographic and cultural space of the Global North. I have no wish to present myself as an objective observer who sits above or apart from the concerns I have outlined.

Disclosure statement

No potential conflict of interest was reported by the author.

Notes on contributor

Mary Phillips is a Reader in Organisation Studies at the University of Bristol, UK. Her research focusses on transformative, and particularly feminist, alternatives to the neo-liberalist agenda on planetary flourishing. Her recent anthology, *Contemporary Perspectives on Ecofeminism*, was published by Routledge in 2015. She is also active in green politics and a member of both the Green Party and Frome Anti-Fracking.

References

Alaimo, Stacey. 2008. "Trans-Corporeal Feminisms and the Ethical Space of Nature." In *Material Feminisms*, edited by Stacey Alaimo and Susan Hekman, 237–264. Bloomington: Indiana University Press.

Alaimo, Stacey. 2009. "Insurgent Vulnerability and the Carbon Footprint of Gender." *Kvinder, Kon & Forskning* 3–4: 22–35.

Barad, Karen. 2003. "Posthumanist Performativity: Toward an Understanding of How Matter Comes to Matter." *Signs* 28 (3): 801–831.

Barad, Karen. 2007. *Meeting the Universe Halfway: Quantum Physics and the Entanglement of Matter and Meaning*. Durham, NC: Duke University Press.

Beasley, Chris, and Carol L. Bacchi. 2005. "The Political Limits of "Care" in Re-Imagining Interconnection/Community and an Ethical Future." *Australian Feminist Studies* 20 (46): 49–64.

Benhabib, Seyla. 1992. *Situating the Self: Gender, Community and Postmodernism in Contemporary Ethics*. Bloomington: Indiana University Press.

Bennett, Jane. 2010. *Vibrant Matter: A Political Ecology of Things*. Durham, NC: Duke University Press.

Borgerson, Janet. L. 2007. "On the Harmony of Feminist Ethics and Business Ethics." *Business and Society Review* 112 (4): 477–509.

Braun, Bruce. 2004. "Querying Posthumanisms." *Geoforum* 35: 269–273.

Castree, Noel. 2008. "Neoliberalising Nature: The Logics of Deregulation and Reregulation." *Environment and Planning A* 40 (1): 131–152.

Colebrook, Claire. 2011. "Earth Felt the Wound: The Affective Divide." *Journal for Politics, Gender and Culture* 8 (1): 45–58.

Cudworth, Erika. 2005. *Developing Eco-Feminist Theory: The Complexity of Difference*. Basingstoke: Palgrave Macmillan.

Cuomo, Chris. 2002. "On Ecofeminist Philosophy." *Ethics and the Environment* 7 (2): 1–11.

Curtin, Deane. 1991. "Toward an Ecological Ethic of Care." *Hypatia* 6 (1): 60–74.

Dobson, Andrew. 2009. "10:10 and the Politics of Climate Change." *Open Democracy*. https://www.opendemocracy.net/article/10-10-and-the-politics-of-climate-change.

Dowling, Emma, and David Harvie. 2014. "Harnessing the Social: State, Crisis and (Big) Society." *Sociology* 48 (5): 869–886.

Eckersley, Robyn. 1992. *Environmentalism and Political Theory*. Albany: State University of New York Press.

Fraser, Nancy. 2009. "Feminism, Capitalism and the Cunning of History." *New Left Review* 56. https://newleftreview.org/II/56/nancy-fraser-feminism-capitalism-and-the-cunning-of-history.

Gaard, Greta. 1993. "Living Interconnections with Animals and Nature." In *Ecofeminism: Women, Animals, Nature*, edited by G. Gaard, 1–12. Philadelphia, PA: Temple University Press.

Gaard, Greta. 2011. "Ecofeminism Revisited: Rejecting Essentialism and Re-Placing Species in a Material Feminist Environmentalism." *Feminist Formations* 23 (2): 26–53.

Gayá, Patricia, and Mary E. Phillips. 2015. "Imagining a Sustainable Future: Eschatology, Bateson's Ecology of Mind and Arts-Based Practice." *Organization*. Advance online publication. doi:10.1177/1350508415619240.

Gibson-Graham, J. K. 2011. "A Feminist Project of Belonging for the Anthropocene." *Gender, Place and Culture* 18 (1): 1–21.

Gilligan, Carol. 1982. *In a Different Voice: Psychological Theory and Women's Development*. Cambridge, MA: Harvard University Press.

Gilligan, Carol. 1995. "Hearing the Difference: Theorizing Connection." *Hypatia* 10 (2): 120–127.

Glazebrook, Trish. 2005. "Gynocentric Eco-Logics." *Ethics and the Environment* 10 (2): 75–99.

Hamington, Maurice. 2004. *Embodied Care: Jane Addams, Maurice Merleau-Ponty, and Feminist Ethics*. Urbana: University of Illinois Press.

Haraway, Donna. 2008. *When Species Meet*. Minneapolis: University of Minnesota Press.

Held, Virginia. 2006. *The Ethics of Care: Personal, Political and Global*. New York: Oxford University Press.

Hoagland, Sarah Lucia. 1991. "Some Thoughts about Caring." In *Feminist Ethics*, edited by Claudia Card, 246–263. Lawrence: University Press of Kansas.

Hopwood, Bill, Mary Mellor, and Geoff O'Brien. 2005. "Sustainable Development: Mapping Different Approaches." *Sustainable Development* 13 (1): 38–52.

Horkheimer, Max. (1947) 1974. *Eclipse of Reason*. New York: Continuum.

Hughes, Bill, Linda McKie, Debra Hopkins, and Nick Watson. 2005. "Love's Labours Lost: Feminism, the Disabled People's Movement and an Ethic of Care." *Sociology* 39 (2): 259–275.

Kheel, Marti. 1993. "From Heroic to Holistic Ethics: The Ecofeminist Challenge." In *Ecofeminism: Women, Animals, Nature*, edited by Greta Gaard, 243–271. Philadelphia, PA: Temple University Press.

Kheel, Marti. 2008. *Nature Ethics: An Ecofeminist Perspective*. Lanham, MD: Rowman and Littlefield.

Lahar, Stephanie. 1991. "Ecofeminist Theory and Grassroots Politics." *Hypatia* 6 (1): 28–45.

Larner, Wendy. 2003. "Neoliberalism?" *Environment and Planning D: Society and Space* 21 (5): 509–512.

Lemke, Thomas. 2001. "'The Birth of Bio-Politics': Michel Foucault's Lecture at The Collège De France on Neo-Liberal Governmentality." *Economy and Society* 30 (2): 190–207.

Littler, Jo. 2013. "The Rise of the "Yummy Mummy': Popular Conservatism and the Neoliberal Maternal in Contemporary British Culture." *Communication, Culture & Critique* 6: 227–243.

MacGregor, Sherilyn. 2006. *Beyond Mothering Earth: Ecological Citizenship and the Politics of Care*. Vancouver: UBC Press.

MacGregor, Sherilyn. 2014. "Only Resist: Feminist Ecological Citizenship and the Post-Politics of Climate Change." *Hypatia* 29 (3): 617–633.

Manning, Rita C. 1992. *Speaking from the Heart: A Feminist Perspective on Ethics*. Lanham, MD: Rowman and Littlefield.

McRobbie, Angela. 2008. *The Aftermath of Feminism: Gender, Culture and Social Change*. London: Sage.

McRobbie, Angela. 2013. "Feminism, the Family and the New "Mediated" Maternalism." *New Formations* 80: 119–137.

Monbiot, George. 2015. "Why We Fight for the Living World: It's about Love, and It's Time We Said So." *The Guardian*. http://www.theguardian.com/commentisfree/2015/jun/16/pope-encyclical-value-of-living-world.

Moore, Niamh. 2008. "Eco/Feminism, Non-Violence and the Future of Feminism." *International Feminist Journal of Politics* 10 (3): 282–298.

Moore, Niamh. 2015. "Eco/Feminist Genealogies: Renewing Promises and New Possibilities." In *Contemporary Perspectives on Ecofeminism*, edited by M. Phillips and N. Rumens, 19–37. Abingdon: Routledge.

Murphy, Joseph. 2000. "Ecological Modernisation." *Geoforum* 31: 1–8.

Neimanis, Astrida, and Rachel L. Walker. 2014. "Weathering: Climate Change and the "Thick Time" of Transcorporeality." *Hypatia* 29 (3): 558–575.

Noddings, Nel. 1984. *Caring: A Feminine Approach to Ethics and Moral Education*. Berkeley: University of California Press.

Phillips, Mary E. 2014. "Re-writing Corporate Environmentalism: Ecofeminism, Corporeality and the Language of Feeling." *Gender, Work and Organization* 21 (5): 443–458.

Phillips, Mary E. 2015. "Developing Ecofeminist Corporeality: Writing the Body as Activist Poetics." In *Contemporary Perspectives on Ecofeminism*, edited by Mary E. Phillips and Nicholas Rumens, 57–75. London: Routledge.

Plumwood, Val. 1991. "Nature, Self and Gender: Feminism, Environmental Philosophy and the Critique of Rationalism." *Hypatia* 6 (1): 3–27.

Plumwood, Val. 1993. *Feminism and the Mastery of Nature*. London: Routledge.

Plumwood, Val. 2002. *Environmental Culture: The Ecological Crisis of Reason*. New York: Routledge.

Plumwood, Val. 2006. "Feminism." In *Political Theory and the Ecological Challenge*, edited by Andrew Dobson and Robyn Eckersley, 51–74. Cambridge: Cambridge University Press.

Porter, Elisabeth. 2006. "Can Politics Practice Compassion?" *Hypatia* 21 (4): 97–123.

Price, Janet, and Margaret Shildrick. 2002. "Bodies Together: Touch, Ethics and Disability." In *Disability/Postmodernity: Embodying Disability Theory*, edited by Mairian Corker and Tom Shakespeare, 62–75. London: Continuum.

Probyn, Elspeth. 2014. "Women Following Fish in a More-Than-Human World." *Gender, Place and Culture* 21 (5): 589–603.

Sandilands, Catriona. 1999. *The Good-Natured Feminist: Ecofeminism and the Quest for Democracy*. Minneapolis: University of Minnesota Press.

Seyfang, Gill. 2005. "Shopping for Sustainability: Can Sustainable Consumption Promote Ecological Citizenship?" *Environmental Politics* 14 (2): 290–306.

Shove, Elizabeth, and Gordon Walker. 2010. "Governing Transitions in the Sustainability of Everyday Life." *Research Policy* 39 (4): 471–476.

Simola, Sheldene. 2010. "Anti-Corporate Anger as a Form of Care-Based Moral Agency." *Journal of Business Ethics* 94: 255–269.

Skeggs, Beverly. 2014. "Values Beyond Value? Is Anything Beyond the Logic of Capital?" *British Journal of Sociology* 65 (1): 1–20.

Stephens, Julie. 2011. *Confronting Postmaternal Thinking*. New York: Columbia University Press.

Sturgeon, Noel. 1997. *Ecofeminist Natures: Race, Gender, Feminist Theory and Political Action*. London: Routledge.

Taylor, Charles. 1995. *Philosophical Arguments*. Cambridge, MA: Harvard University Press.

Thompson, Charis. 2006. "Back to Nature? Resurrecting Ecofeminism after Poststructuralist and Third-Wave Feminism." *Isis* 97 (3): 505–512.

Tronto, Joan C. 1987. "Beyond Gender Difference to a Theory of Care." *Signs: Journal of Women in Culture and Society* 12 (4): 644–663.

Tronto, Joan C. 1993. *Moral Boundaries: A Political Argument for an Ethic of Care*. New York: Routledge.

Tronto, Joan C. 2013. *Caring Democracy: Markets, Equality and Justice*. New York: New York University Press.

Twine, Richard T. 1997. "Masculinity, Nature, Ecofeminism." *Ecofem.org/journal*. http://www.lancs.ac.uk/staff/twine/ecofem/masc.pdf.

Warren, Karen. 2000. *Ecofeminist Philosophy: A Western Perspective on What It Is and Why It Matters*. Lanham, MD: Rowman and Littlefield.

Whatmore, Sarah. 1999. "Human Geographies: Rethinking the "Human" in Human Geography." In *Human Geography Today*, edited by Doreen Massey, John Allen, and Philip Sarre, 22–39. Cambridge: Polity Press.

Whatmore, Sarah. 2002. *Hybrid Geographies: Natures, Cultures, Spaces*. London: Sage.

Whatmore, Sarah. 2004. "Humanism's Excess: Some Thoughts on the "Post-Human/ist" Agenda." *Environment and Planning A* 36: 1360–1363.

Wood, Glenice J., and Newton Janice. 2006. "Childlessness and Women Managers: 'Choice', Context and Discourses." *Gender, Work & Organization* 13 (4): 338–358.

World Wildlife Fund. 2014. *Living Planet Report*. http://assets.worldwildlife.org/publications/723/files/original/WWF-LPR2014-low_res.pdf?1413912230&_ga = 1.230044959.269800605.1426861329.

Postmaternal Times and Radical Feminist Thinking

Alison Bartlett

ABSTRACT
Linking the postmaternal to postfeminism as products of late twentieth-century neoliberal capitalism, postmaternal thinking is defined in this article by its historical time period, from the early 1980s onwards, and by its legacy of radical feminist thinking which was critical in messing up traditional understandings of maternity. This is demonstrated through research and resources related to the women's peace movement, with specific reference to the women-only peace camps at Greenham Common (U.K.) and Pine Gap (Australia). The intellectual legacies of these complex and compelling debates around the social practices of maternity, the politics of family, collective domesticity and activism are often occluded in social memory, as Stephens argues in *Confronting Postmaternal Thinking* (2011). This paper extends Stephens' working definition of postmaternity to argue for an interconnected structural social analysis of postmaternal times, and contests modernist categories of knowing to consider postmaternity as postmodernist in its multiple and shifting array of politics. In this way postmaternity becomes a time in which maternity is open to redefinition through a proliferation of meaning and possibilities, and this is demonstrated by concluding in the form of a manifesto.

Prologue: mothers and daughters at the sink

In 1970 a group of women formed the Sydney Women's Film Group, one of the first women's liberation groups in Australia. They started making a film as a means of engaging women in liberationist discussion and also as an act of cultural intervention: of taking the means of production to produce a women's culture. Shot mostly in 1970, it was released in 1973 as *Film for Discussion*. This black and white experimental film is structured through montage and then classical cinematic narrative to follow a young woman's day moving between work and home. The montage uses: text by Marx; stills and moving advertisements for make-up, bras, washing powder, sex, and wedding gowns; poetry and linocut illustrations from the feminist magazine *MeJane*; footage of women working in offices as secretaries and in factories as machinists and with children marching in street protests to the tune of 'Don't be Too Polite, Girls'. After this chaotic and sonally intense prelude, the realist narrative follows a young office worker, Jeni, through her monotonous day at the office, driving home with her boyfriend who is the office manager, and having a family dinner with him at her parents' house. After dinner she is washing the dishes with her mother, in a scene that is a visual extension of the monotony of office and factory work. Their conversation, like many of the conversations in this narrative, registers the everyday discourses and social practices of the day and finds them frustratingly inadequate:

> Mother: Can you imagine the complete chaos that would be here if I didn't come home to cook the meal? And everything else? Your father would be ropeable. Heavens, he's bad enough now. The problem lays, I think, with this drinking every night with the boys. Drinking so much every night that he comes home half P-I-S-S-E-D, and this seems to cause the problem and the trouble.
> Jeni: No but it's more than that. It's the way that you put up with it that is causing it.
> Mother: I wonder if you're going to be any different if you marry John. Although John's a different personality to your father.
> Jeni: Oh I don't know, I think they're all the same.
> Mother: Why, do you think he could change?
> Jeni: I think John wants to become like Dad. He's already started ... he just gives me all this extra work at the office.
> Mother: What, typing?
> Jeni: Yes, after hours. I don't get paid for it or anything.
> Mother: Well you wouldn't expect to get paid for it, pet, if he's asked you to do it.
> Jeni: Well that's just the point. Why should I have to do it when I've got all my own work to do? Just because I'm his girlfriend?
> Mother: Men seem to expect this of women.
> Jeni: But that's what I mean.
> Mother: You're never ever supposed to get tired, we're there for their beck and call.
> Jeni: But that's what I'm saying. If we start to ... if we can ...
> Mother: But we've always been like this. I couldn't imagine it being any different. And I think there is a slight need, deep down, there's a need to be needed.
> Jeni: It would have to be different. Look, I don't want to get married and do what you do, or stay in the office and do the same sort of work I'm doing.
> (Sydney Women's Film Group 1973)

This scene was not scripted, so can be understood to constitute some of the common parlance about gendered labour at the time. It also articulates a family relation between mother and daughter that is impacted by the shifting social values generated by the women's liberation movement. Akin to the dynamics of consciousness raising practices at the time, women's relations in a heterosexual model of family life are articulated and questioned, even as they are being performed in this scene. As mother and daughter stand washing and drying dishes at the sink, their discussion lacks vitriol or violence but keenly establishes the differences between what has always been and what has to be different in their life trajectories. The daughter no longer finds 'what has always been' acceptable, while the mother seems to have performed those expectations without questioning them and finding some consolation in feeling needed. The lack of animosity or even conflict in this scene is noteworthy, and yet the generational difference emerging is quite clear in their divergent expectations and thinking around maternity, work, and women's lives.

I consider this scene a prelude to postmaternalism. It suggests the need for a shift in the patriarchal legacies of a mother–daughter continuum whereby mothers model for daughters the experience of marriage and the management of men in a compulsorily heterosexual environment of unequal opportunity and male privilege. It locates this scene in the mundanity of white Australian middle-class suburbia. It articulates the daughter's insistence that something is wrong and it cannot continue. It insists that the daughter does not want the same as the mother, and yet she still wants the same mother. She may even want maternity, but the maternal can never be the same.

Postmaternal times

The postmaternal is a relatively new term introduced by Stephens in her book, *Confronting Postmaternal Thinking: Feminism, Memory, and Care* (2011), in which she develops a renewed call to value maternity at a broad cultural level. Stephens' premise is that the work of caring and the idea of dependency and vulnerability are considered shameful and penalised in public policy and cultural representations, and that this paradigm impoverishes social relations and denigrates maternity. It is distinguished from 'maternalism', which publicly values and celebrates maternity and care, albeit from a conservative understanding of gender difference (Stephens 4). This work is founded on four decades of feminist critique of the ways in which maternity has been both idolised and reviled as a form of labour, knowledge, practices, and values associated with women. Since the 1970s, around the time when *Film for Discussion* was made, much feminist critique around maternity and its inevitable entanglement in the ideology of family took place on a local level (in small magazines, pamphlets, in consciousness raising groups, theatre and poetry for example). Key texts also emerged to ground the study of maternity as an academic subject: motherhood was critiqued as a social institution and ideology (Rich 1976; Wearing 1984), as oppressively medicalised (Katz Rothman 1982) and through particular disciplinary perspectives like psychoanalysis and sociology (Chodorow 1978), anthropology (Kitzinger 1978), history and politics (Reiger 1985), and philosophy (Ruddick 1989). This foundational work in the seventies and eighties meant that Umansky (1996) was able to reflect on the impact of feminists theorising motherhood since the 1960s, heralding a new surge in maternal studies that was consolidated in the textbook, *Maternal Theory: Essential Readings* (O'Reilly 2007). Stephens' contribution to this ongoing feminist engagement with maternity is to provocatively suggest that we regard current social understandings of care, nurture, and dependency as 'postmaternal thinking':

> Postmaternal thinking refers to a process where the ideals intimately bound up with the practices of mothering are disavowed in the public sphere, and conflicted in the private. In my view this is a profoundly regressive development with significant political and social effects. What unfolds then is the proposition that postmaternal thinking is a prevailing cultural logic, central not only to policy debates but also to contemporary understandings of feminism and to the role that care, nurture, and dependency inevitably plays in all our lives. (Stephens 2011, x)

Stephens argues that this is evident in widespread cultural hostility to the idea of dependency, in which neoliberal values of individualism, independence, and self-made success are valorised while care and nurturing are regarded as services that can be outsourced: this 'can be seen as a kind of unmothering of society as a whole. The postmaternal therefore becomes a fantasy of self-sufficiency' (Stephens 7).

If the postmaternal is a time in which maternity is diminished in value and has little political authority, as Stephens argues, it arises in a particular time period, akin to postfeminism, in which the maternal and feminism are strained through late capitalist neoliberalism. Postfeminism has been largely discussed as a 'sensibility' deriving from a set of discourses refracted through mainstream media and social technologies that celebrate self-made identities that are highly visual and sexualised and have a dubious relation to second-wave feminism (Gill 2007; McRobbie 2009). While there is much in postfeminism that might also characterise postmaternal thinking, I intend to take my cue from Henderson, however, who argues that we can define postfeminism as 'a historical period – as that which comes after the organised grassroots movement of second-wave feminism (so dating from around the early 1980s)' (2016, 2). If the postmaternal is relocated in terms of its periodicity, then postmaternal thinking follows on from the contestation of maternity by the women's movement in the 1970s and early 1980s. It follows Jeni's prescient suggestion in *Film for Discussion* that 'it would have to be different'. The scene from that film at the beginning of this article represents one particular cultural moment in Australian social life when maternity is contested by generational and social change, and when it is recognised as not only involving care, nurture, and (financial and social) dependency, but also exploitation and the threat of violence. The debates and intellectual ideas of the seventies and early 1980s that critiqued the patriarchal nuclear family model produced complex and sometimes divisive formulations of alternative ideologies and living arrangements; as Barrett Meyering notes, from 1969 'motherhood had become a major preoccupation of activists both within women's liberation groups and the reform-oriented Women's Electoral Lobby (WEL) as they deliberated over the nature of female oppression' (2013, 1). In her research Barrett Meyering reflects on the negotiations and thinking involved in forging new feminist lifestyles and child-rearing practices in the early 1970s, noting that contemporary literature for feminist mothers on child-raising and maternal practice 'owes much to the efforts of mothers who were active in the women's movement during the 1970s and early 1980s [when] … a distinct set of feminist child-rearing practices emerged out of the second wave' (2013, 14). This article seeks to extend this work in conjunction with Stephens' by re-aligning the postmaternal as a timely extension of radical feminist thinking around maternity.

Social memory and modernism

Stephens' analysis of postmaternal thinking as a cultural logic in which professional work is valued over mothering work links it to feminism through the unpredictable exigencies of social memory. Postmaternal thinking, Stephens argues, 'relies on an elaborate process of cultural forgetting' (xi): forgetting about mothering, and forgetting about feminism. Feminism becomes congealed around the career woman: 'the dominant, contemporary public image of feminists is one of career-obsessed free-market individuals' (93). This paradoxically renders second-wave feminism 'synonymous with the neoliberalism of late capitalism' (94) in social memory. Interestingly, Stephens' analysis diametrically opposes Campo's argument (2009) that the popular press selectively use feminism when it needs to account for women's increased participation in the public sphere while also using it as a point of disagreement or ridicule. Campo argues that, following a culmination of events in the late 1990s in Australia, 'by 2001, the narrative about feminism that held it responsible for denigrating motherhood and ruining women's lives had become a "common sense", providing a conceptual framework within which women's experiences were understood'. (330). In contrast to Stephens, Campo argues that 'family values' have dominated Australia's conservative politics for the last two decades and have hinged on a narrative that 'feminism has failed': that women want to stay at home, perhaps working part time for some pocket money. Taking a broader structural position, Campo concludes that: 'it is not feminism that has failed mothers but rather workplaces and government policies, which continue to be structured around the "care-free" worker' (338). Campo's argument directly references radical feminist objections to the liberal reformist strategy of 'equality'; while equity discourses retain currency, the opposing arguments that women may not want to be inserted into the existing world of work, that ideas of work needed transforming to include domestic work, and that workplaces needed reimagining to accommodate people's needs (e.g. workplace daycare), are rarely remembered. Disagreements over whether the career woman is 'neglecting' her family is a sorely reduced figure of a social movement whose goal was the fundamental transformation of society in all of its social, political and cultural manifestations (Grahame 1998, 55). What both writers attest to, however, is public resistance to feminist thinking.

While the collective memory of feminism is found to be reductive, Stephens' use of oral histories demonstrates the more 'diverse motivations and desires' (94) of feminism thinking and maternity, offering a 'counterhistory' to social memory (94). The oral narratives she uses are a collection of interviews with feminist activists about their memories of the movement when they were active in it from the 1960s and 1970s, held in the National Library of Australia. Their memories 'reveal a maternalist ethos that has been overlooked in the way much of feminism has been remembered' (Stephens, 72). While feminists might breathe a sigh of relief here, at the point where a complex intellectual heritage is given credence, for me this is compromised by a reassertion of maternalism. Stephens notes:

> maternalism does resurface in oral history recollections of an activism that had, as one of its central aims, to transform the concerns of mothers and children from a private responsibility into public policy. The nurturing impulses of this kind of activism seem to have been overshadowed or buried in the collective memory of the women's movement. (88)

I suggest that while feminist activists may or may not have been nurturing, this kind of activism was grounded in a structural social analysis that sought to overturn the privatisation of the nuclear family and its violent secrets into the concerns of the state, in order to provide women with opportunities for financial independence and therefore opportunity to pursue lives in public. Maternalist or not, this impulse fundamentally sought to mess up the very idea of the nuclear family (Greer 1971, 263), whose ideologies were found to underpin capitalism, consumerism, imperialism, and militarisation, as well as reinforcing ideologies of race, class, sexuality through the proper performance of gender (Ferrier 2006, 7). Rather than celebrate nurturing and care *per se* which, as Beasley and Bacchi argue, is not always just nor is it always 'laudable or predictable' (2005, 60), I'm interested in the ways that postmaternal thinking can be figured to include the intellectual legacies of the 1970s and early 1980s. As a counter-strategy, then, I want to look for a postmaternalist ethos that can argue multiple positions and still be understood as feminist without necessitating one understanding of maternity as necessarily valuing care, nurture, and dependency. I want a counter-history that offers alternatives to both a dissipated social memory and a diminished feminist agenda around maternity.

A valuable thread of Stephens' analysis of postmaternal thinking rests on identifying the residue of modernism that underpins the social understanding of 'liberation' in the public sphere. This modernist humanist understanding of liberal notions of equality proposes that 'if women were to become modern, emancipated subjects, certain things would have to be left behind. The so-called ancient maternal ties were seen to be the first to go' (Stephens 94). Stephens calls this the 'celebratory narrative of feminist modernity, the women-as-nation-builders cultural script' (94), and clearly attributes it to the disavowal of mothering in favour of paid work and careerism. Yet to look to feminist activist memories for glimpses of maternalism as an antidote to this modernist script misses an opportunity to disrupt it altogether with multiple, complex, postmodernist understandings of fluid subjectivities and competing discursive positions, within structural relations of power and political ecologies. Feminism doesn't have to be either pro- or anti-maternalist (or maternal/postmaternal); rather, as an ongoing project of social change it is more likely to invest in destabilising entrenched conservative understandings of maternity through proliferating multiple positions and possibilities. As an historical period post-early 1980s, postmaternal thinking might usefully be imagined as a constellation of discursive positions that flow from the radical feminist thought which precedes it historically.

This article takes up this challenge to offer further counter-histories from the archive of texts, pamphlets, banners, lyrics, diaries, and analyses of the women's peace movement of the early 1980s. These events sit at the cusp of the turn from the second-wave women's movement to what we understand as postfeminism (Henderson 2016). As such, they also sit at the cusp of postmaternity, and so form an immediate intellectual precursor that both contribute to and complicate what postmaternal thinking might mean. Looking for 'an alternative feminist maternalism' in her last chapter (xiii), Stephens finds that the 'intersection between feminism, environmentalism, and peace politics can … be portrayed not as a trace of the old but as a site through which an alternative feminist politics can be imagined' (143). These fields are potent sites of thinking and so I too draw on those intersections through my research on the women's peace movement to offer further counter-histories of postmaternal thinking. As I argue elsewhere, the women's peace movement in Australia is largely located only in archives and memories due partly to its ephemerality as a lived protest (Bartlett 2013, 179), so using feminist materials from archival collections offers another form of intervention in social memory which has the potential to refigure postmaternal thinking. Much of the Australian material I draw on here was found in the Jessie Street National Women's Library, a volunteer-run library in Sydney which holds one of the largest dedicated collections of archives of second-wave feminism and notably the women's peace camps. Material on the British women's peace camps was found in the Feminist Archives South, currently under the guardianship of Bristol University Library Special Collections. These invaluable resources offers potent reminders of the ways feminist thinking extends beyond the neoliberalism of postmaternal times.

Thinking about women's peace camps

While Sara Ruddick's ground-breaking book *Maternal Thinking: Towards a Politics of Peace* (1989) is a key text yoking maternity and peace activism, it was the perhaps the women's peace movement during the early 1980s that thought through the relations between maternalism and militarism, peace and protest, women and war. The Greenham women's peace camp is 'a model for peace politics' (Cresswell 1996, 104), beginning in 1981 when a group called Women for Life on Earth marched from Cardiff to Greenham Common to demand a debate around war and militarisation as American and British governments made agreements for nuclear missiles to be placed around the world as a deterrent to Russia in the nuclear arms race. As Jolly notes, this action was initially understood as 'a mother's movement for peace' (2003, 1) and this is repeatedly evident in the other peace camps worldwide. In Australia, at the Women for Survival peace camp at Pine Gap in 1983 a banner titled 'A Letter to all Army, Navy & Air Force Personnel' is written in the name of 'mothers all over the world':

> Throughout history you obeyed the order: the order was always the same and wars always prevailed. Many millions of innocent victims have been killed in the massacres you always claimed necessary for peace
> The weapons are different now and your role is limited – but a nuclear war cannot be limited and your destruction along with the lives of the children of this planet is inevitable unless you start to obey a different kind of order ... the order of sanity and of your own conscience.
> Along with other mothers all over the world we implore you to reconsider the sentence of death nuclear energy has placed up the children of the earth.
> Disarm our world now.
> Global peace.

The plea for peace from women as mothers is a longstanding device that was utilised at the turn of the twentieth century in what became known as maternalist politics (Roseneil 1995, 4) but the use of maternalism as a position in late twentieth-century radical feminism was arguably just as effective in its rhetorical appeal to the media as well as for participants. An activist at the Pine Gap women's peace camp notes 'I am beginning to feel the threat of nuclear war as a personal threat to myself and my family. I'm surprised to realise that this feeling is new to me. Up till now it has been a theory' (Poussard 1984, 39). As Roseneil points out, 'maternalism is a discourse which resonates with many women's socially constructed material experience' (1995, 5). Ways in which to live according to feminist theory was a major legacy of the second-wave slogan, the personal is political.

In another set of discourses, maternalism roused criticism within the women's movement due to its valorisation of care and nurturing and its implicit association with women's place in the heterosexual family. Thiele railed against the presumption 'that women have a unique contribution to make to the peace movement because our reproductive capacity "naturally" provides us with critical qualities, such as peacefulness and protectiveness' (1984, 13). A British pamphlet titled *Breaching the Peace* savages the way the women's peace movement has become the 'acceptable' face of the women's movement by

> falling into women's traditional role of concern for future generations, pacifying etc. ... So it's OK to link arms and hold hands around a military base in the cause of peace, but do it on the streets for the love of it and it's another matter. (Green 1983, 8)

The exclusion of lesbians in the family-nurturing discourses of peace politics thus positioned the women-only activism as conservative amid the intersection of feminism, peace, and Cold War politics. Later work by scholars like Roseneil (2000) however recast the gender and sexual politics to read the event as queering feminism and protest through the 'experimentations with values, politics and ways of living ... the destabilisations, disruptions and transformations of gender, sexuality and political order they set in train' (2000, 1). Arguably even maternity can be queered at the peace camps as roles are messed up, as children are both visible and left behind at home, as domesticity is made public, and the women-only camps resist hegemonic social relations and state-enforced social order. As Cresswell argues, women were 'out of place' (1996, 105), thus troubling established hierarchies and intervening in established relations of family and the state. Maternalism in the women's peace movement can thus be understood variously as embraced and rejected, conservative and radical, normative and queer.

Maternity was not the only motivation of the women's peace movement of course, which sought to exercise women's political voice through principles of non-violence direct action and collective decision-making. While attributes of cooperation and negotiation were often attributed to women as biological attributes, these conscious and principled processes were integrally linked to feminist thinking. The Australian peace camp at Pine Gap involved the creation of 'affinity groups' and training in non-violence, in legal rights, in media relations and in racism, as well as regular group meeting to decide on actions and discuss involvement. One of the intense debates was how long to stay non-violent and how far that definition can be stretched. In their book *Greenham Women Everywhere*, Cook and Kirk stress that 'confrontation is a central part of non-violence, but confrontation without recourse to violence or aggression' (1984, 65), indicating the fuzzy borders debated around what non-violence can include. While the camps themselves acted to turn military installations into homely domestic campsites, many of the support actions were also highly creative and engaging: like staging a 'die-in' outside the London Stock Exchange where women just fall to the ground and lie still, giving away 'peace pies' outside the Bank of England to engage passersby in discussion, dancing on the nuclear missile silos at Greenham, and keening at the Houses of Parliament in order to touch people emotionally (Cook and Kirk 64–67). Actions often involved artwork, singing, street theatre, so rather than aiming for traditional strength through numbers feminist peace protests aimed 'to produce a change in consciousness, a questioning of violence as a valid option, opening up channels of debate' (Cook and Kirk 67). The form of the protest could not feed into the repertoire of acts used in war, militarism, and violence, whose critique formed the foundation of protest politics.

Thinking outside the family

The feminist critique of violence paralleled the international model of military relations to the micro model of family relations, thus alternative ways of living communally were sought. This is evident in Australian Senator Susan Ryan's address in 1982 when she argues that

> it is only by a recognition of the values of feminism that a wider women's disarmament movement could develop, and it is essential to link the revulsion for war with a rejection of the political, social and economic structures that leave women in a powerless position. (9)

Senator Ryan's attention to structural analysis explicitly calls for 'a movement that challenges the very basis of capitalism in the west and totalitarianism in the east; a movement which has a clearly defined alternative view of the world' (9). The decision to make the peace camps women-only is one example of an alternative worldview. Highly controversial, and the source of ongoing debate (Poussard 1984; Roseneil 1995; Bartlett 2011), the women-only peace camps were part of an ongoing commitment to both value women's agency and build collectivity and also to withdraw energy from men and male governance (Cook and Kirk 1984, 80). These political commitments to being women-centred were entwined with rethinking the nuclear family as a model for collective living. As Roseneil explains,

> Greenham was a liminal place, outside many of the structures and routines of everyday life under patriarchy and capitalism. In going to Greenham, particularly for any length of time, women were leaving home both physically and emotionally ... they were thereby displacing themselves, and relocating themselves into a new environment in which new ways of thinking and being became possible. (1995, 143)

Sometimes these new ways of being included relationships with other women and building new homes rather than returning 'home'. Alternatives were also in the form of housing cooperatives, squatting, informal share housing, and the development of rural communities which were often separatist and lesbian. The concerns of maternity were still not far from these alternate lifestyles. Principles of collective parenting and social mothering (by those who were not the biological mother) were ideologically embedded in feminist and other counter-cultural housing arrangements. Feminists challenged the assumptions that children needed their mothers, that mothers needed their children, and that mothering was innate and innately good. Social movement historian Verity Burgmann notes the argument that,

> the total dependence of a child on his or her mother is not healthy and that interaction with other caring adults and other children is valuable for the child's development; and that all women had the right to choose how to combine mothering with other activities. (1993, 105)

While childcare was invariably incorporated into feminist events up until the late 1980s, the material conditions of living with children often caused fault lines in the capacity and will to live the theory. As Rebecca Jennings explains, there were discomforting ramifications for single mothers and lesbians who had boy children, and were subject to the conflicting allegiances to women-centred, community child-raising (2016). Barrett Meyering notes that 'feminist mothers also confronted uncomfortable questions about their son's access to male privilege, placing pressure on their relationship with other women in the feminist community' (14). Boy children were sometimes subject to censure and exclusion from feminist events and locations, depending on their age, but were also regarded with hope for a new generation of men who were caring and respectful (Jennings 2016). Feminist child-raising stressed the dissolution of gender socialisation on an individual level, championed the broad responsibility for caring for children on a community level, and sought reform at a state level for 24-hour childcare and workplace reform (Sawer 1990; Lake 1999), all of which might be considered important developments in postmaternal thinking.

The development of alternative living communities did not just replicate the nuclear family home in its practices but involved a wholesale rethinking of how to live outside of capitalist patterns of consumption and mass production. Winter notes that 'in communal houses cooking, eating and childcare were shared, as were political analysis and activism. There were rituals around shopping and eating – where to shop, what to buy, which brands were more responsible for capitalist patriarchal oppression than others' (2013, 197).

Partially from poverty but also in a desire to remake the world outside of parental traditions and the repetition of meat-and-three-veg meals, Winter's remembered feminist food praxis involved 'a feminist DIY ethic ... evident in home-made and grown food – bread, yoghurt, tofu, vegie patches and compost heaps' (200). And yet, she notes, contradictions emerged in feminist households around what sort of ethical labour was most valuable:

> although its proponents regard cooking and creating from scratch as resisting mass production and consumption, serious feminist dedication to vegetarian or vegan DIY eating practices risks reproducing the historical status quo in terms of the domestic division of labour, as well as a withdrawal of energy from, arguably, bigger picture civil or political rights. (2013, 200)

Carol Adams's influential book *The Sexual Politics of Meat: A Feminist-Vegetarian Critical Theory* (1990) provided an important critical analysis of food that connected the principles discussed by feminists in the peace movement and applied them to personal food patterns. Novelist Coetzee reviews the twentieth anniversary edition in 2010 by noting that 'the connections traced between rampant masculinity, misogyny, carnivorism, and militarism operate as powerfully today as when Carol Adams first diagnosed them twenty years ago'. Adams' analysis is not just about an alternative lifestyle or a maternalist care for animals, but a political and ethical analysis of the interconnectedness of hierarchical social systems of oppression, which also informs ecofeminism. Initially founded on the common connection between the exploitation of women and the exploitation of the environment, (Instone 1997, 135), ecofeminism adds another vector to postmaternal times through attending to environmental ethics.

Ecofeminism extends the scale of feminist thinking beyond human society to other species and forms on a planetary level (thus meeting up more recently with feminist posthumanism), but is important also for its inclusion of the relations between environmentalism and competing indigenous positions. Plumwood draws attention to the way 'the category of "nature" has been above all a political category, one which has allowed its [indigenous] occupants to be erased from consideration' (1994, 77), citing the doctrine of *terra nullius* by which the British claimed Australia as unoccupied in 1788. While feminism is often remembered for being focussed on white middle-class concerns, reminders like Plumwood's draw attention to the history of colonisation and its imperialising ideologies whose legacies remain in contemporary state policy-making and cultural representations. Ferrier routinely points out the 'systematic destruction of Indigenous family life through white Australian history' (2006, 7) evident in Indigenous literature, and Gisela Kaplan tables the contrasting demands of the state by Anglo-Celtic women and Aboriginal mothers (1996, 147). Partially due to its location in the central Australian desert, much work was put into aligning the Pine Gap peace camp event with local Aboriginal women who lead the march on the first day. Many of the Indigenous women who came from the nearby homelands attended because they remembered the British Government's nuclear testing that decimated Maralinga (Lloyd 1988, 70). While the Aboriginal women wanted to protest nuclear missiles and American military bases on the basis of their responsibilities as mothers, they disapproved of direct action due to the antagonistic relations with the local police (Lloyd 74), and were uncomfortable with the public displays of lesbian affection. On the other hand, Sydney Aboriginal activist MumShirl who led the first day parade produced a surprise speaker in the form of Aboriginal man Shorty O'Neil, when men had been expressly banned from the ceremony. Additionally, MumShirl introduced another unexpected discourse into the scene when she 'talks about the Virgin Mary ... "I'm a mad Roman Catholic and I'm black and don't your forget it", she says' (Poussard 1984, 27). Catholicism, Indigenous politics and feminism make for an unusual set of positions, and yet are part of the constellation of discourses that made up the peace camp. For many of the white urban women at the camp this event was their first encounter with Aboriginal women and profoundly affected their understanding of the controversial topic of land rights and indigenous relations to the land. Similarly Roseneil argues that women at Greenham Common 'developed a collective ethos of concern for the ecology of the Common and a wider ecofeminism' that 'worked both on an emotional level and an intellectual level' (1995, 148). Chants like *'For the Earth'* work on this level: 'We are women/we are crying/we are singing/for the earth' (1983). Roseneil draws a similar connection with 'the experience of living and working in a women-only community ... many women came to realise that they had learnt not to value other women's company, and that their social orientations had been constructed as heterorelational' (1995, 146). The intersection of all these levels of feminist thinking thus requires a complete re-evaluation of every aspect of life. The maternal can never be the same.

Maternalism reconfigured?

My research on the culture of the women's peace movement and its complex engagement with feminist debates around women's agency and critique of traditional liberal humanist social structures demonstrates the proliferation of maternal positions developed in postmaternal times since the early 1980s. What emerges is an array of often competing positions: of personal conflicts with theory and theoretical conflicts with privilege, of disconcerting intersections between race and religion, between sexuality and maternity, between communal and individual obligations. The ways in which they can all coexist as feminist discourses is through the prism of feminist postmodernism. Indeed, Tong notes the defining feature of postmodern feminism is its refusal of binary thinking (1989, 217), and Roseneil identifies Greenham as 'historically one of the first and major instances of postmodern feminist politics' (1999, 166). If postmodernism is a time in history that questions modernist narratives of universality and progress, which favours ambivalence, contingency, multiplicity, and ambiguity, and values reflexivity (Roseneil 1999, 164), then Greenham embraced all of these qualities in its refusal to conform to any singular feminism (like maternalism or queer or radical or ecofeminism) and yet its inclusion of all of them. Roseneil notes the playfulness of Greenham women's resistance through spectacles like 'dancing on the missile silos, picnicking on the runway, cutting down the fence, and just living a rather chaotic domesticity in front of a Cruise missile base defended by razor wire, watchtowers and thousands of soldiers' (1999, 169). These wilful acts of disobedience open up other civic possibilities of resistance, contest hegemonic codes of gender and sexuality, and publicly doubt the modernist teleological narrative of scientific and technological progress amid the threat of nuclear annihilation.

Towards the end of *Confronting Postmaternal Thinking* Stephens presents an array of maternal activist communities that embody for her the hope of a return to maternal values. These are largely U.S. organisations that claim to be transnational in their social media reach, and include specific examples: Code Pink, who encourage their members to dress in pink slips and underwear to rally against the Iraq war and to redirect resources to healthcare and green jobs deploying humour and joy; and Cindy Sheeran, who spearheaded anti-war campaigns after her son was killed in U.S. military service in Iraq and draws on an emotional rhetoric of maternalism and 'matriotism' (maternal patriotism). These worthy causes embody hope for Stephens because they rest on maternal values and, through this rhetoric, unite women (116), and yet I wonder who else they alienate besides critics like myself. I have serious critical conniptions about the politics of wearing pink slips to protest (reminding me of the very different politics of the slut walks), and I also mourn the loss of structural social analysis that can identify and articulate the relations of power that cross gender and sexuality, race and class, the domestic and the state, war and peace, and which still apparently leave women protesting for peace pretty in pink while the associations between masculinity, violence and military invasion go unchecked. Despite my reservations, the hope Stephens draws from such examples shall not go unheeded in postmaternal thinking. If pink petticoats can presage peace, then they ought to be included in connecting women's peace activism in postmaternal times. Zillah Eisenstein wrote in 2004 that 'remembering at this moment is subversive and stands against the erasure of political history' (Eisenstein 149 as quoted in Ferrier 11); by remembering the complex intersections of competing discourses and positions around maternity in the women's peace movement, postmaternal times must surely resist such erasure and be made infinitely more interesting.

Epilogue: a manifesto for postmaternal times

The maternal can never be the same
After Dad comes home P-I-S-S-E-D and John keeps demanding more typing
After the 'organised grassroots movement of second wave feminism'
After state sanctioned military violence is likened to the secrets of family violence
After mothers leave their children to live in communal households
After mothers bring their children to live in communal households
After lesbians and single women want children and married women don't
After masculinity and militarism are in the same sentence as carnivore and misogyny

The maternal can never be the same
After no fault divorce
After the single mother's pension
After childcare is available
And the marriage bar is lifted
After university is free and learning is thrilling and employment is enriching

The maternal can never be the same
After the pill
After women find their clitoris
After *Our Bodies Ourselves* and then *Ourselves Our Babies*
After someone finds the address of a women's refuge
After someone finds the address of an abortionist

After Adrienne Rich tells us about the collective fantasy of infanticide
After *The Female Eunuch* and *The Dialectic of Sex*
After gender performativity and the heterosexual hegemony and Dolly the Sheep
After sperm can be bought and eggs can be harvested and IVF is so expensive
After amniocentesis demands a decision
After forced sterilisation and the stolen children and the forgotten generations

The postmaternal is undecidable
Is it caring nurturing and dependency
Is it late capitalism, consumption, caesarean, celebrity
It is wearing pink slips with a wink to femininity
Is it leaning in or opting out of corporations
Is it neoliberal or radical feminist or conservative or new labour or green
Is it intensive/intimate, cuddly/claustrophobic, limiting/liberating
One or the other or all of the above
Is it startups or radical homemaking or can we still do it all
Would it include slut walks in big cities and donating fertilised eggs
And is surrogacy for free or paid, domestic or overseas
And how about childcare: can grandparents do it for free or should we pay them
Is it a scheduled caesarean just to be safe or homebirth or birthing suite or what?
And can I breastfeed or am I not allowed to pump and what about formula
It must be a pregnant man and infertile women
It surely can't still be forced sterilisation and stolen children
And what about sperm donor dads and virgin mothers
And girls who don't know they're pregnant and birth in bed one morning and throw the baby out with the laundry
While fostering and family courts and custody arrangements are contested and so is carbon pricing and domestic footprints, solar energy and dirty coal and vegans and femivores and bureaucrats and feminazis and neo-Nazis and coalitions and marginal seats and climate change and refugees fleeing torture and murder and rape and terrorism and technology and the posthuman postmodern postmaternal on a genetic level, a cellular memory, a social memory, going viral or bacterial, proliferating or birthing now hush little baby don't say a word.

Acknowledgements

This article benefitted from time and thinking at the University of Bristol as Benjamin Meaker Visiting Professor in 2015, and work in the Feminist Archives South in the Special Collections Library at Bristol University.

Disclosure statement

No potential conflict of interest was reported by the author.

Notes on contributor

Alison Bartlett teaches at The University of Western Australia. She has widely published on maternity, 1980s peace camps and Australian feminist histories. She is the author of *Breastwork: Rethinking*

Breastfeeding (2005) and recently edited *Things That Liberate: an Australian Feminist Wunderkammer* (with M. Henderson, 2013).

References

"A Letter to all Army, Navy & Air Force Personnel." Banner. 1983. Jessie Street National Women's Library, Pine Gap Collection.
Adams, Carol J. 1990. *The Sexual Politics of Meat: A Feminist-Vegetarian Critical Theory*. London: Continuum.
Barrett Meyering, Isobelle. 2013. "'There Must Be a Better Way': Motherhood and the Dilemmas of Feminist Lifestyle Change." *Outskirts* 28: 1–18.
Bartlett, Alison. 2011. "Feminist Protest and maternity at Pine Gap Women's Peace Camp, Australia 1983." *Women's Studies International Forum* 34 (1): 31–38.
Bartlett, Alison. 2013. "Feminist Protest and Cultural Production at the Pine Gap Women's Peace Camp, Australia, 1983." *Women: A Cultural Review* 24 (2–3): 179–195.
Beasley, Chris, and Carol Bacchi. 2005. "The Political Limits of 'Care' in Re-imagining Interconnection/Community and an Ethical Future." *Australian Feminist Studies* 20 (46): 49–64.
Burgmann, Verity. 1993. *Power and Protest: Movements for Change in Australian Society*. North Sydney: Allen & Unwin.
Campo, Natasha. 2009. "Feminism Failed Me: Childcare, Maternity Leave and the Denigration of Motherhood." *Australian Feminist Studies* 24 (61): 325–342.
Chodorow, Nancy. 1978. *The Reproduction of Mothering: Psychoanalysis and the Sociology of Gender*. Berkely: University of California Press.
Coetzee, J. M. 2010. *Back Cover of the Sexual Politics of Meat: A Feminist-Vegetarian Critical Theory. 20th Anniversary Edition, by Carol J. Adams*. London: Continuum.
Cook, Alice, and Gwyn Kirk. 1984. *Greenham Women Everywhere: Dreams, Ideas and Actions from the Women's Peace Movement*. Clevedon: South End Press.
Cresswell, Tim. 1996. *In Place/Out of Place: Geography, Ideology, and Transgression*. Minneapolis: University of Minnesota Press.
Ferrier, Carole. 2006. "So, What Is to Be Done About the Family?" *Australian Humanities Review* 39–40: 1–16.
For the Earth. 1983. Roneoed Song Lyrics Sheet. Jessie Street National Women's Library. Canberra Women's Archive Box 0023 File 15.
Gill, Rosalind. 2007. *Gender and the Media*. Cambridge: Polity.
Grahame, Emma. 1998. "Cultural Politics." In *Australian Feminism: A Companion*, edited by Barbara Caine et al., 48–56. Melbourne: Oxford University Press.
Green, Frankie. 1983. "Not Weaving but Frowning." In *Breaching the Peace: A Collection of Radical Feminist Papers*, 7–10. London: Onlywomen Press.
Greer, Germaine. 1971. *The Female Eunuch*. London: HarperCollins.
Henderson, Margaret. 2016. "Retrovisioning Chicko Rolls: *Puberty Blues* as Postfeminist Television Adaptation and the Feminization of the 1970s." *Continuum*. doi:10.1080/10304312.2016.1166559.
Instone, Lesley. 1997. "Denaturing Women: Women, Feminism and the Environment." In *Contemporary Australian Feminism 2*, edited by Kate Pritchard Hughes, 134–160. South Melbourne: Longman.
Jennings, Rebecca. 2016. "The Body-Child in Australian Lesbian Feminist Discourse and Community." *Cultural and Social History*. doi:10.1080/14780038.2015.1093283.
Jolly, Margaretta. 2003. "Writing the Web: Letters from the Women's Peace Movement." In *The Feminist Seventies*, edited by Helen Graham, Ann Kaloski, Ali Neilson, and Emma Robertson, 1–6. York: Raw Nerve Books.
Kaplan, Gisela. 1996. *The Meagre Harvest: the Australian Women's Movement 1950s – 1990s*. St Leonards: Allen & Unwin.
Katz Rothman, Barbara. 1982. *In Labor: Women and Power in the Birthplace*. New York: Norton.
Kitzinger, Sheila. 1978. *Women as Mothers*. Oxford: Martin Robinson.

Lake, Marilyn. 1999. *Getting Equal: The History of Australian Feminism*. Sydney: Allen & Unwin.

Lloyd, Jane. 1988. "Politics at Pine Gap: Women, Aborigines and Peace." Honours thesis. Deakin University.

McRobbie, Angela. 2009. *The Aftermath of Feminism: Gender, Culture, and Social Change*. Los Angeles: Sage.

O'Reilly, Andrea, ed. 2007. *Maternal Theory: Essential Readings*. Toronto: Demeter.

Plumwood, Val. 1994. "The Ecopolitics Debate and the Politics of Nature." In *Ecological Feminism*, edited by Karen J. Warren, 64–87. London: Routledge.

Poussard, Wendy. 1984. *Outbreak of Peace: Poems and Notes from Pine Gap*. East St Kilda: Billabong Press.

Reiger, Kerreen. 1985. *The Disenchantment of the Home: Modernizing the Australian Family 1880–1940*. Melbourne: Oxford University Press.

Rich, Adrienne. 1976. *Of Woman Born: Motherhood as Experience and Institution*. New York: WW Norton.

Roseneil, Sasha. 1995. *Disarming Patriarchy: Feminism and Political Action at Greenham*. Buckingham: Open University Press.

Roseneil, Sasha. 1999. "Postmodern Feminist Politics: the Art of the (Im)Possible?" *European Journal of Women's Studies* 6: 161–182.

Roseneil, Sasha. 2000. *Common Women, Uncommon Practices: The Queer Feminisms of Greenham*. London: Continuum.

Ruddick, Sara. 1989. *Maternal Thinking: Towards a Politics of Peace*. London: Women's Press.

Ryan, Susan. 1982. "Women and Disarmament." Roneoed copy. James Cook University Archives Cairns WELC00291 Box 46 Series 15.

Sawer, Marion. 1990. *Sisters in Suits: Women and Public Policy in Australia*. North Sydney: Allen & Unwin.

Stephens, Julie. 2011. *Confronting Postmaternal Thinking: Feminism, Memory, and Care*. New York: Columbia University Press.

Sydney Women's Film Group. 1973. *Film for Discussion*. Reissued by Ballad films as DVD (n.d.) and this scene online http://aso.gov.au/titles/documentaries/a-film-for-discussion/clip3/.

Thiele, Bev. 1984. "Women, Nature and the Peace Movement." *Social Alternatives* 4 (3): 13–16.

Tong, Rosemarie. 1989. *Feminist Thought: A Comprehensive Introduction*. Colorado: Westview Press.

Umansky, Lauri. 1996. *Motherhood Reconceived: Feminism and the Legacy of the Sixties*. New York: New York University Press.

Wearing, Betsy. 1984. *The Ideology of Motherhood: a Study of Sydney Suburban Mothers*. Sydney: Allen & Unwin.

Winter, Alexandra. 2013. "Tofu." In *Things That Liberate: an Australian Feminist Wunderkammer*, edited by Alison Bartlett and Margaret Henderson, 195–203. Cambridge-Upon-Tyne: Cambridge Scholars.

Shape-shifting Around the Maternal: A Response

Julie Stephens

ABSTRACT
This article provides a considered response to all the contributions in this special issue on 'Refiguring the Postmaternal'. It reflects on the new possibilities of postmaternalism as advanced and extended by each contributing author. It also attempts to reassert the idea of the postmaternal as a cultural anxiety about care and dependency and the need for 'maternal thinking'. These are reinforced as important interpretive frames, while at the same time as paying particular attention to the limitations of these conceptions. Some of the recent literature on maternalism is discussed and this in turn raises questions about the widespread feminist discomfort around maternalism and its many historical and contemporary associations. A notion of the maternal as limit is introduced as a possible rich area for further investigation. The article ends with some policy examples of what a re-maternalised public sphere might look like. It calls for a cultural remembering of maternalist activism, alongside striving to develop alternative feminist visions for these postmaternal times.

Two moments. The first is from a recent final year celebration evening in a small private girls' school in Melbourne. Twelve talented young women from the drama club, stood in defiant stances on the stage and performed a piece they had written called 'The Girl Next Door'. This involved shouting challenges to the audience (complete with accompanying choreographed movements) about the lies this imagined girl had been told during her life. These included being told not to walk at night alone, to dress modestly and avoid certain streets but not being told that the real danger of violence was at home; being told that her life partner would be a man but not being told it could be a woman; being told that just because she had female parts she was a girl but not being told that she could change her parts and be a boy if she wanted to; being told that she was equal to men but not being told that her wage could be 16% less than a man working in the same position. It was powerful activist theatre in the making and we all cheered and clapped. There was one reference to maternity in this performance, where half the actors mimed rocking a baby while the other half mimicked a baby wailing. The audience laughed uncomfortably at this, perhaps because it was unimaginable that any of these high achieving young women could be so restricted. The rhetoric of the evening in every speech and award, including a speech from the Victorian Sex

Discrimination Commissioner was that these girls were remarkable, exceptional, magnificent and outstanding and that they could do and be anything. No limits here.

The second moment concerns my discovery of Xenofeminism (XF), described as a politics for alienation, its radical principles and non-programme outlined in the XF Manifesto (http://www.laboriacuboniks.net/). In this collectively written declaration, form and content are mixed and the digital text moves in a fluid, colliding and non-linear fashion. For instance, a line crossing out the word 'manifesto' appears when you hover over the text with the computer mouse. XF defines itself as 'vehemently anti-naturalist', 'gender abolitionist' and with a new abolitionist spirit that extends to racialised and classed identities. There is nothing that cannot be manipulated technologically. Everything can be transformed and re-engineered, including bodies. The other frameworks underpinning XF are more elusive and multiform, a bewildering tangle of high postmodern theory, technoscience, second-wave feminist terminology around gender justice and feminist emancipation, queer politics and an accelerationist call for an end 'to futureless repetition on the treadmill of capital' and 'no more submission to the drudgery of labour, productive and reproductive alike' (XF Manifesto, http://www.laboriacuboniks.net/#zero/1). No limits here either.

These two fragments provide a way into responding to the nuanced and generous readings of the concept of postmaternal thinking in the contributions to this special issue of *Australian Feminist Studies*. The snapshots of XF and 'The Girl Next Door' bring postmaternalism into sharp focus: old dichotomies are challenged, the subject is infinitely malleable and represented as freely choosing, the body is de-linked from biology, and reproductive work is called into question. All good on the one hand, but on the other, it should be noted that the very same undermining of established binaries (public/private, production/reproduction, natural/fabricated) is the stuff of neoliberal policy and the bio-economy market. The point is not to argue to uphold these dichotomies. The problem rather lies in the conviction that there are no limits; no limits to the choices one can make and no limits to accumulation of enjoyment, identities, commodities and capabilities, or to the market encroachment in intimate life. The notion of desire without limits is of course crucial to the capitalist imaginary, as it is essential to its economic growth and the maintenance of social consent and political dominance. It is an ethos that has also been linked to the care crisis, or what Nancy Fraser calls a more thoroughgoing crisis in social reproduction itself (Fraser 2014, 2016): a depleted capacity for 'birthing and raising children, caring for friends and family members, maintaining households and broader communities, and sustaining connections more generally' (2016, 99). Fraser posits this as one of the key crises of our time, on par with the environmental crisis and intersecting with current political and economic emergencies. She warns that 'no society that systematically undermines social reproduction, can endure for long' (2016, 99). So, following Fraser, when we talk about care, much is at stake.

The high stakes are recognised by each contributor to this special issue on *Refiguring the Postmaternal*. The wide horizons of the authors' perspectives, the different disciplinary approaches to the concept and the deep level of engagement with my book *Confronting Postmaternal Thinking: Feminism, Memory and Care* (2011) have certainly expanded my own understanding of new possibilities of postmaternalism as an idea and an interpretive frame and also its shortcomings. I am grateful to the editors, Maria Fannin and Maud Perrier for providing the opportunity for this timely reflection on feminism, neoliberalism and maternal studies scholarship and for the spirit of scholarly dissent expressed in these articles. Given that my role is to provide a brief response rather than review each contribution, I will concentrate only on selected aspects of the work collected here, with a view to enlarging what I hope will be an ongoing discussion.

Postmaternal vocabularies

The concept of the postmaternal appears in different guises in this collection of articles. New definitions are proposed, rich counter-readings are developed and significant omissions identified by different authors in novel ways. These include excursions into the feminist film archive (Bartlett), interviewing 'mumpreneurs' in Bristol about their businesses providing care for mothers (Fannin and Perrier), ecofeminist metaphysical analyses (Phillips), rejections of the postracialism in breastfeeding and maternal and child health policies in the UK (Hamilton) and putting the postmaternal alongside autonomist speculation about a postwork society (Baraitser). Postmaternalism is given a positive inflection by some contributors: for Lisa Baraitser it conjures the clearing of a space for reparation, the repetitive time required for love and hate to be in proximity with one another, and for Junko Yamashita, it represents the possibility for fathers to be institutionally supported to acquire 'maternal thinking'. Often surprising in their reach, each contribution develops the concept of postmaternalism in productive and provocative ways.

While there seems to be broad agreement about postmaternalism's link with the cultural logic of neoliberalism (Phillips 2017, 468), all authors express varying degrees of unease with the idea of a reconfigured feminist maternalism (Stephens 2011, 131–144). I will return to this point later. In the different conceptions of the postmaternal developed here, Alison Bartlett gives a temporal interpretation of the phenomenon, situating it in an historical period post-early 1980s, and suggesting that 'postmaternal thinking might usefully be imagined as a constellation of discursive positions that flow from the radical feminist thought which precedes it historically' (Bartlett 2017, 491). This genealogy traces our current 'postmaternal times' to the problematising of the maternal role and reproduction that was so crucial to mid-century liberal and radical feminism. To talk of 'postmaternal times' in this way seems particularly valuable. Bartlett also reiterates the phrase that 'the maternal can never be the same', first in her 'Prelude to Postmaternalism' in reference to the 1973 *Film for Discussion* and then as a refrain, underlining how women's peace camps changed the meaning and experience of maternity and finally as a chorus in her concluding manifesto. Bartlett's compilation of social and cultural shifts and ruptures going back to the 1970s does put the maternal and postmaternal firmly in question. Yet, the maternal is in danger of being formulated as both everything and nothing. In Bartlett's list, it is in danger of being only a reductive category. My book is an attempt to mobilise the concept and highlight its productive elements. Moreover, this shape-shifting around the constitution of the maternal, only resonates if the dependency needs of newborns and infants are erased from view. There are limits here. What is the reason for such unease with the idea that there are some elements of the maternal that are less mutable than we may desire? As D. W. Winnicott puts it, 'human infants cannot start to *be* except under certain conditions' (1960, 589). Sara Ruddick's comments are also apposite, that infants are vulnerable no matter what their social and cultural circumstances. They are 'small, powerless, imperfectly made, subject to illness and abuse', and demand 'what we call mothering' (Ruddick cited in Stephens 2011, 11). As argued in *Confronting Postmaternal Thinking*, if we follow Ruddick's conception, a particular moral vantage point is not ascribed to mothers but to mothering. The material and affective labour required for a baby to survive and flourish (a labour Ruddick calls mothering and I call maternal) is necessary regardless of the gender(s) of the persons performing it and regardless of different family and caring constellations. In this respect, and perhaps in this respect only, *the maternal has to be the same*.

Alison Bartlett, like other contributors, points to omissions in my formulation of the postmaternal. In her discussion of women's peace camps in Britain and Australia, she reminds us of the different ways feminist thinking can extend far beyond the times in which it is situated. This is an important point, although I would disagree that in the striking examples she uses – the Greenham Common peace camp and the Pine Gap protests – this thinking went beyond 'the neoliberalism of postmaternal times' (491). There were prefigurative elements, yet in the 1980s, both in the UK and in Australia, welfare support for women as the expected primary carer for children had not been fully dismantled (Cain 2016, 2). Nor were neoliberal values of individual responsibility, personal risk management, entrepreneurship and the citizen as a genderless, rational economic agent, as dominant at this time. Nonetheless, her more general point stands that there are and continue to be countless examples of feminism thinking beyond itself and beyond the limits of its time.

Maud Perrier and Maria Fannin rightly identify another form of forgetting in *Confronting Postmaternal Thinking*, in the focus on care in the private sphere, outside the workplace. Their article provides a timely reminder of the care and social reproduction often performed by women in paid work. The authors suggest that spaces of work can be a struggle for the politics of feminism rather than a forgetting of maternalism (Perrier and Fannin 2017). By interviewing women who make claims as mother-workers and run small businesses providing services to mothers, they found examples of maternalism being transformed from outside the home. They argue that this less visible group of working women can be linked to (and indeed some see themselves as part of) a long feminist tradition of building alternative and community spaces for women. These provide emotional support to mothers and equip women with knowledge about their bodies and their reproductive capacities (449). Notably, the practices of the maternal entrepreneurs they interviewed cannot be fully captured by the 'logics of the commodification of commercial practices around birth and mothering'. Neither can this 'mothering of mothers' be 'necessarily subsumed by the neoliberal project of the self and its accompanying technologies' (464). Perrier and Fannin demonstrate new relationships between work and care expressed in their interviewees' narratives. It would be interesting to identify what may also be masked in these narratives. As the authors recognise, these entrepreneurs represent a gendered form of self-employment that mirrors but is not entirely captured by austerity rhetoric in the UK about personal responsibility and work-focused activities. As such, these activities are the expected neoliberal priority for the model of the self-sufficient family. This would be worthy of further investigation both empirically and theoretically.

Patricia Hamilton takes the concept of postmaternalism in a different direction. She does this is unexpected ways. She links the postmaternal and what she calls postracial thinking in neoliberal state policy in Britain around breastfeeding and preferred styles of parenting (Hamilton 2017, 412). She draws attention to the often overlooked 'absent presence' of race in the political imaginary and her article brings these two forms of cultural forgetting together. Like other contributors, the theme of cultural forgetting is given a distinctive articulation by Hamilton. Her article prompts us to remember that 'race continues to play a significant role in the construction of the ideal neoliberal citizen' (413) and that racial difference is mobilised in UK policy in ways that make it difficult for marginalised women to meet the cultural demands of 'good' motherhood (413). It also demonstrates the insights gained by adopting an intersectional feminist approach that pays attention to multiple and mutually constitutive oppressions. Less persuasive is the link she makes between postmaternal thinking and attachment parenting (AP), as I will discuss below. However, the critique Hamilton offers about the individualising, gendering and privatising of maternal responsibility in AP goes beyond the more familiar criticisms (see Faircloth 2013; Lee et al. 2014) in a number of ways. She underscores the extent to which cultural discourses around mothering and race are often completely contradictory by showing, on the one hand, how race is a signifier of failed citizenship in the UK in the figure of the 'welfare mother' but on the other, a mark of good, natural motherhood (as long as these non-white mothers are elsewhere).

> AP enthusiasts often problematically conflate instinctual desires with the current parenting practices of people in the Global South. From Mongolia to Kenya, racialised women in the Global South are constructed as better mothers because they continue to (naturally) be attuned to their babies' desires, unlike their European and North American counterparts (Hamilton 2017, 416).

In my view, this is a critical contribution to the literature.

My unease with the link between postmaternalism and AP is that the latter is an approach to parenting that stands in stark contrast to neoliberal precepts about autonomy, self-sufficiency and the outsourcing of care as the solution to work/life balance (Stephens 2015). The more fundamentalist forms of AP are profoundly anti-market. More convincing needs to be done about the extent to which AP permeates UK policy around breastfeeding and maternal and child health. In Australia, this parenting ideology represents a marginal set of practices, adopted by small groups of economically and culturally privileged women or some alternative communities. At a policy level, maternal and child health advice still revolves around the opposite of AP in the form of feeding timetables, anti-co-sleeping and an almost magical value ascribed to controlled crying. A relative new ingredient to this list is advice about obesity prevention (Laws et al. 2014). So, if AP has infused popular consciousness, it has not done so very effectively. The fact that according to the Australian National Infant Feeding Survey,[1] Australian breastfeeding rates have remained static since 1995, with only 39% of babies being exclusively breastfed at 4 months of age, looks like testimony to the failure of these ideas. Analyses of the link between intensive mothering rather than AP – given the two are related but not synonymous – and the neoliberal management of risk, seem to be more consistent with a view I have attempted to advance where postmaternal thinking is a cultural anxiety around maternal care, vulnerability and dependency. Deborah Lupton's research (2011, 2014) points one way forward here. Through sensitive and theoretically attuned analyses of the concerns expressed by contemporary mothers, cultural fears around risk and the vulnerability of children seem to be present in a generalised form regardless of the specifics of particular parenting approaches.

Mary Phillips offers another take on the postmaternal. She argues for a concept of care that that encompasses but is not reduced to maternalism (Phillips 2017, 468). She carefully builds a case for an alternative model of care founded on what she calls 'embodied relatedness' to the human and more than human world (468). She argues that this model is anti-anthropocentric, and as such, better supports the radical restructuring of social and political institutions required for life on the planet to survive and flourish. Her article meticulously details the contours of ecofeminist thought, thereby contesting what she views as the inadequate treatment of the philosophical complexities of ecofeminism in my book. This is a fair charge. My final chapter engaged in 'speculation about a form of remembering that has emerged in *some* feminist responses to the environmental crisis' (Stephens 2011, 131). This speculation, preliminary in its reach, involved reading certain ideas through the lens of a hypothetical, reconfigured ecofeminist maternalism.

Spectres of maternalism past

Phillips does not reject maternalism outright and is careful to point out that maternalism does not need to be transcended by an ecofeminist politics. Rather, her concern is with the relationships between mothers and children being seen as exemplars of care (482) and the issue of this form of care being too narrow to address social and environmental crises. This is also a source of unease for others, such as Baraitser and Yamashita, in this special issue of *Australian Feminist Studies*. It is important to say again that the imperfect work of mothers and children is not the understanding or model of a new feminist maternalism I attempt to advance. As I delimit from the outset, 'the concrete experiences of specific mothers or the contexts that shape the particular ways they may or may not relate to their children's needs' is not my focus (2011, xii). Without revisiting the debates about maternalism covered in *Confronting Postmaternal Thinking*, it is worth highlighting three key and defining elements: recognition of the public importance of mothering and the care of children; extending the social and political value given to the *ideals* and *ethics* associated with maternal care, and a politics that, at its best, challenges the boundaries between public and private, men and women, state and civil society (Koven and Michel 1993, 6).

Despite these qualifications on my part, the fact remains that maternalism appears to be a much less acceptable idea than that of postmaternalism. The merest mention of maternalism seems to carry the residue of either pronatalist policies of the past or the spectre of benevolent, affluent, white women instructing poor mothers about frugality and hygiene. Obviously, neither of these is pertinent to a new maternal feminism for 'postmaternal times', but the residue remains. How can political activism in a consciously maternal idiom or in the name of mothers and children, cast off the shadow of maternalisms' past? Baraitser's article throws light on the hate and love aroused by the figure of the mother and certainly this is evident in public discourse. It may be one factor explaining the often knee-jerk reaction to the idea of maternalism. Pejorative readings of maternalism as fundamentally conservative, seem to predominate current feminist discussion on the topic (see Cummins and Blum 2015). Even the relatively new interdisciplinary area of maternal studies is haunted by older ideas of maternalism, bypassing the expression itself in favour of such phrases as 'activist mothering', 'maternal activism' (Logsdon-Conradsen 2011), 'feminist mothering practice' or 'matricentric feminism', an approach developed and fully theorised by O'Reilly (2016). While

I may see this as confirmation of the pervasiveness of postmaternal thinking, Plant and van der Klein (2010) and Plant (2015) use the stronger expression of 'anti-maternalism', in her work on an earlier era. Her description of motherhood becoming 'too freighted with political meaning and too laden' (2015, 287) seems just as relevant to the discussion we are conducting here as it is to scholarship today.

The maternal as limit

In a finely crafted and enigmatic contribution, Lisa Baraitser opens up meanings of the maternal in what she describes as a 'space clearing' exercise. Thinking with and against the postmaternal, she introduces a very carefully drawn idea of 'reparation'. This is the desire to repair the psychic damage done to the loved object, in the mother–child relationship, a damage caused by destructive states of mind that are always at play, and always in unresolvable tension with love. As she indicates, she is speaking to an impossibility here. One imagines that Baraitser is also referring to broader psychosocial damage as she cites Joan Tronto and Berenice Fisher's earlier notion of care as a 'species activity' involving an attempt to 'repair our world' (Fisher and Tronto in Baraitser 2016, 16). Time is an essential requirement for these reparative desires to emerge, as they necessitate returning again and again to the scene of love and hate. Time is crucial for the two to be brought into a bearable proximity with each other and there are dangers lurking if we fail to remember, that in social and psychic life, there is the impossibility of love without hate.

Baraitser's densely textured and evocative reflections require a much more detailed response than I am able to provide here. Familiar feminist axioms and accustomed reference points are disrupted. Maternal care is given a different name, that of the 'public management of hate'. This is an uncommon and de-familiarising phrase. Given her ongoing concern with temporality, I would like to profess that I need more time to think about such propositions before being able to give them the serious and considered attention they deserve. Aside from the Kleinian certainties about the object relation, the speaking of love and hate together is fundamental to psychoanalytic theory and clinical practice. The 'death drive' (Freud) and the drives (Lacan) unyieldingly work against the service of life. So the notion of a 'maternal death drive', what appears to be an original conception by Baraitser is complicating something life-giving and sustaining (the maternal in its ideal sense) by placing it with its opposite, as part of hate and the drive toward death. I can see the dialectic at work here but remain uneasy. The maternal has always been an unstable category and the maternal death drive perhaps more so. Almost as dislocating is Baraitser's poetic return to the anecdote about a mother–child pair, waving ambivalently hello and goodbye to each other as a sign of reparation and acceptance of the intermingling of love and hate that is integral to the time it takes for a child's life to unfold. Being able to tolerate this departure (and the return) without celebrating or mourning is offered as a new understanding of the postmaternal. Accordingly, the maternal and postmaternal are conceived of as subjectivities we inhabit simultaneously.

Reparation, through the desire to 'make good the damage done' (397) may achieve what Baraitser calls 'a temporary state of ambivalence'. And complex and ambivalent accounts of mothering have been a staple of mid-twentieth century feminism and beyond, as she asks us to recall.

> This work was influential for a whole generation of feminist scholarship – literary, sociological, psychological – that took up maternal ambivalence as a crucial way to de-idealize motherhood, and draw attention to the anxieties and aggressions that it mobilizes. (400)

I wonder if we need to be reminded of this, given it is a history in which arguably we are still embedded. The maternal ambivalence explored in this foundational scholarship remains a dominant strand in both feminist and postfeminist conceptions of motherhood. It is one of the areas where feminism may not have moved to a new stage or 'wave'. The lure of the idea of ambivalence is evident always in conjunction with the maternal and the matricidal tendencies unleashed in feminisms' second wave have not dissipated over time. While ambivalence is by definition a double-sided phenomenon, as Baraitser shows so deftly, and it is impossible to talk about one without the other, nonetheless, a one-sided use of the term as negative prevails in scholarly and popular discussion. In public discourse, the dark, repudiating side of ambivalence is firmly ingrained as the recognisable face of maternal subjectivity, experiences of mothering and to a lesser extent the mother–child bond. Possibly the whole area of maternal studies has emerged in response to this partiality. In this respect, *Confronting Postmaternal Thinking* could be seen as a reparative act on the side of love becoming more fully included (without sentimentality) in our contemporary understanding of this ambivalence. If Baraitser is proposing that some kind of cultural repair is needed, then I fully agree but we may differ on what this might look like.

Extending this sense of reparation as 'repair', Baraitser argues for a more radical model in order to rethink a feminist maternalism that includes but is not subsumed by a politics of care. She turns to the notion of 'postwork', a utopian imaginary that uncouples the relationship between wage and labour and promises a future premised on other ideals. Baraitser draws attention to the compelling vision explored by Weeks (2011) who argues for an end to work as we know it in order to address economic inequality, the subordination of life to the requirements of the workplace and to end the cycle of meaningless consumption. Significantly, as Baraitser (following Weeks) confirms, wage labour is a key 'mechanism through which gender is enforced, performed, and endlessly recreated' (402). I am particularly drawn to such imaginaries as reflected in earlier research on the anti-work ethic of counterculture of the 1960s (Stephens 1998). Unfortunately, full engagement with this postwork narrative goes beyond the scope of this response. Just to note briefly that these important ideas have been promoted since the 1960s and more recently have been incorporated into accelerationist thinking of Srnicek and Williams (2016). The fear of mass unemployment driven by automation has also made postwork options more mainstream in the last 10 years. The future that Weeks brings into view is premised on an end to capitalism. Unhappily though, visions of a universal basic income or postwork future are being embraced by Silicon Valley entrepreneurs and free-market thinktanks such as the Cato Institute (Tanner 2015). These neoliberal versions of postwork are advocated as a way of consolidating, if not saving capitalism. Also, according to this marketised scenario, robotics and technoscientific developments will transform care, remove the care deficit, release labour from production and end the crisis in social reproduction. Reproduction will in turn be further reshaped by biotechnology. This ideal market future would include a small universal basic income as this would be essential to prevent political instability from all those who become workless as they are replaced by technology. This is a very different future to a more radical imagining where we will be released from repetitive and alienating wage labour to live a 'full life' that 'will include but not be subsumed by reproduction or work' (Baraitser 2017, 405). However, the market version of postwork is not so different to the XF I sketched at the opening to this article. Even though XF represents itself as a radical, queer, postwork, anti-market, gender abolitionist movement, it shares with neoliberalism a notion of desire without limits and the fantasy of an endlessly malleable individuated self. Could a reconfigured maternal for the twenty-first century or what Fannin and Perrier call 'new collective imaginaries around mothering' (2017, 388) signify a limit to the ravaging cultural superegoic injunction of capitalism, ever demanding 'more'? Could we call this a 'maternal not-all'[2] as one small way of countering new tendencies in capitalist commodification? Would this challenge or reinforce postmaternal thinking? These are questions for future research and debate.

Junko Yamashita's discussion of the need for policies that institutionalise 'men's experience of maternal practice' (2017, 433) further extends the meanings of postmaternalism. I appreciate the very close reading of the literature she provides covering both approaches to parental leave and different caregiver models. Much is also to be learned from the examples of South Korea, Japan, Spain, Italy, Iceland or Sweden. There is wide agreement with her fundamental argument that to achieve gender equality, the redistribution of what is considered primarily women's work, namely care work, is vitally necessary (445). She calls on us to 'envisage a postmaternalism that does not abandon care, nature and human dependency'. This picture of a future where care and caregiving is valued would need, she argues, to include a universal basic income and 'a raft of other measures' (438). More particularly, it would ensure that men are involved, and obliged to be involved, in the labour of care. Yamashita critiques the different earner/caregiver models on offer and promotes an alternative version of postmaternalism where maternal practice is not only restricted to women. She argues that solely maternalist policies would not open this possibility. In this respect she sees maternalism itself as a limit. She also suggests that if men are required to become engaged in caregiving, and this requirement is institutionalised, it will mean that men have the opportunity to better acquire maternal thinking. This is in keeping with the view that maternal thinking is a practice-based form of reasoning that emerges from acts of caregiving and is not confined to mothers (Ruddick in Stephens 2011, 37). Illustrations of existing universal caregiving policies and provisions that are targeted toward men, include equipping fathers with the longest non-transferable period of parental leave in the world as in Iceland, and the practice of father's quotas in other Nordic countries (441). She also draws our attention to Paul Kershaw's interesting work, which even though it reinforces a neoliberal framework, advocates *carefair*, a system of penalties and obligations that equally bind men and women to engage in caring activities as a civic duty (Kershaw 2006). I imagine that Yamashita would resist linking these policy frameworks with maternalist ideas, nevertheless, they satisfy the three defining elements of maternalist policy that I outline above: recognition of the public importance of mothering and the care of children; social and political value given to the *ideals* and *ethics* associated with maternal care, and challenging the boundaries between public and private, men and women, state and civil society.

Conclusion

What might a re-maternalised public sphere look like or a social policy framework founded on maternal thinking? I do not think it would be alarming, reactionary or compromise our feminist principles. While I am not a policy specialist and have always resisted going down this path, a few comments seem to be in order. In many ways a maternal feminist approach would resemble already accepted mild measures that have been implemented in some of the Nordic countries. This would certainly be true of generous, government paid family leave arrangements, gender equity bonuses for men who take their full parental leave (Carlson 2013), special financial and service support for sole mothers and full and free provisions for pregnant, birthing and postpartum women. It would ensure ease of access for prams on public transport and in all buildings and commercial areas, open, safe public areas for children's play and a child rights' framework built into relevant legislation. It would have to include policy around paid leave for parents to care for sick children when they cannot go to school or childcare. Adequate support for refugee mothers and newly arrived families would also have to be a priority. It would not include locking up children of asylum seekers in off-shore processing detention centres. Equally essential would be high wages and social recognition for those working in childcare, disability services or eldercare. These uncontroversial and far from radical measures would not in my view, be in any danger of reproducing the problems of the maternalism of the past, of undermining gender equality, or taking us back to a pre-feminist era.

Returning to Plant's (2015) comments quoted above, it is clear that motherhood has somehow become 'too freighted with political meaning and too laden' (287) for it to be invoked without discomfort in the public, political domain. This appears to be just as true of maternalism (regardless of any feminist or postfeminist reconfiguring), as the articles in this special issue attest. Strangely, we are more accepting of expressions of maternalist politics if they emerge in the global South. Hamilton's (2017) comments cited above about the 'absent presence' of race in our political imaginary are pertinent here. Nonetheless, I remain hopeful, as I have argued in *Confronting Postmaternal Thinking* (2011), that these culturally laden meanings can be still be put to good political use in feminist, ecological and peace politics. This ladenness with all the weighty and conflicted associations around the name 'mother' is precisely what makes maternalism such a potent instrument for activism in the twenty-first century. Consequently, I will end with a description of a photograph that appeared in the Melbourne newspaper *The Age*. It is of women protesting against the slaughter of civilians and the subsequent evacuation of Aleppo. The action was held in Sarajevo on 14 December 2016, the city itself having considerable symbolic meaning for any protest around peace. The photograph shows a group of Bosnian women marching together. Those at the front have gaffer tape on their mouths. In contrast to their mostly dark clothes, they cradle baby dolls wrapped in a stark white swaddling splattered with red, as though covered in blood.[3] This is a maternalist form of activism that crosses class, religious and geographic boundaries. It is decidedly and profoundly feminist in its force. It speaks to the silencing of mothers, to male violence in war and to a maternal limit in not being able to always protect one's children. It is an activism that carries moral authority and weight. It is important to remember this as one of the many faces of maternalism, as we strive for alternative feminist visions in a postmaternal future.

ORCID

Julie Stephens http:\\orcid.org\0000-0002-6446-2218

Notes

1. See http://www.aihw.gov.au/publication-detail/?id=10737420927 last accessed on December 13, 2016.
2. The idea of a 'not-all' is borrowed from Lacan's (1975) seminar on feminine sexuality and knowledge Book XX Encore, 1972–1973. I am using the 'not-all' in a much more general sense here.
3. See Basham et al. (2015).

Disclosure statement

No potential conflict of interest was reported by the author.

Notes on contributor

Julie Stephens is an Honorary Professor in Humanities and Social Sciences at Victoria University, Australia. She is author of *Confronting Postmaternal Thinking: Feminism, Memory, and Care* (2011) and *Anti-Disciplinary Protest: Sixties Radicalism and Postmodernism* (1998). Her research is informed by feminist theory, social movement theory, memory studies and the emerging area of maternal studies. She also has a research and clinical interest in the theory and practice of psychoanalysis.

References

Baraitser, Lisa. 2017. "Postmaternal, Postwork and the Maternal Death Drive." *Australian Feminist Studies* 31 (90): 393–409.
Bartlett, Alison. 2017. "Postmaternal Times and Radical Feminist Thinking." *Australian Feminist Studies* 31 (90): 486–500.
Bassam, Leila, Suleiman al-Khalidi, and Perry Tom. 2015. "Aleppo Evacuation Stalls as UN Says Bombardment Likely a War Crime." *The Age*. Accessed on 16 December 2016. http://www.theage.com.au/world/aleppo-evacuation-stalls-as-un-says-bombardment-likely-a-war-crime-20161214-gtbhat.html.
Cain, Ruth. 2016. "Responsibilising Recovery: Lone and Low-paid Parents, Universal Credit and the Gendered Contradictions of UK Welfare Reform." *British Politics* 11 (3): 1–20.
Carlson, Juliana. 2013. "Sweden's Parental Leave Insurance: A Policy Analysis of Strategies to Increase Gender Equality." *Journal of Sociology & Social Welfare* 40 (2): 63–76.
Cummins, Emily, and Linda Blum. 2015. "Suits To Self-sufficiency: Dress for Success and Neoliberal Maternalism." *Gender and Society* 29 (5): 623–646.
Faircloth, Charlotte. 2013. *Militant Lactivism? Attachment Parenting and Intensive Motherhood in the UK and France*. Oxford: Berghahn Books.
Fannin, Maria, and Maud Perrier. 2017. "Introduction: Refiguring the Postmaternal." *Australian Feminist Studies* 31 (90): 383–392.
Fraser, Nancy. 2014. "Can Society Be Commodities All the Way Down? Post-Polanyian Reflections on Capitalist Crisis." *Economy and Society* 43 (4): 541–558.
Fraser, Nancy. 2016. "Contradictions of Capital and Care." *New Left Review* 100: 99–117.
Hamilton, Patricia. 2017. "The 'Good' Attached Mother: An Analysis of Postmaternal and Postracial Thinking in Birth and Breastfeeding Policy in Neoliberal Britain." *Australian Feminist Studies* 31 (90): 410–431.
Kershaw, Paul. 2006. "Carefair: Choice, Duty, and the Distribution of Care." *Social Politics* (13): 341–371.

Koven, Seth, and Sonya Michel. 1993. "Introduction: 'Mother Worlds'." In *Mothers of a New World: Maternalist Politics and the Origins of Welfare States*, edited by Seth Koven, and Sonya Michel, 1–43. London: Routledge.

Lacan, Jacques. 1975. *The Seminar of Jacques Lacan, Book XX Encore, 1972–1973*. Translated by Bruce Fink. New York: WW Norton & Company.

Laws, R., K. Campbell, G. Russell, K. Ball, D. Crawford, J. Lynch, R. Taylor, and E. Denney-Wilson. 2014. "Obesity Prevention in Early Life: The Role and Practice of Maternal and Child Health Nurses in Victoria, Australia." http://compare-phc.unsw.edu.au/content/obesity-prevention-early-life-role-and-practice-maternal-and-child-health-nurses-victoria.

Lee, Ellie, Jennie Bristow, Jan Macvarish, and Charlotte Faircloth. 2014. *Parenting Culture Studies*. Basingstoke: Palgrave.

Logsdon-Conradsen, Susan. 2011. "From Maternalism to Activist Mothering: The Evolution of Mother Activism in the United States Environmental Movement." *Journal of the Motherhood Initiative* 2 (1): 9–36.

Lupton, Deborah A. 2011. "'The Best Thing For the Baby': Mothers' Concepts and Experiences Related to Promoting Their Infants' Health And Development." *Health, Risk and Society* 13 (7–8): 637–651.

Lupton, Deborah A. 2014. "The Reproductive Citizen: Motherhood and Health Education." In *Health Education: Critical Perspectives*, edited by K. Fitzpatrick, and R. Tinning, 48–61. London: Routledge.

O'Reilly, Andrea. 2016. *Matricentric Feminism: Theory, Activism, Practice*. Toronto: Demeter Press.

Perrier, Maud, and Maria Fannin. 2017. "Belly Casts and Placenta Pills: Refiguring Postmaternal Entrepreneurialism." *Australian Feminist Studies* 31 (90): 448–467.

Phillips, Mary. 2017. "Embodied Care and Planet Earth: Ecofeminism, Maternalism and Postmaternalism." *Australian Feminist Studies* 31 (90): 468–485.

Plant, Rebecca Jo. 2015. "Anti-maternalism: A New Perspective on the Transformation of Gender Ideology in the Twentieth-century United States." *Social Politics: International Studies in Gender, State & Society* 22 (3): 283–288.

Plant, Rebecca Jo, and Marian van der Klein. 2010. "Introduction: A New Generation of Scholars on Maternalism." In *Maternalism Reconsidered: Motherhood, Welfare and Social Policy*, edited by Marian van der Klein, Rebecca Jo Plant, Nichole Sanders, and Lori R. Weintrob, 1–21. Oxford: Berghahn Press.

Srnicek, Nick, and Alex Williams. 2016. *Inventing the Future: Postcapitalism and a World Without Work*. London: Verso.

Stephens, Julie. 1998. *Anti-disciplinary Protest: Sixties Radicalism and Postmodernism*. Cambridge: Cambridge University Press.

Stephens, Julie. 2011. *Confronting Postmaternal Thinking: Feminism, Memory, and Care*. New York: Columbia University Press.

Stephens, Julie. 2015. "Reconfiguring Care and Family in the Era of the 'Outsourced Self'." *Journal of Family Studies* 21 (3): 208–217.

Tanner, Michael. 2015. "The Pros and Cons of a Guaranteed National Income." Policy Analysis, Cato Institute. Accessed December 16, 2016. https://www.cato.org/publications/policy-analysis/pros-cons-guaranteed-national-income.

Weeks, Kathi. 2011. *The Problems with Work: Feminism, Marxism and Antiwork Politics and Postwork Imaginaries*. Durham, NC: Duke University Press.

Winnicott, Donald W. 1960. "The Theory of the Parent–Infant Relationship." *International Journal of Psycho-Analysis* 41: 585–595.

XF Manifesto. http://www.laboriacuboniks.net/.

Yamashita, Junko. 2017. "A Vision for Postmaternalism: Institutionalising Fathers' Engagement with Care." *Australian Feminist Studies* 31 (90): 432–447.

Index

21st century feminist theory: socialist feminism state-funded childcare 3–4

activism: maternal advocacy groups 91; see also ecofeminism
Adams, Carol 113
adult worker model 50–54
advocacy groups 91
Aleppo evacuation protest 128
alternative living communities 111–114
ambivalence 18, 125–126
Anthropocene 88
anxieties: cultural about mothering 18
AP (attachment parenting): attachment theory 29; birth bonding 35–39; breastfeeding 39–40; emotional resources 33; financial resources 33; intensive mothering comparison 33; lack of support for participation in workforce 42–43; nature 34; nature versus work choices 40–41; neoliberal devaluation of maternal care 30; physical resources 32–33; popular culture 29; postmaternalism link 123; Sears definition 28; tools 34; traditional gender-based division of labour 32
Appiah, Kwame Anthony: postmodernism 16
Archive Fever 17
The Attachment Parenting Book 34
attachment parenting see AP
attachment theory 29
autonomy: caregiver parity model 54–55; natural birth as response to medicalisation 36–37; natural birth essential to public health 37–39

basic income 23, 56
Beauvoir, Simone de: *The Second Sex* 18
Bion, Wilfred: reverie 19
birth bonding 35–39; natural birth as essential to public health 37–39; natural birth as response to medicalisation 36–37
breastfeeding: justifications for promoting 39; length of time recommendations 42; nature versus work choices 40–41; socio-economic inequalities 40
Bristol birth and parenting economies/cultures 68–69; commodification of motherhood 69–72; community economies 74–77; self-care 77–81
Britain: breastfeeding campaigns 39–40; Nationality Act 40; neoliberal austerity measures 29

care: alternative living communities 111–114; caregiver parity model 54–55; deficit 80–81; devaluation of maternalist role 67; dual-earner dual-caregiver model 56–57; embodied 94–97; embodied relatedness 124; ethics 93–94; familialism 54; gender equality 55, 127; maternal inclination 18–19; maternal practice 58–59; more-than-human connectivities 88, 98–99; new relationships between work and care 122; paternal leave 59–62; political/social subordination 97–98; radical/liberatory 98; receiving/giving care relationship 98–99; reparation 125; self-care 77–81; social representation of mothers 17–19; universal carer model 55–57; women's predisposition to care 97; see also ecofeminism
carefair 127
caregiver parity model 54–55
Cavarero, Adrianna: inclined self/maternal inclination 18–19
choice: convergence of neoliberalism and feminist demands 42–43
commodification of motherhood 69–72
communal childcare 76
community economies 74–77
Confronting Postmaternal Thinking: Feminism, Memory, Care 1–2, 5
connecting professional and personal lives 76–77
contemporary culture: commodification of motherhood 69–72; community economies 74–77; devaluation of maternalist role 67; postfeminism 109; postmodernism feminism 114–115; self-care 77–81; see also mumpreneurs

INDEX

convergence of neoliberalism and feminist demands for choice and autonomy 42–43
Costa, Mariarosa Dalla: *The Power of Women and the Subversion of the Community* 21–22
Cox, Nicole: *Counter-Planning from the Kitchen: Wages for Housework, A Perspective on Capital and the Left* 21–22
culture: anxieties of mothering 18; AP dominance 29; devaluation of maternalist role 67; formation of postmaternalism 5; postracial thinking 122–123; professional work valued over mothering work 107; shifts 121; welfare state influence 52–53; *see also* contemporary culture; liberation movement

daddy's month 59–60
death drive 14, 23–24, 125
de-commodification 54
dependency: social representation of mothers 17–19
depressive position 19
Derrida, Jacques: *Archive Fever* 17
devaluation of maternal care 30, 67
dignity of dependence 13
domestic labour: dual-earner dual-caregiver model 56–57; paternal leave 59–62; professional work valued over 107; redistribution 127; universal carer model 55–57; wages for housework 21–22
dual-earner dual-caregiver model 56–57; *see also* universal carer model

ecofeminism 87; alternative living communities 113; dualisms 90; embodied care 88–89, 94–97; emergence 89; ethics of care 93–94; maternalism association 91–92; more-than-human relationships 98–99; neoliberalism focus on individualism/pursuit of individual advantage 90–91; political/social subordination 97–98; radical/liberatory care 98; rationality 90; receiving/giving care relationship 98–99; women's predisposition to care 97
economics: basic income 56; breastfeeding campaigns 39–40; commodification of motherhood 69–72; community economies 74–77; marketisation of nature 87; *see also* labour market
embodied care 88–89, 94–97
embodied motherhood 61
embodied relatedness 124
emotional resources: AP 33
entitlements for women's participation in labour market: welfare-to-work program 67
ethics of care: ecofeminism 93–94; non-human others 12; work ethic 20–21

EU (European Union): gender equality 55
extended breastfeeding 42

familialism 54
family values 108
family-friendly work 70–71
farewell to maternalism: adult worker model 51; paternal leave 62–63
father's quota 59
Federici, Silvia: *Counter-Planning from the Kitchen: Wages for Housework, A Perspective on Capital and the Left* 21–22
femininity: maternal thinking 58
feminism: engagement with maternity 106; maternalism shift 2–3; socialist state-funded childcare 3–4; technology of confidence 79–80; thinking beyond itself/limits of its time 122; *see also* postfeminism
'Feminism, the Family and the New 'Mediated' Maternalism' 3
Film for Discussion 104–105
financial resources: AP 33
forgetting nurturing mothers 17

gender equality: AP division of labour 32; caregiver parity model 54–55; dual-earner dual-caregiver model 56–57; European Union 55; intersectionality with race 31; paternal leave 59–62; predisposition to care 97; redistribution of care 127; regendering public cultures 67–68; universal breadwinner model 53–54; universal carer model 55–57; welfare state influence 52–53; *see* liberation movement
'The Girl Next Door' performance piece 119
giving care 98–99
Greenham women's peace camp 110

hate: infantile experiences 14–15; public management of 125

Iceland paternal leave 59
identity as a mumpreneur 73–74
inclined self 18–19
income security 56–57
infants: love and hate experiences towards maternal figures 14–15
influence: welfare states 52–53
informal care work support 54–55
intensive mothering 123; AP comparison 33
interdependence of care 98–99
intersectionality of gender and race 31

James, Selma: *The Power of Women and the Subversion of the Community* 21–22

Klein, Melanie: depressive position 19; *Love, Guilt, and Reparation* 14–15

INDEX

labour as a form of maternal thinking 17–18
labour market 20–21; adult worker model 50–51; caregiver parity model 54–55; community economies 74–77; conflicting with natural choices 40–41; dual-earner dual-caregiver model 56–57; family-friendly work 70–71; gender and liberation movement 104–105; glorifying 52; lack of support for demands on participation 42–43; new relationships between care and work 122; politics of feminism 122; postwork 126–127; universal breadwinner model 53–54; universal carer model 55–56; valued over mothering work 107; welfare-to-work programs 67
liberation movement: feminist engagement with maternity 106; gendered labour 104–105; modernism 109; peace movement 109–111; postfeminism 107; social memory 107–109
life: substituting for value 23
life-work balance 22–23
London Stock Exchange die-in 111
Love, Guilt, and Reparation 14–15
love and hate towards maternal figures: infantile experiences 14–15

marketisation: nature 87
Marxist feminism: waged/unwaged labour 21
maternal advocacy groups 91
maternal alterity 12
maternal death drive 23–24, 125
maternal inclination 18–19
maternal practice 58–59
maternal thinking 17–18, 51; 58–59
Maternal Thinking: Towards a Politics of Peace 17
maternalism: ecofeminism association 91–92; past ideas of 124–125; shift in feminist scholarship 2–3
maternalist policies 61–62
maternalist politics 110
McRobbie, Angela: 'Feminism, the Family and the New 'Mediated' Maternalism' 3; postfeminist sexual contract 16–17
medicalisation: natural birth as response 36–37
men: dual-earner dual-caregiver model 56–57; paternal leave 59–62; redistribution of care 127; social policies 51; universal carer model 55–56
modernism *see* contemporary culture
moral vantage point of mothers 122
more-than-human connectivities 88, 98–99
mumpreneurs: community economies 74–77; difficulties 72; family-friendly work 70–71; future of their business 73; label/identity 73–74; link between motherhood and entrepreneurial activities 71; motivations 79; new relationships between work and care 122; self-care 77–81

National Institute for Health and Care Excellence *see* NICE
Nationality Act 40
natural birth: essential to public health 37–39; response to medicalisation 36–37
nature: AP 34; conflicting with work choices 40–41; marketisation 87; more-than-human connectivities 88; *see also* ecofeminism
neoliberalism: austerity measures 29; birth bonding 35–39; devaluation of maternal care 30; focus on individualism/pursuit of individual advantage 90–91; glorifying paid work 52; justifications for promoting breastfeeding 39–40; lack of support for participation in workforce 42–43; nature 87–88; nature *versus* work choices 40–41; race 31
new father 60
NICE (National Institute for Health and Care Excellence) 35; birth bonding 35–39; breastfeeding 39–40
non-human others 12
Nourishing Start for Health 29
nurture: forgetting nurturing mothers 17; social representation of mothers 17–19

Oakley, Ann 2–3
Osborne, Peter: postmodernism 16

paid labour *see* labour market
parental leave policies 51; paternal leave 59–62
past ideas of maternalism 124–125
paternal leave 59–62
peace movement 109–111
personal and professional life connections 76–77
physical resources: AP 32–33
Pine Gap peace camp 111
political subordination of care 97–98
politics: feminism in labour market 122; peace movement 109–111; postmodernism feminism 114–115; social policies founded on maternal thinking 127–128
The Politics of Time 16
post prefix 16
postfeminism: alternative living communities 111–114; counter-histories 108; defined 107; ecofeminism 113; focus on family values 108; manifesto 115–116; modernism 109; peace movement 109–111; postmodernism 114–115; social memory 107–109
postfeminist sexual contract 16–17
post-industrial welfare state: caregiver parity model 54–55; universal breadwinner model 53–54; universal carer model 55–56; visions 53
postmaternal thinking 1–2, 5
postmaternal times 121

INDEX

postmaternalism: cultural formation 5; feminist engagement with maternity 106
postmodernism 16
postmodernism feminism 114–115
postracial: intersectionality of gender and race 31; thinking 122–123
postwork 13, 126–127; basic income 23; death drive 14; life-work balance 22–23; love and hate towards maternal figures 14–15; maternal death drive 23–24; reparation 13–14; substitute life for value 23; waged labour 20; work ethic 20–21
The Power of Women and the Subversion of the Community 21–22
prefix post 16
privatising caregiving in public sphere 54
The Problem with Work: Feminism, Marxism, Antiwork Politics and Postwork Imaginaries 20
professional and personal life connections 76–77
professional work valued over mothering work 107
public health: natural birth as essential 37–39
public management of hate 125
public time 22–23

race: cultural forgetting 122–123; intersectionality with gender 31; lack of support for participation in workforce 42–43; natural birth as response to medicalisation 36–37; natural birth essential to public health 37–39; nature *versus* work choices 40–41; neoliberalism 31; political/social subordination of care 97–98; socio-economic inequalities in promoting breastfeeding 40
radical feminism: alternative living communities 111–114; peace movement 109–111; postmodernism feminism 114–115
radical social enterprises 74–77
rationality: ecofeminism 90
receiving care 98–99
redistributing of domestic work 127
regendering public cultures 67–68
re-maternalised public sphere 127–128
reparation 13–14; ambivalence 125–126; maternal death drive 24; public management of hate 125; time 125
reverie 19
Rich, Adrienne 2–3
Ruddick, Sara 2–3; *Maternal Thinking: Towards a Politics of Peace* 17

Sarajevo Aleppo evacuation protest 128
Sears, William: attachment parenting (AP) 28; *The Attachment Parenting Book* 34
The Second Sex 18

second-wave feminism *see* postfeminism
self-care 77–81; costs 80–81; maternalist rationale 78–79; self-knowledge 79; technologies 79–80
self-employment *see* mumpreneurs
self-knowledge 79
Sennett, Richard: dignity of dependence 13
sexual contract 16–17
The Sexual Politics of Meat: A Feminist-Vegetarian Critical Theory, 113
social memory 107–109
social policies: adult worker model 50–51; familialism 54; founded on maternal thinking 127–128; glorifying paid work 52; income security 56–57; opportunities for men 51; parental leave 51; paternal leave 60–61; welfare state influence 52–53; women's liberation movement 104–105
social representation of mothers: care and dependency 17–19
social reproduction: maternal death drive 23–24; postwork 13; wages for housework 21–22
social shifts 121
social subordination of care 97–98
socialist feminism: state-funded childcare 3–4; waged/unwaged labour 21
socio-economic inequalities: breastfeeding campaigns 40; community economies 77
South Korea paternal leave 59–60
state-funded childcare 3–4
Stephens, Julie: *Confronting Postmaternal Thinking: Feminism, Memory, Care* 1–2, 5
Sweden: adult worker model 53; paternal leave 59
Sydney Women's Film Group 104–105

technologies of self-care 79–80
time: life-work balance 22–23; reparation 125
total work 21
Tronto, Joan: caring 19
tyranny of maternity 98

universal breadwinner model 53–54
universal carer model 55–56
unpaid work *see* domestic labour
U.S. adult worker model 53

value: substituting life for 23

waged labour 20–21
wages for housework 21–22
Weeks, Kathi: *The Problem with Work: Feminism, Marxism, Antiwork Politics and Postwork Imaginaries* 20
welfare states: adult worker model 53–54; caregiver parity model 54–55; dual-earner

INDEX

dual-caregiver model 56–57; familialism 54; influence 52–53; post-industrial visions 53; universal breadwinner model 53–54; universal carer model 55–56
welfare-to-work programs 67

work *see* labour market
work ethic 20–21

Xenofeminism (XF) 120

Yummy Mummies 70